THE BEST PLACES TO BUY
A HOME IN SPAIN

by

Joanna Styles

SURVIVAL BOOKS • LONDON • ENGLAND

First published 2002
Reprinted 2003

Survival Books Limited, 1st Floor, 60 St James's Street
London SW1A 1ZN, United Kingdom
☎ +44 (0)20-7493 4244, 📄 +44 (0)20-7491 0605
✉ info@survivalbooks.net
🖥 www.survivalbooks.net

British Library Cataloguing in Publication Data.
A CIP record for this book is available from the British Library.
ISBN 1 901130 96 7

Printed and bound in Finland by WS Bookwell Ltd

ACKNOWLEDGEMENTS

My sincere thanks to all those who contributed to the successful publication of this book, in particular Joe and Kerry Laredo (editing, proof-reading and desktop publishing) and Graeme Chesters (editing). Also many thanks to the following people for providing information and photographs: Katy Roque (REMAX, Gran Canaria), David Wood and Vanessa Gilbert (Horizon, Tenerife), Franz (Interalkem), Carlos Alonso, Jayne & Peter Mitchel-King (Molino Villas, Costa Blanca), Eric Schroder (Balearics, 💻 www.balearics.com), Katy Stjernström (Gran Canaria), Dennis and Jan Kelsall (Milestones) and Patrick Hickey (Costa del Sol). Finally a special thank you to Jim Watson for the superb cover, illustrations and maps.

Patrick Hickey, who provided the pictures of the Costa del Sol, is a Danish documentary and feature photographer. He can be contacted by e-mail at ✉ pahiphoto@hotmail.com or ☎ +34-952 115 081.

What Readers and Reviewers

When you buy a model plane for your child, a video recorder, or some new computer gizmo, you get with it a leaflet or booklet pleading 'Read Me First', or bearing large friendly letters or bold type saying 'IMPORTANT – follow the instructions carefully'. This book should be similarly supplied to all those entering France with anything more durable than a 5-day return ticket. It is worth reading even if you are just visiting briefly, or if you have lived here for years and feel totally knowledgeable and secure. But if you need to find out how France works then it is indispensable. Native French people probably have a less thorough understanding of how their country functions. – Where it is most essential, the book is most up to the minute.

Living France

We would like to congratulate you on this work: it is really super! We hand it out to our expatriates and they read it with great interest and pleasure.

ICI (Switzerland) AG

Rarely has a 'survival guide' contained such useful advice. This book dispels doubts for first-time travellers, yet is also useful for seasoned globetrotters – In a word, if you're planning to move to the USA or go there for a long-term stay, then buy this book both for general reading and as a ready-reference.

American Citizens Abroad

It is everything you always wanted to ask but didn't for fear of the contemptuous put down – The best English-language guide – Its pages are stuffed with practical information on everyday subjects and are designed to complement the traditional guidebook.

Swiss News

A complete revelation to me – I found it both enlightening and interesting, not to mention amusing.

Carole Clark

Let's say it at once. David Hampshire's *Living and Working in France* is the best handbook ever produced for visitors and foreign residents in this country; indeed, my discussion with locals showed that it has much to teach even those born and bred in l'Hexagone. – It is Hampshire's meticulous detail which lifts his work way beyond the range of other books with similar titles. Often you think of a supplementary question and search for the answer in vain. With Hampshire this is rarely the case. – He writes with great clarity (and gives French equivalents of all key terms), a touch of humour and a ready eye for the odd (and often illuminating) fact. – This book is absolutely indispensable.

The Riviera Reporter

Have Said About Survival Books

What a great work, wealth of useful information, well-balanced wording and accuracy in details. My compliments!

Thomas Müller

This handbook has all the practical information one needs to set up home in the UK – The sheer volume of information is almost daunting – Highly recommended for anyone moving to the UK.

American Citizens Abroad

A very good book which has answered so many questions and even some I hadn't thought of – I would certainly recommend it.

Brian Fairman

A mine of information – I may have avoided some embarrassments and frights if I had read it prior to my first Swiss encounters – Deserves an honoured place on any newcomer's bookshelf.

English Teachers Association, Switzerland

Covers just about all the things you want to know on the subject – In answer to the desert island question about the one how-to book on France, this book would be it – Almost 500 pages of solid accurate reading – This book is about enjoyment as much as survival.

The Recorder

it's so funny – I love it and definitely need a copy of my own – Thanks very much for having written such a humorous and helpful book.

Heidi Guiliani

A must for all foreigners coming to Switzerland.

Antoinette O'Donoghue

A comprehensive guide to all things French, written in a highly readable and amusing style, for anyone planning to live, work or retire in France.

The Times

A concise, thorough account of the DOs and DON'Ts for a foreigner in Switzerland – Crammed with useful information and lightened with humorous quips which make the facts more readable.
American Citizens Abroad

Covers every conceivable question that may be asked concerning everyday life – I know of no other book that could take the place of this one.

France in Print

Hats off to *Living and Working in Switzerland*!

Ronnie Almeida

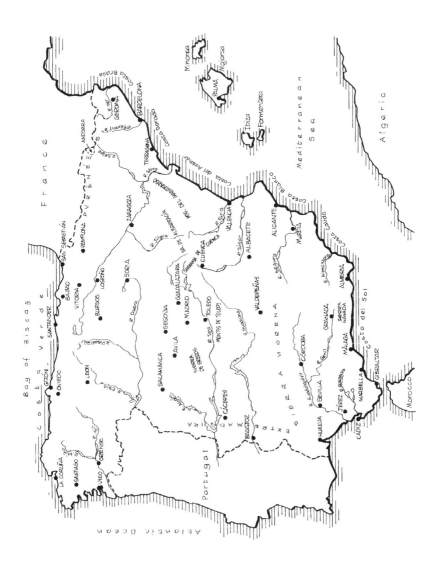

CONTENTS

WATERSTONE'S

1/5 Bridlesmith Gate
NOTTINGHAM
NG1 2GR
Tel.No: 0115 948 4499
For refunds and exchanges please see
our Customer Satisfaction Guarantee
displayed instore.

128 CASH-1   1416 0352 010

EST PLACES TO BUY	QTY 1	11.95
9781901130126		
EST PLACES TO BUY	QTY 1	11.95
9781901130966		
FTER THE ICE	QTY 1	10.99
9780753813928		
TOTAL GBP		34.89
BOOK TOKEN		25.00
BOOK TOKEN		5.00
CASH		10.00
CHANGE		5.11

VAT No GB 710 6311 84

29/02/04   16:40

IMPORTANT NOTE

Readers should note that the laws and regulations concerning buying property in Spain aren't the same as in other countries and are liable to change periodically. I cannot recommend too strongly that you always check with an official and reliable source (not always the same) and take expert legal advice before paying any money or signing any legal documents. Don't, however, believe everything you're told or read – even, dare I say it, herein!

To help you obtain further information and verify data, useful addresses and references to other sources of information have been included in all chapters and in appendices A to C.

AUTHOR'S NOTES

- Property prices should be taken as estimates only, although they were mostly correct at the time of publication.
- His/he/him also means her/she/her (please forgive me ladies). This is done to make life easier for both the reader and (in particular) the author, and isn't intended to be sexist.
- All spelling is (or should be) English and not American.
- Warnings and important points are shown in **bold** type.
- The following symbols are used in this book: ☎ (telephone), 🖷 (fax), 🖥 (Internet) and ✉ (e-mail).
- Lists of **Useful Addresses**, **Further Reading** and **Useful Websites** are contained in **Appendices A, B and C** respectively.
- For those unfamiliar with the Metric system of weights and measures, imperial conversion tables are included in **Appendix D**.
- A map of Spain showing the regions and provinces is included in **Appendix E**, and a map showing the major cities and geographical features is on page 6. Maps of each region and sub-region showing the major towns and developments are also included in the relevant chapters.

Estepona

INTRODUCTION

If you're planning to buy a home in Spain but aren't sure where you would like to live, or just wish to compare towns in your chosen area – this is **THE BOOK** for you! The purpose of *The Best Places to Buy a Home in Spain* is to provide you with the information necessary to help you choose the most appropriate region or town **to satisfy your family's requirements**. Most important of all, it will help you to avoid buying a home in the wrong area and having to uproot yourself after a few years.

Spain offers something for everyone, but where should *you* buy *your* home? Perhaps you wish to live on an island in the Balearics or Canaries? Or maybe you fancy a home in one of Spain's many coastal regions, such as the Costa Brava, Costa Blanca or Costa del Sol? On the other hand, you may prefer the faster pace of life in a Spanish city such as Barcelona, Madrid or Seville? With so many inviting regions and towns to choose from it can be a difficult decision, particularly as the climate, lifestyle and cost of living can vary considerably from region to region, and even within a region.

Where you buy a property in Spain will depend on a range of factors, including your preferences, your financial resources and, not least, whether you plan to work. If you intend to look for employment or start a business, you must live in an area that allows you the maximum scope. On the other hand, if you're looking for a holiday or retirement home, the whole of Spain is your oyster.

For many people, choosing the location for a home in Spain has previously been a case of pot luck. However, with a copy of *The Best Places to Buy a Home in Spain* to hand you'll have a wealth of priceless information at your fingertips – information derived from a variety of sources, both official and unofficial, not least the hard-won experiences of the author, her friends, colleagues and acquaintances. This book will also reduce your risk of making an expensive mistake that you may bitterly regret later and help you to make informed decisions and calculated judgements, instead of costly mistakes and uneducated guesses (forewarned is forearmed!). **Not least, it will save you money and repay your investment many times over.**

Buying a home in Spain is a wonderful way to make new friends, broaden your horizons and revitalise your life – and it provides a welcome bolt-hole to recuperate from the stresses and strains of modern life. I trust this book will help you choose the most appropriate area and smooth your way to many happy years in your new home in Spain, secure in the knowledge that you've made the right decision.

¡Mucha suerte!   **David Hampshire (Editor)**
                                                    August 2002

Binibeca Vell

1.

WHY BUY A HOME IN SPAIN?

Spain is one of the world's top holiday-home and retirement destinations (over 1.5 million foreigners live there). The British *Economist* magazine recently ranked Spain as the world's third-most attractive country with regard to social, political, economic and cultural criteria. Spain's premier tourist destinations such as the Costa del Sol, Costa Blanca, Majorca and Tenerife frequently top the list of the world's favourite retirement destinations. Many thousands of Europeans, particularly Britons and Germans, have settled permanently in Spain and in several towns foreign residents actually outnumber locals! Foreigners are the main property buyers in resort and *costa* areas; for example in the province of Malaga in 2001 some 80 per cent of all property was purchased by foreigners (it's estimated that a third of the total amount spent by foreigners on property in Spain is spent in the province of Malaga alone).

There are many excellent reasons for buying a home in Spain, although it's important to ask yourself *exactly* why you want to buy a home there. For example, are you primarily looking for a sound investment or do you plan to work or start a business in Spain? Are you seeking a holiday or retirement home? If you're seeking a second home, will it be mainly used for long weekends or for lengthier stays? Do you plan to let it to offset the mortgage and running costs? If so, how important is the property income? You need to answer these and many other questions before deciding on the best (and most appropriate) place to buy a home in Spain.

Often buyers have a variety of reasons for buying a home in Spain; for example, many people buy a holiday home with a view to living there permanently or semi-permanently when they retire. If this is the case, there are many more factors to take into account than if you're 'simply' buying a holiday home that you will occupy for just a few weeks a year (when it's usually wiser not to buy at all!). If, on the other hand, you plan to work or start a business in Spain, you will be faced with a completely different set of criteria. An increasing number of people also live in Spain and work in another European country, commuting back and forth by air.

Property values in Spain generally increase at an average of less than 5 per cent a year or in line with inflation (with no increase in real terms). In some fashionable resorts and developments, however, prices rise faster than average, although this is usually reflected in much higher purchase prices. For example, prices have increased by over 25 per cent in some parts of the Costa del Sol in the last few years. Generally, however, there's a stable property market in most of Spain, which acts as a discouragement to speculators wishing to make a fast buck, particularly when you consider that capital gains tax can wipe out much of the profit made on the sale of a second home. You also need to recover the costs associated with buying a home in Spain when you sell.

*Benaque Gave Billede,
Costa del Sol
(© Patrick Hickey)* ▶

▲ *Albarracín, Aragón
(© Dennis Kelsall)*

▲ *Ronda, Costa del Sol (© Patrick Hickey)*

▲ *Fisterra, Galicia
(© Dennis Kelsall)*

◀ *Puerto Rico Muelle,
Gran Canaria
(© Katy Stjernström)*

Casca Antiguo, Majorca
(© Marc Castejon)

▲ *Cabo Vilan, Galicia (© Dennis Kelsall)*

▲ *Istan, Costa del Sol (© Patrick Hickey)*

▲ *Loarre, Aragón*
(© Dennis Kelsall)

Cabo de Gata, ▶
Costa de Almeria
(© Patrick Hickey)

Herradura, Costa del Sol
(© Patrick Hickey)

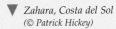

Mojacar, Almeria
(© Patrick Hickey)

Cuenca, Castilla-La Mancha
(© Dennis Kelsall)

Zahara, Costa del Sol
(© Patrick Hickey)

Sepúlveda, Castilla y León
© Dennis Kelsall

Casares, Costa del Sol ▶
(© Patrick Hickey)

▲ *Muros, Galicia (© Dennis Kelsall)*

▼ *Villa, Costa Blanca*
(© Molino Villas)

▼ *S'Algar, Majorca*
(© Marc Castlejon)

▲ *Mount Teide, Tenerife*
(© Horizon)

ADVANTAGES & DISADVANTAGES

There are both advantages and disadvantages to buying a home in Spain, although for most people the benefits far outweigh any drawbacks. Spain has many attractions: much of the country enjoys a sunny and warm climate all year round, with over 300 days of sunshine annually and high temperatures (in some areas, all year round); the country has many modern airports with frequent, inexpensive flights to most international destinations, particularly major European cities, most of which are less than three hours away; there has been widespread investment in the country's infrastructure during the last two decades and most regions can now be reached by good dual-carriageways or motorways; high-speed trains have been introduced in the last decade or so and are being expanded to link up with a Europe-wide network; and the country's telecommunications are among the best in Europe.

Spain is famous for the huge variety of its cultural and leisure activities and the friendliness and hospitality of its people. The standard of living is generally high, with the added advantage of one of the lowest costs of living in Western Europe, including relatively good value homes (if you avoid fashionable areas). Although prices have risen on many of Spain's *costas* and islands in recent years, property remains far cheaper than its equivalent in the UK, for example, with the added bonus that the sun shines almost every day.

Among the many other advantages of buying a home in Spain are: good rental possibilities (in many areas); good local tradesmen and services (particularly in resort areas); fine food and wine at reasonable prices; a slow, relaxed pace of life; one of the least polluted regions in the world; and the dramatic and rugged beauty of Spain on your doorstep. When buying property in Spain, you aren't simply buying a home but a lifestyle, and in terms of quality of life, the country has few equals.

Naturally, there are also a few disadvantages, including: the relatively high purchase costs associated with buying a home in Spain; unexpected renovation and restoration costs (if you don't do your homework); the dangers of buying a property with debts and other problems (if you don't take legal advice); a high rate of burglary in some areas; overcrowding in popular tourist areas during the peak summer season; traffic congestion and pollution in many towns and cities; relatively high taxes for non-resident homeowners; severe water shortages in some regions (particularly during the summer); and the expense of getting to and from Spain if you own a holiday home there and don't live in a nearby country with good air connections.

CHOOSING THE REGION

Spain is a huge country (the third-largest in western Europe after Germany and France) with a vast array of landscapes ranging from flat desert-like terrain to rugged mountain peaks, from tiny medieval villages to lively cosmopolitan cities. Some parts of Spain remain practically uninhabited, while others are a melting pot of foreigners from all corners of the world. You can choose from an authentic Spanish village where you can immerse yourself in the Spanish way of life, an expatriate community where you will live among your own countrymen and other foreigners, and an area where you can enjoy the best of both worlds. Alternatively, you may prefer the hustle and bustle of city life in dynamic Barcelona or Moorish Granada, complete isolation in the Sahara-like dune landscape of Fuerteventura, nautical life in Majorca with some of the world's best sailing on your doorstep, the freshest mountain air in Europe in the Alpujarras, or mixing it with the jet-set in Marbella or package tourists in Benidorm.

Spain is a world unto itself, and deciding where to live can be difficult and the choice overwhelming. Many people's choice is based on previous holidays, friends' recommendations or simply an area's reputation. However, how do you know whether an area is a good investment and what you can expect to get for your money? Where can you find expatriate services, good hospitals or lively nightlife? Which areas and resorts are quieter in summer and offer a more relaxed way of life? What are the local roads and public transport system like?

This book has been written to help answer these questions by providing comprehensive information about the most popular areas among foreign homebuyers in Spain and giving an accurate picture of what everyday life is *really* like in a certain area. The 'best' place to live in Spain obviously depends on your preferences and it's impossible to specify a best location for everyone. The aim of this book is to identify the positive and possible negative aspects of each of the selected areas in order to help you to choose the part of Spain that suits you and your family best.

The book is divided into six chapters, each dealing with a region (or regions) where the majority of foreigners choose to buy property or settle permanently in Spain:

- The Balearics
- The Canaries
- Cities (Barcelona, Granada, Madrid, Seville and Valencia)
- Costa Blanca
- Costa del Sol & Las Alpujarras
- Other Costas and The Cantabrian Coast

Each chapter examines the area in detail with a description of the most popular towns and communities in the area, the advantages and disadvantages of living there, the climate, language and cost of living, local services and amenities, the property market including the average prices of different kinds of properties and land (note that prices change continually and those quoted in this book were accurate in mid-2002), rental rates and typical homes, communications and transport, and other useful information to help you choose the best place to buy a home.

Once you've decided on a preferred region or area, you need to consider the type of home you want to buy and the location that suits you best.

LOCATION

The most important consideration when buying a home anywhere is usually its location – or as the old adage goes, the *three* most important points are location, location and location! A property in a reasonable condition in a popular area is likely to be a better investment than an exceptional property in a less attractive location. There's usually no point in buying a dream home in a terrible location. Spain offers almost everything that anyone could want, but you must choose the right property in the right place. **The wrong decision regarding location is one of the main causes of disappointment among foreigners who purchase property in Spain.**

There are many points to consider regarding the location of a home, and you should take into account the present and future needs of all family members.

Climate: Do you want or need winter *and* summer sunshine? If you want it to be really warm all year round, the only choice is the Canaries. Note that although the Costa Blanca and Costa del Sol are mild and pleasant in winter with daytime temperatures around 15 to 20°C (60 to 68°F), this may seem cool if you're accustomed to the blazing heat of high summer (when air-conditioning is a blessed relief). In winter, it's too cold for sea bathing anywhere in Spain except the Canaries. Bear in mind both the winter and summer climate, position of the sun, average daily sunshine, plus the rainfall and wind conditions. The orientation or aspect of a building is vital, and if you want morning or afternoon sun (or both) you must ensure that balconies, terraces and gardens are facing the right direction (take a compass when house hunting).

Natural Phenomena: Check whether an area is liable to natural disasters such as storms, floods, volcanic eruptions or forest fires. If a property is located near a waterway, it may be expensive to insure against floods (or flash floods), which are a threat in some areas. Note that in areas with little rainfall there may be frequent droughts, severe water restrictions and high water bills.

Noise: Noise can be a considerable problem in Spain, the noisiest country in Europe and the second-noisiest in the world after Japan! Although you cannot choose your neighbours, you can at least ensure that a property isn't located next to a busy road, industrial plant, commercial area, building site, discotheque, night club, bar or restaurant (where revelries may continue into the early hours). Look out for objectionable neighbouring properties and check whether nearby vacant land has been zoned for commercial activities. In community developments (e.g. apartment blocks) many properties are second homes and are let short-term, which means you may have to tolerate boisterous holiday-makers as neighbours throughout the year (or at least during the summer months). In towns, traffic noise, particularly from motorcycles, can continue all night!

Tourists: Bear in mind that if you live in a popular tourist area, i.e. almost anywhere on the Mediterranean coast or the islands, you will be inundated with tourists in the summer. They won't just jam the roads and pack the beaches and shops, but will also occupy your favourite table at your local bar or restaurant (heaven forbid!). Bear in mind that while a 'front-line' property sounds attractive and may be ideal for short holidays, it isn't always the best solution for permanent residents. Many beaches are hopelessly crowded in the peak season, streets may be smelly from restaurants and fast food outlets, parking will be impossible, services stretched to breaking point and the incessant noise may drive you crazy. You may also have to tolerate water shortages, power cuts and sewage problems. Some people prefer to move inland to higher ground, where it's less humid, you're isolated from the noise and can also enjoy excellent views. On the other hand, getting to and from hillside properties can be difficult, and the often poorly-maintained roads (usually narrow and unguarded) are for sober, confident drivers only.

Community: Do you wish to live in an area with many other expatriates from your home country or as far away from them as possible (you won't get very far away on many parts of the Mediterranean coast)? If you wish to integrate with the local community, you should avoid the foreign 'ghettos' and choose a Spanish village or an area or development with mainly local inhabitants. However, unless you speak fluent Spanish or intend to learn it, you should think twice before buying a property in a village, although residents who take the time and trouble to integrate into the local community are invariably warmly welcomed. If you're buying a permanent home, it's important to check on your prospective neighbours, particularly when buying an apartment. For example, are they noisy, sociable or absent for long periods? Do you think you will get on with them? **Good neighbours are invaluable, particularly when buying a second home in a village.**

On the other hand, if you wish to mix only with your compatriots and don't plan to learn Spanish, living in a predominantly foreign community will be ideal. Note that many developments and towns in popular tourist areas are inhabited largely by second homeowners and are like ghost towns for most of the year. In these areas, many facilities, businesses and shops are closed outside the main tourist season, when even local services such as public transport and postal collections may be severely curtailed.

Town or Country: Do you wish to be in a town or do you prefer the country? Inland or by the sea? How about living on an island? Life on an island is more restricted and remote, e.g. you cannot jump into your car and drive to Barcelona or Madrid or 'pop' over the border into Andorra, France, Gibraltar or Portugal. Bear in mind that if you buy a property in the country you will have to tolerate poor public transport, long travelling distances to a town of any size, solitude and remoteness, and the high cost and amount of work involved in the upkeep of a country house and garden. You won't be able to pop along to the local shop for fresh bread, drop into the local bar for a glass of your favourite tipple with the locals, or have a choice of restaurants on your doorstep. In a town or large village, the weekly market will be just around the corner, the doctor and chemist's close at hand, and if you need help or run into any problems, your neighbours will be near by.

On the other hand, in the country you will be closer to nature, will have more freedom (e.g. to make as much noise as you wish) and possibly complete privacy, e.g. to sunbathe or swim *au naturel*. Living in a remote area in the country will suit those looking for peace and quiet who don't want to involve themselves in the 'hustle and bustle' of town life (not that there's a lot of this in Spanish rural towns). If you're seeking peace and quiet, make sure that there isn't a busy road or railway line nearby or a local church within 'DONGING' distance. Note, however, that many people who buy a remote country home find that the peace of the countryside palls after a time and they yearn for the more exciting city or coastal life. If you've never lived in the country, it's wise to rent before buying. Note also that while it's cheaper to buy in a remote or unpopular location, it's usually much more difficult to find a buyer when you want to sell.

Garden: If you're planning to buy a country property with a large garden or plot, bear in mind the high cost and amount of work involved in its upkeep. If it's a second home, who will look after the house and garden when you're away? Do you want to spend your holidays mowing the lawn and cutting back the undergrowth? Do you want a home with a lot of outbuildings? What are you going to do with them? Can you afford to convert them into extra rooms or guest accommodation?

Employment: If you will be working in Spain, how secure is your job or business and are you likely to move to another area in the near future? Can you find other work in the same area, if necessary? If there's a possibility that you will need to move in a few years' time, you should rent a home or at least buy one that will be relatively easy to sell and recoup the cost. You should consider also your partner's and children's present or future job requirements.

Schools: What about your children's present and future schooling? What is the quality of local schools? Note that even if your family has no need or plans to use local schools, the value of a home may be influenced by the quality and location of schools.

Services: What local health and social services are provided? How far is the nearest hospital with an emergency department? Are there English-speaking doctors and dentists and private clinics or hospitals in the area?

Shopping: What shopping facilities are provided in the neighbourhood? How far is it to the nearest large town with good shopping facilities, e.g. a super/hypermarket? How would you get there if your car was out of commission? Note that many rural villages are dying and have few shops or facilities, and they aren't usually a good choice for a retirement home.

Sports & Leisure Facilities: What is the range and quality of local leisure, sports, community and cultural facilities? What is the proximity to sports facilities such as beaches, golf courses, ski resorts or waterways? Bear in mind that properties in or close to ski and coastal resorts are considerably more expensive, although they also have the best letting potential. If you're a keen skier, you may want to be close to the Sierra Nevada (Granada) or the Pyrenees, although there are smaller skiing areas in other regions.

Public Transport: Is proximity to public transport, e.g. an international airport, port or railway station, or access to a motorway important? Don't believe all you're told about the distance or travelling times to the nearest airport, station, motorway junction, beach or town, but check for yourself .

Parking: If you're planning to buy in a town or city, is there adequate private or free on-street parking for your family and visitors? Is it safe to park in the street? Note that in Spanish cities it's important to have secure off-street parking if you value your car. Parking is a problem in cities and most large towns, where private garages or parking spaces are unobtainable or expensive. Traffic congestion is also a problem in many towns and tourist resorts, particularly during the high season. Bear in mind that an apartment or townhouse in a town or community development may be some distance from the nearest road or car park. How do you feel about carrying heavy shopping hundreds of metres to your home and possibly up several flights of stairs? If you're planning to buy an apartment above the ground floor, you may wish to ensure that the building has a lift.

Crime Rate: What is the local crime rate? In many resort areas the incidence of burglary is high, which also results in more expensive home insurance. Check the crime rate in the local area, e.g. burglaries, stolen cars and crimes of violence. Is crime increasing or decreasing? Note that professional crooks love isolated houses, particularly those full of expensive furniture and other belongings that they can strip bare at their leisure. You're much less likely to be the victim of thieves if you live in a village, where crime is virtually unknown – strangers stand out like sore thumbs in villages, where their every move is monitored by the local populace.

Administration: Is the local council well run? Unfortunately many are profligate and simply use any extra income to hire a few more of their cronies or spend it on grandiose schemes. What are the views of other residents? If the municipality is efficiently run, you can usually rely on good local social and sports amenities and other facilities. In areas where there are many foreign residents, the town hall may have a foreign residents' department (*departamento de extranjeros*).

This book will provide you with answers to many of the above questions. However, although the information about each area is comprehensive and up-to-date, it isn't intended as a substitute for personal research.

RESEARCH

It's essential to spend time looking around your areas of interest. If possible, you should visit an area a number of times over a period of a few weeks, both on weekdays and at weekends, in order to get a feel for the neighbourhood (it's better to walk rather than drive around). A property seen on a balmy summer's day after a delicious lunch and a few glasses of *vino tinto* may not be nearly so attractive on a subsequent visit *sin* sunshine and the warm inner glow. If possible, you should also visit an area at different times of the year, e.g. in both the summer and winter, as somewhere that's wonderful in summer can be forbidding and inhospitable in winter (or vice versa if you don't like extreme heat). This is particularly important when choosing a holiday resort, which may be bustling and lively during the summer months but deserted in winter. If you're planning to buy a winter holiday home, you should view it in the summer, as snow can hide a multitude of sins! In any case, you should view a property a number of times before deciding to buy it. If you're unfamiliar with an area, most experts recommend that you rent for a period before buying. This is particularly important if you're planning to buy a permanent or retirement home in an unfamiliar area. Many people change their minds after a period and it isn't unusual for buyers to move once or twice before settling down permanently.

Before looking at properties it's important to have a good idea of the type of property you want and the price you wish to pay, and to draw up a short list of the areas and towns of interest. Most importantly make a list of what you want and don't want – if you don't do this, you're likely to be overwhelmed by the number of properties to be viewed. You should consider a property's proximity and travelling time to your place of work, schools, bars and restaurants, countryside or towns, shops, public transport, beaches, swimming pools, entertainment, sports facilities, etc. If you buy a country property, the distance to local amenities and services could become a problem, particularly if you plan to retire to Spain. If you live in a remote rural area, you will need to be much more self-sufficient than if you live in a town. Don't forget that Spain is a **BIG** country and if you live in a remote area you will need to use the car for everything (which will increase your cost of living).

If you wish to live near a particular town, airport or facilities, such as a beach, sports or other amenities, obtain a large scale map of the area and decide the maximum distance you will consider travelling. Mark the places that you've seen on the map, at the same time making a list of the plus and minus points of each property. If you use an estate agent, he will usually drive you around and you can then return later to the properties that you like best at your leisure (provided you've marked them on your map!). Note, however, that agents may be reluctant to give you the keys to visit a property on your own.

IMPORTANT NOTE

Unless you know exactly what you're looking for and where, it's best to rent a property until you're familiar with an area. As when making all major financial decisions, it's never wise to be too hasty. Many people make expensive (even catastrophic) errors when buying homes abroad, usually because they do insufficient research and are in too much of a hurry, often setting themselves ridiculous deadlines, such as buying a home during a long weekend break or a week's holiday. Not surprisingly, most people wouldn't dream of acting so rashly when buying property in their home country! It isn't uncommon for buyers to regret their decision after some time and wish they'd purchased a different property in a different region (or even in a different country!).

The decision to purchase property, retire or relocate to Spain (or any other country) should only be taken after careful consideration and extensive research. You should also consider learning Spanish, particularly if you intend to live in Spain permanently, although there are many parts of Spain where the *lingua franca* is English. There are numerous books about Spain (see **Appendix B**), including ***Buying a Home in Spain*** and ***Living and Working in Spain***, written by David Hampshire and published by Survival Books, which are packed with important information about property purchase and daily life in Spain. **Note that the cost of investing in a few books or magazines (and other research) is tiny compared with the expense of making a big mistake.** Numerous websites (see **Appendix C**) also provide free information about Spain.

Windmills on the Mallorcan central plain

2.

THE BALEARIC ISLANDS

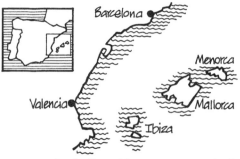

The Balearic Islands (or Balearics) are one of Europe's top tourist destinations and attract millions of visitors every year. They're located in the Mediter- ranean Sea off the east coast of Spain (approximately 200km/ 120mi south-east of Barcelona) and consist of three main islands – Majorca, Minorca and Ibiza – and several smaller ones, including Formentera and the uninhabited Cabrera. The islands' landscape is magnificent, comprising woodlands, almond and olive groves, fertile plains and impressive coastlines, with numerous sandy coves separated by craggy cliffs.

The largest and most popular island is **Majorca** (Mallorca in Spanish, also known as the 'Isle of Dreams'), which has been a retreat for the rich and famous since the 19th century; Chopin and his lover George Sand lived there for many years. It's the administrative capital of the Balearics and an island of contrasts, with brash, bustling holiday resorts and tranquil rural villages. **Minorca** (Menorca in Spanish), the second largest island, is by far the quietest of the main three; rich in relics of its ancient history, it has strong connections with Britain dating from Admiral Nelson's stay on the island. **Ibiza** is famous for its lively nightlife and is a Mecca for Europe's jet set, although it also has peaceful corners. A narrow channel separates Ibiza from Formentera, the smallest inhabited island with a population of just 5,000 and very few homes for sale, making it of little interest to foreign homebuyers.

The Balearics attract many foreign residents, the majority of whom are German and British, although it should be noted that the islands are considering introducing residence quotas in order to limit the number of immigrants. Tourism is the most important industry, although farming (principally citrus fruits and olives) remains an important source of income for many.

A general overview of the three main islands is given below, followed by individual island directories.

Advantages & Disadvantages

The Balearics' main advantages are their pleasant climate (for most of the year) and their natural beauty, each island having a different landscape. The islands have good air connections with most parts of the world, although flights are reduced in the winter months. Inter-island communication is also excellent. Apart from a few areas such as the Bay of Palma in Majorca and San Antonio in Ibiza, the Balearics are generally unspoilt by the ravages of mass tourism, and strict regulations ensure that new building is usually in keeping with the natural surroundings.

The islands do, however, have some drawbacks: the massive influx of tourists, especially in the summer, can be daunting and makes some regions almost impossibly crowded; island life can be claustrophobic and, during the winter months especially, some people feel isolated and trapped. Despite this, however, the Balearics remain one of Spain's top attractions, both for tourists and foreign property buyers.

Population

Along with the Canary Islands, the Balearics are the only part of Spain where foreigners account for over 5 per cent of the total population. In 2000, there were around 46,000 official foreign residents on the islands, mainly German followed by British, although unofficial figures are much higher. Foreign residents tend to be concentrated in the main towns.

Language

The Balearics have two official languages, Spanish and Catalan. The latter has three dialects, one on each island – Mallorquín is spoken on Majorca, Menorquín on Minorca and Ibiçenco on Ibiza – although all are similar and can be understood by speakers of the others. The regional government has a policy of 'implanting' Catalan into daily life and education (the state school system is bi-lingual), and there are Catalan newspapers and television stations. Most islanders are bi-lingual and signs and notices tend to be in both Spanish and Catalan. While it isn't essential to learn Catalan, if you choose to live inland or in remoter parts of the islands, the ability to speak it will greatly ease your integration into the local community. German and English are also widely spoken, so much so that in some places it can be difficult to find a menu written in Spanish or Catalan!

Climate

The Balearics enjoy a temperate, Mediterranean climate. Summers are hot, although maximum temperatures aren't excessive, as they're moderated by sea breezes, while winters are mild and fairly dry. Winter temperatures rarely fall below freezing, although snow on Majorca's mountains isn't unknown. The islands have an average of 11 hours of sunshine per day in summer and around five in winter. Some parts of the islands, particularly in Minorca and Formentera, can be windy.

Cost of Living

The Balearics have the highest cost of living in Spain, and Calvia in Majorca lays claim to being the second-richest town in Europe. With the exception of Minorca, property on the islands is the most expensive in Spain.

Crime Rate & Security

The crime rate on the Balearics has risen alarmingly in recent years and is now among the highest in Spain. Some parts of the islands – such as Magaluf on Majorca and San Antonio on Ibiza – suffer from 'lager lout' violence, particularly during the high season. Drug-related crime is also common, although an increased police presence and stricter licensing laws are expected to reduce these problems. Inland and in more isolated parts of the islands, on the other hand, the crime rate is very low and there's a strong sense of community, meaning that neighbours keep an eye out for each other.

Amenities

Sports: Sailing is by far the most popular sport in the Balearics, where anybody who's anybody owns a boat. The islands have numerous marinas, and sailing along the Balearics' beautiful coastlines and mooring in secluded coves is considered to be one of the world's great sailing pleasures. Note, however, that mooring prices are the most expensive in Spain, considerably higher than on the mainland. There are also many opportunities to practise water-sports other than sailing, including windsurfing and scuba diving in pristine diving areas, particularly around the island of Cabrera. Back on land, most large municipalities have a sports centre at which activities and membership are often subsidised; these usually have extensive facilities, including an indoor pool. There are also numerous private sports centres and an abundance of tennis and riding clubs.

Golf is a major island sport, especially on Majorca, and the Balearics have become one of Europe's main golfing destinations. Majorca has several world-class courses set in beautiful surroundings, and more are planned. Ibiza and Minorca have just one course each, but there are plans for more. Most of the islands' courses offer a 'pay-and-play' facility.

Leisure: There's usually plenty to enjoy on most of the islands – Formentera is the most underdeveloped and makes a virtue of it – although outside the high season many attractions are closed. Palma de Majorca maintains a lively cultural scene all year round and there's a surprising amount to do on Ibiza during the winter. Concerts, recitals and plays are held throughout the year in the islands' main towns and there are several important festivals, including Majorca's Chopin Festival. Summer brings a wealth of leisure opportunities, particularly nightlife (which is when Ibiza comes into its own), and is the time when the islands' marinas buzz with activity. Majorca and Ibiza have the best choice of aquarium-type attractions and water parks.

All of the islands' towns and villages, however small, have colourful annual fairs and festivals. Of particular note are the Saint Sebastian festivities held in Palma in January and those at Ciudadela on Minorca in June, in honour of Saint John. Other leisure activities involve making the most of the islands' spectacular scenery, with walking particularly popular.

English-language Cinema & Theatre: Palma has the only English-language cinema, while expatriate theatre groups perform in Majorca and Ibiza.

Shopping Centres & Markets: The Balearics enjoy a wide range of shopping facilities, and Palma's shops are as good as those in any major European city. Resort areas generally have a good choice of shops, although in more remote parts of the islands they may close out of season. Weekly markets are held in the larger towns and resorts on the three main islands.

Foreign Food & Products: Most supermarkets offer a selection of foreign produce, with the emphasis on British and German goods, although availability is limited outside the main resorts out of the high season and prices are high.

Restaurants & Bars: There are numerous restaurants and bars in the Balearics, serving local cuisine or international fare, which in resort areas tends to be limited to fast food. The islands are noted for their excellent cuisine, which includes sea food, mayonnaise (invented in Mahon), *coca* (a vegetarian pizza-type dish) and *ensaimada* (a cake in the shape of a snail's shell). Majorca also produces some good-quality wines, Minorca is known for its gin and Ibiza offers a potent herb liqueur.

Services

International & Private Schools: There are five international schools in Majorca, one in Ibiza and one in Minorca. For further information on accredited international schools with a British curriculum, consult the ECIS website (🖳 www.ecis.org) or the National Association of British Schools in Spain (NABSS) website (🖳 www.nabss.org). All three main islands have private schools, located in their respective capitals, offering a Spanish curriculum and bi-lingual lessons in Catalan and Spanish. Many private schools are run by religious orders and are single-sex.

Language Schools: Most major towns have language schools at which Spanish, Catalan, English and German are taught. In main tourist areas, the local town council may provide subsidised Spanish lessons for foreign residents. The University of La Palma offers an extensive range of courses for foreign students, and private lessons are also available.

Hospitals & Clinics: Each of the three main islands has a large public hospital in the capital, although public medical facilities are insufficient and waiting lists for non-emergency treatment are long. Palma also has several private hospitals. Most main towns have at least one public health centre, where you can see a general practitioner, and some of the larger centres also offer emergency treatment, x-rays, family planning advice and physiotherapy. There are also many private clinics, where the majority of doctors and medical staff speak English.

Doctors & Dentists: There's a large number of English-speaking doctors and dentists in the Balearics, particularly in the main towns and resorts.

Retirement Homes: There are few nursing or residential care homes in the Balearics.

Tradesmen: The Balearics' expatriate population is well served by foreign workers providing a vast range of services, from boat repairs to website design. Many advertise in the English-language press or in local bars and restaurants. While most are hard-working professionals, you should take care and ensure that you check references and obtain personal recommendations. Spanish tradesmen are generally excellent and many speak some English.

English-language Radio: None.

English-language Press: Most English newspapers are printed in Madrid and available daily at international newsagents throughout the islands. Some English and other foreign newspapers may arrive later in the day, or in the case of some US newspapers, the following day. The main local English-language publications are: *The Ibiza Sun*, published weekly, distributed free; *Mallorca Daily Bulletin*, published daily, price €0.90; *The Reader*, published weekly, price €1.50.

Consulates: Consular representation is generally available only in Majorca. See individual directories below for further details.

Churches: The main islands have churches from a variety of denominations – mainly Anglican and Protestant – and there are Catholic services in Spanish in churches everywhere. Information about meetings and services can be found in the local press and on notice boards.

Clubs: The large number of foreign residents on the Balearics has generated a wide range of clubs and activities, catering for everything from bridge to walking and theatre. There are branches of global social clubs, such as the Lions Club and Rotary International, while charitable and self-help groups such as Alcoholics Anonymous and animal welfare groups are also represented. Further details can be found in the local press and on notice boards. Spanish speakers can also join local Spanish clubs, of which there's a wide variety. The local town council will provide information about them.

Property

The Balearics' property market has been booming in recent years and is one of the healthiest in Spain. There's a wide variety of properties for sale, prices have been rising steadily (in common with the rest of Spain) and property on Majorca and Ibiza in particular is among the most expensive in Spain. Prices are expected to continue to rise and the islands' authorities have imposed strict building regulations. In some areas of Majorca, new construction has been halted, a policy which will eventually lead to a shortage of resale properties. There's also a lack of building land on the islands (because of the strict building regulations) and many areas are either protected or part of national parks. Property in the Balearics is generally considered to be a good investment and there's an excellent rental market.

A wide range of properties is available, including small studios in apartment blocks, huge villas on luxury developments and typical Majorcan stone mansions set in spectacular countryside. The cheapest property is found on Minorca in apartment blocks in the tourist resorts in the west of the island, the most expensive on Majorca and Ibiza. Inland, you can buy old houses and land reasonably cheaply, although restoration costs will push the price considerably higher.

Typical Homes: Property on the Balearics comes in all shapes and sizes, although the three main islands all have an abundance of apartment blocks in and around the resort areas, often with communal gardens and swimming pools. Luxury villas tend to be on the outskirts of resorts, around golf courses and in up-market developments near the main cities. Typical architecture depends on the particular island (see below for details).

Land: Land *can* be bought on the Balearics, although it's in short supply and in view of the strict building regulations it's essential to take professional advice before committing yourself to a purchase. Many buyers have found themselves with land on which they either cannot build or may only build a small property. Generally, the minimum plot size is at least 1,000m², but this varies with the area. Make sure that you have an official copy of all the land regulations from the local authorities before purchasing land, including the regulations concerning the type of construction permitted.

Rental Property: The Balearics' popularity with holidaymakers ensures that there's a thriving rental market on the islands, particularly for short-term lets (under six months), and many foreign property owners let their properties. Long-term rentals are generally difficult to find at short notice and you will need to plan ahead. Rents are high for most of the year, and during the high season they rocket. For rental costs in individual islands and areas, see the directories below.

Communications

Air: Majorca, Minorca and Ibiza all have international airports, well served by inexpensive charter flights from Britain, Germany and other European countries. Flights are also available from many airports on the Spanish mainland, although these can be expensive. Majorca's airport is Spain's busiest and receives some 20 million passengers per year, and both Ibiza's and Minorca's airport passenger numbers run to millions each year. Flights are reduced in winter, particularly to Minorca, and there are no inter-island flights. The islands' airports are well served by bus services to nearby resorts and the main towns. Taxis also provide a relatively inexpensive service and car hire is available at airports. Formentera has no airport and must be reached by sea – see below.

Sea: There are frequent ferry crossings to the Balearics from mainland Spain (Barcelona and the Costa Blanca), with an increased service during the summer (for details of crossing times, see island surveys below). There are also weekly sailings to Marseilles (France) and Genoa (Italy). Inter-island ferries are available, the ferry from Ibiza to Formentera being the only way to reach the island. Crossings can, however, be rough at any time of the year, particularly in winter, and services are sometimes suspended because of bad weather. Balearics' residents are often entitled to discounts on air and sea travel between the islands and mainland Spain.

Public Transport: Majorca boasts the Balearics' only train services. They're leisurely, run through beautiful scenery and are more of a tourist attraction than a means of getting around. Buses to and from the main towns and resorts provide an average service, although bus services to remoter areas tend to be infrequent. The islands' authorities plan to improve bus services and wish to encourage the use of public transport, although for now the best way to get around is by private transport.

Roads: The Balearics generally have good, well maintained roads, especially on the major routes. Majorca enjoys the best road system, with several stretches of dual carriageway around the capital and major resorts. Inland and in more inaccessible areas, roads may be little more than tracks suitable only for four-wheel drive vehicles. Petrol stations are plentiful around the resorts and in the main towns, but are few and far between in remote areas, and petrol is considerably more expensive than on the mainland.

Planned Developments

The islands' authorities and residents invariably agree that the Balearics, Majorca in particular, won't stand further development and there's growing support for a more ecological approach to tourism. Public opinion is moving away from mass tourism and towards conservation of the Balearics' unique scenery. Indeed, the islands' authorities have implemented an 'eco-tax' on all tourist stays in hotels and holiday apartments. This is a highly controversial move and was contested by the Spanish national government in the High Court. The tax was approved, however, and implemented in May 2002, the revenue being used for conservation projects. Therefore major developments seem unlikely in the future and construction will probably be limited to improving the existing infrastructure and essential services such as new roads and hospitals.

Employment Prospects

Job opportunities are plentiful in the high season, when there's an abundance of work available in the tourist sector, although hours can be long and pay modest or poor. Out of season, finding employment is more difficult and limited to the tourist and service sectors in the main towns and resorts. The ability to speak German and Spanish will greatly improve your chances of finding work.

Further Information

Useful Websites

🖳 www.balearics.com (a good general guide to the islands)
🖳 www.balearic-jobs.com (online seasonal job opportunities on the islands)

MAJORCA

Majorca (Mallorca in Spanish and pronounced 'ma-yorca') lies 150km (93mi) off the east coast of Spain and is the largest of the Balearics, covering an area of 3,640km^2 (1,405mi^2) and 95km (60mi) across at its widest point. A rugged mountain range (the Sierra de Tramontana) covers a fifth of the island, extending for 100km (62mi) along the north-western coast, from Isla Dragonara to Cabo Formentor. It has seven peaks over 1,000m (3,280ft), the highest of which is Puig Mayor (1,445m/4,750ft). In contrast with parts of the over-developed coastline, Majorca's rugged interior is empty, peaceful and unspoilt. Much of the island is beautiful, with a wide variety of landscapes, ranging from high mountains to extensive citrus groves and secluded coves.

Majorca is trying (with some success) to live down its reputation as a cut-price haven for lager louts on package tours, even going so far as to bulldoze some of its cheap hotels to discourage the louts from coming. Today, the ugly, low-quality, high-rises of the 1960s have fallen out of favour and new developments are mainly low-rise, low-density buildings. Majorca is also popular with the international jet set, and some of the world's rich and famous have homes there.

Advantages & Disadvantages

One of Majorca's main attractions is that it's an island of contrasts, with lively, dynamic resorts, unspoilt beaches and coves, spectacular natural areas and the Balearics' only real city, Palma, which has a rich cultural and architectural heritage. Other advantages are the pleasant climate and the wide variety of leisure activities, including the vibrant nightlife.

Drawbacks include overcrowding during the high season and a high cost of living, including some of Spain's most expensive property. Some people also find island life restrictive and parochial, although communications between Majorca and mainland Spain are generally good. Bear in mind that many resorts, particularly those in the north and east, close down either partially or completely in outside high season, when they become virtual ghost towns. Village life on the island has a reputation for being closed and unwelcoming to newcomers.

Major Towns & Places of Interest

Bay of Palma: The Bay of Palma, the wide and sheltered bay surrounding Palma, is home to several of Majorca's most popular resorts. The 'capital' of the Balearics and its only real city, **Palma de Majorca** (pop. 325,000) is home to over half of Majorca's population. It has a vibrant, cosmopolitan atmosphere and offers a wide range of cultural and leisure activities. The city also has several important monuments, including its Gothic castle and limestone cathedral, which dominates the skyline overlooking the bay. Palma's yacht club is one of the best in Spain, and the prestigious King's Sailing Cup regatta is held there every summer. (The Spanish royal family's summer residence is at the Marivent Palace, to the west of the city.) Palma has a large English-speaking population, many connected with the yachting industry.

Calvia lies to the west of the capital and claims to be the second-richest region in Europe (it was formerly a principality). Together with the Bay of Palma, the area boasts several of Majorca's most popular resorts. At the western end of the Bay are the resorts of **Peguera** and **Santa Ponça**, both attractive towns with extensive amenities. Inland is the town of **San Ferrer**, popular with permanent residents, partly because its property is cheaper than that on the coast.

At the eastern end of the Bay is **Magaluf**, which was marshland just a few decades ago but is now a prime example of the worst kind of 1960s over-development, with a plethora of ugly high-rise buildings. Despite this, it's Majorca's most popular resort, particularly with young people, and has a good beach and extensive facilities. East of Magaluf lies the popular resort of **Palmanova,** which also has many high-rise buildings, although fewer than Magaluf, and several of the capital's best residential suburbs, including **Portal Nous**, which is considered by many to have the finest marina in the Mediterranean. To the east of Palma are more residential suburbs and the popular resort of **S'Arenal**, with its many high-rise apartment blocks.

Although the Bay of Palma is highly developed, there are still a number of quiet beaches, coves and forested areas.

North-west Coast: In stark contrast to the excesses of Palma Bay, the mountainous north-west coast remains undeveloped. It's characterised by plunging cliffs and tiny coves, and there are also some attractive towns, including **Andratx**, smart and exceptionally beautiful and set in a valley of pine and almond trees. Nearby **Port d'Andratx**, likened to Saint Tropez, has many luxury homes, and the marina provides mooring for some of the Mediterranean's most spectacular craft. The area's lack of good beaches has meant that mass tourism has had little effect and the town has preserved much of its original character.

Cala Deià (home of the late British poet Robert Graves) is popular with the rich, famous and arty during the summer months, although it's deserted for the rest of the year. Inland lies the small town of **Valldemossa**. Further north up the coast lie **Sóller** and **Port de Sóller**, which together form the largest and most important town in the area. Sóller's vast olive groves and citrus orchards have brought prosperity to the town, which for centuries was practically cut off from the rest of Majorca by the surrounding mountainous terrain. Port de Sóller is the only natural harbour on the north side of the island and its inhabitants traditionally found it easier to sail to France than to cross the mountains to other parts of the island. This accounts for the area's decidedly French atmosphere. Railway enthusiasts can enjoy a trip on the vintage (circa 1900) train running from Palma to Sóller (the only other train in the Balearics runs from Palma to Inca) through tunnels, mountains and some of the island's best scenery. From Sóller, an equally ancient tram runs through orange and lemon groves to Port de Sóller.

North-east Coast: The Bays of Pollença and Alcudia in the north are home to several attractive towns and popular resorts. **Pollença** is an interesting town with a rich Roman architectural legacy and an auditorium, and the Port de Pollença is the largest resort in the area, with a popular marina. The medieval town of **Alcudia** lies on the opposite side of the bay and the surrounding villa developments are among the island's most exclusive. In the neighbouring bay is **Port d'Alcudia**, which is popular with British tourists, offering excellent beaches lined with hotels, apartment blocks and extensive amenities. Inland is the national park of S'Abufera, whose marshlands are famous for their rich bird life. Further south on the bay lies the resort of **Can Picafort**, which has seen extensive development over recent years and is popular with German visitors. Note that many of the resorts in this part of the island close out of season.

East Coast: Much of the east coast is unspoiled, with many isolated beaches and coves (only around 10 per cent of the coast has been 'sacrificed' to tourism). Resorts include **Portopetro**, a quiet fishing town, which has preserved much of its original character and is home to a Club Méditerranée resort. **Cala d'Or** is a busy, attractive, purpose-built resort with few high-rise buildings and is popular with British tourists. **Portocolom** is one of the island's most picturesque coastal towns and has experienced a lot of recent development. **Portocristo** is home to the spectacular Cuevas del Drac caves, one of the island's principal tourist attractions. **Cala Millor** and **Cala Bona** are two busy resorts which merge into one. Note that although amenities in these resorts are generally excellent, many close out of season.

Inland: The main inland towns are **Inca**, which lies in the centre of the island and is famous for its craft market, and **Manacor**, situated inland from Portocristo, and the centre of the island's artificial pearl industry (which was threatened by bankruptcy in early 2002).

Islands: The Cabrera island chain off the south coast of Majorca is a highly protected, uninhabited area of great ecological and natural significance. Majorca also has several small islands off its coasts. None of these is habitable.

Population

The total population of Majorca is around 660,000, with some 25,000 official foreign residents, mostly German and British. Unofficial figures, however, suggest that there are some 30,000 Britons living either permanently or for most of the year on Majorca. The island also plays host to millions of tourists every year and in 2000 nearly 3.5 million Britons and 4 million Germans visited it.

Climate

Majorca has a typical Mediterranean climate, with hot summers and mild winters. The average annual temperature is 21°C and the island has around 2,400 hours of sunshine per year. Although winters are generally mild on the coast, it isn't unusual for the inland mountains to be snow-covered during the coldest months. The south-west corner of the island is the warmest in the winter. Rainfall can be torrential, particularly during the autumn and winter, the southern part of the island being the driest. Note that tap water has a high mineral content and many people prefer to drink bottled water.

Cost of Living

Majorca has Spain's highest cost of living, exceeding that of both Madrid and Barcelona, although many would argue that it also has the highest standard of living. The Majorcan district of Calvia claims to be the richest in Spain and the second-richest in Europe after Monaco.

Crime Rate & Security

Official figures for 2001 show an increase of almost 40 per cent in crime on Majorca. Pick pocketing is rife on the island, particularly at markets and bus queues, and you must take particular care of your belongings in crowded places. Theft from hire cars is also common and Magaluf has problems with 'lager lout' violence in the summer. Inland and in more remote areas the crime rate is generally very low.

Amenities

Sports: Majorca has some of the Mediterranean's (if not the world's) best facilities for water-sports, particularly sailing, with over 40 marinas, ranging from small moorings in remote coves to large, bustling developments. The marina at Portals is considered to be the best, home to many exclusive and expensive craft. There are also numerous water-sports clubs along the coast offering just about every water-sport, including scuba diving (the diving around the small islands is considered to be of unique interest) and windsurfing. There are also numerous land-based sports clubs, and racket sports (e.g. tennis) are especially popular. Horse riding is available and the flat terrain of much of the island means that cycling is popular. Majorca is renowned for its golf courses, which comprise five 18-hole courses and one 9-hole. Most offer a 'pay-and-play' option, although a few are private. Further courses are planned.

Leisure: The island has a wide range of cultural and leisure activities, especially in Palma, where there's an extensive programme of recitals, concerts, ballets and plays throughout the year. The annual Chopin Festival is of particular note. Palma and many resorts have bustling nightlife and an endless choice of night spots, particularly at Portal Nous, although choice can be limited (or indeed non-existent) out of season.

Majorca's scenery and dramatic coastline make for interesting day or weekend trips, and rural tourism is growing in popularity. Walking and hiking are also popular. In true Spanish tradition, most towns and villages have an annual *fiesta*, usually based on a maritime or agricultural theme. Of particular note are the Saint Sebastian celebrations in Palma during January and the Saint John festivities throughout the island in June.

Majorca has several theme parks, including Marineland at Magaluf with its dolphin shows, the Aquarium at Portocristo, Natura Parc near Santa Eugenia and Safari Zoo near Sa Coma. Magaluf also has a Western (i.e. Wild West) theme park and a pirate adventure centre. The island has three water-parks, at Alcudia, El Arenal and Magaluf, all of which are open only during the summer.

English-language Cinema & Theatre: One cinema in Palma shows one film a week in English with Spanish sub-titles.

Shopping Centres & Markets: Palma has excellent shopping facilities, including the El Corte Inglés department store and many chain stores and international boutiques. Most resorts are well provided with supermarkets and small shops, although many close out of season. The island has several important markets, the craft markets at Inca being of particular note. Markets are held on Mondays in Calvia and Manacor, Tuesdays in Alcudia and Can Picafort, Wednesdays in Andratx and Porto Pollença, Thursdays in Inca and Arenal, Saturdays in Palma and Sóller, and on Sundays in Alcudia.

Foreign Food & Products: A wide range of foreign food is available at supermarkets and specialist shops, particularly British and German products.

Restaurants & Bars: Majorca has numerous restaurants and bars, particularly in resort areas and Palma, which, along with Portal Nous, is considered to have the best restaurants on the island. All types of cuisine are offered, although fast food outlets are most prevalent in resorts. Many restaurants specialise in local cuisine, based mainly on pork, seafood and rice.

Services

International & Private Schools: Majorca is the best served of the Balearic islands for international schools, of which four offer a British curriculum and one an American. All are located in or near the capital. There are numerous private schools on the island, the vast majority in or near Palma. Several are run by religious orders and most offer a bi-lingual curriculum (Spanish and Catalan).

Hospitals & Clinics: The Son Dureta Hospital in Palma is the main public hospital for the Balearics, a prestigious university hospital. The only other public hospital on Majorca is at Manacor. Palma also has a few private hospitals. Most main towns and resorts have a public health centre, sometimes offering emergency treatment. There are also several private clinics, situated mainly in Palma and the main resort and residential areas.

Doctors & Dentists: Many English-speaking medical professionals are available on the island, mainly in Palma and resort areas.

Tradesmen: The island has many foreign companies and workers, serving most needs, the majority based in the Bay of Palma.

English-language Radio: None.

English-language Press: *Mallorca Daily Bulletin*, published daily, price €0.90; *The Reader*, published weekly, price €1.50; *Santa Ponça Scene*, a free guide to the town, published monthly in the summer and once during the winter.

Consulates: Consulates representing several countries, including Austria, Belgium, France, Germany, Ireland, Italy, Netherlands, the UK and the USA, are located in Palma.

Churches: A few services are held in English, e.g. the Anglican service at Santa Ponsa. Details of service times and venues can be found in the local press and on notice boards.

Clubs: A variety of expatriate clubs operate on Majorca, including several bridge and sports clubs, including (surprisingly) cricket.

Property

Majorca has some of Spain's most expensive property and prices have been rising steadily over the last decade, a tendency that looks set to continue. Property on the island is therefore regarded as an excellent investment, particularly typical Majorcan houses near the capital. Apartments and villas are also good investments for rental accommodation, which is in great demand on the island.

The island's most expensive property is found inland near Palma and around Andratx, where large villas and typical Majorcan mansions can reach € millions. Majorca's cheapest property is generally found on the western side of Palma Bay, particularly in the small town of San Ferrer, which is favoured by foreign residents because of its relatively inexpensive property. All property on Majorca, however, is expensive compared with the rest of Spain.

Construction on the island has been extensive in recent years, and in 2000 the average price for construction was around €1,250 per m², which is much higher than the national average. In common with all of Spain's islands (and indeed, with most of Spain's tourist resorts), the Majorcan authorities are now dramatically reducing the number of building licences issued, and there are strict regulations in force regarding the size and type of construction permitted. In several areas of the island, including most resorts around Palma Bay, new construction isn't currently allowed at all. This will inevitably lead to a shortage of resale property, which will add to the area's investment potential.

Typical Homes: Majorca is famous for its palatial villas, built from local sandstone and found mainly inland and in the capital. They're popular with foreign buyers, although prices tend to be high because restoration work is invariably carried out by hand, by highly specialised craftsmen. Prices for a typical stone house start at around €400,000 (the sky's the limit for an old castle or palace set in acres of countryside). There's also a plentiful supply of village houses needing restoration, with prices starting at around €75,000. You should, however, bear in mind that restoration costs will greatly inflate the initial price.

Cost of Housing: The following prices are intended only as a guide and were current in mid-2002.

- **Palma**

  Properties in the old town are popular and in great demand, and they're generally considered to have good rental potential. Prices range from around €150,000 for a small two-bedroom apartment to over €1,800,000 for a 'palace'. In the suburbs, two-bedroom apartments cost from €150,000 and three-bedroom apartments start at €200,000.

- **Bay of Palma**

  Two-bedroom apartment: from €120,000;
  Three-bedroom apartment: from €170,000;
  Small villa: from €450,000.

- **Andratx**

  Two-bedroom apartment with sea view: from €200,000;
  Three-bedroom apartment with sea view: from €250,000;

Townhouse: from €300,000;
Large villa: from €800,000.

- **North-east Coast**
  Three-bedroom apartment: from €190,000;
  Small semi-detached villa: from €270,000 to €470,000;
  Villa: from €500,000.

Land: Land is expensive on Majorca, where strict building controls and quotas have been imposed by the authorities. The number of annual building licenses has been drastically reduced and it's becoming increasingly difficult to build you own home. You should avoid purchasing land without a building permit. Plots with a building permit cost around €285 per m^2.

Rental Accommodation: As in most popular tourist destinations, there's an abundance of holiday and short-term rental accommodation on the island. The choice is wide, ranging from small studio apartments to palatial villas. Long-term rentals are more difficult to find, although easier than in some parts of Spain. Rents on the island are high, and monthly rates for a one-bedroom apartment start at €750, a two-bedroom apartment at €1,100 and a villa at €1,800. Short-term and holiday rates are considerably higher, particularly during the summer.

Communications

Air: Majorca's San Juan airport (situated 11km/7mi east of Palma) is Spain's busiest and in 2001 handled almost 20 million passengers. Flights are available to and from most major European cities, particularly in Britain and Germany, and most flights are charter. Flights from mainland Spain are also available, the least expensive from Barcelona and Valencia (☎ 971-789-099 for information).

Sea: Palma has frequent ferry services to and from Alicante (around ten hours), Barcelona (eight hours in a conventional ferry or four hours by catamaran) and Valencia (six hours by fast ferry), and to Ibiza, Mahon and Cabrera, plus Genoa (Italy) and Marseilles (France) in summer. There are also ferries from Alcudia (on the north-east coast) to Minorca. Boats and water taxis operate between some Majorcan resorts during summer.

Public Transport: Public transport on the island ranges from excellent in the capital and the southern resorts to unreliable and infrequent in other regions. Palma has a comprehensive bus service and there are daily services from the main towns and resorts to Palma, which run several times a day to the main towns. Note that buses are often very crowded, especially on market days, and may not run outside high season. Bus services in the rest of the island can be infrequent or non-existent and private transport is often essential. Train services connect Palma with Inca and Sóller, although the latter route is primarily a tourist attraction. Taxis are plentiful and usually inexpensive, particularly if there are several passengers.

Roads: Roads from the capital to the main resorts are generally excellent and there are dual-carriageways running the length of the Bay of Palma and from the capital to Marratxi and Inca inland. The journey from Palma to Sóller has been improved by the Sóller tunnel, although it has been subject to much controversy due to political corruption surrounding its construction. Roads to remoter areas and along the north coast are often tortuous and driving can be dangerous. Although the island is small and distances appear short, journey times on many roads are relatively long. Allow 90 minutes for journeys from the airport to resorts on the east side of the island and two hours to those in the north. Resorts on the Bay of Palma can be reached in around an hour. Note also that in the more remote areas, petrol stations are few and far between.

Planned Developments

Majorca has seen vast development in recent years, over a third of which has been concentrated around Palma. This has caused alarm bells to be sounded by locals and ecologists, who claim that the island's energy and water resources will soon be stretched to the limit. Many also feel that the island's quality of life is in danger of being compromised. Majorca's authorities have responded to these concerns by introducing strict building controls, as well as the controversial 'eco-tax' for all tourists and visitors (see page 35). It therefore appears that future development on the island will be severely limited.

Employment Prospects

Majorca has one of Spain's lowest unemployment rates (around 6 per cent) and job prospects are generally very good, although limited to the service sector, which employs over 70 per cent of the working population. The ability to speak German (as well as Spanish) is a distinct advantage.

Further Information

Useful Publications

- *AA Essential Mallorca*, T. Kelly (AA Publishing)
- *A Woman Unknown*, L. Graves (Virago Press)
- *Landscapes of Mallorca*, V. Crespi-Green (Sunflower Books)
- *Rough Guide to Mallorca*, P. Lee (Rough Guides)

Useful Websites

🖳 www.mallorcanow.com (tourist and general information)
🖳 www.mallorcaonline.com (useful tourist and general information)

MINORCA

Minorca (Menorca in Spanish) lies 40km (25mi) north-east of Majorca and is the second-largest of the Balearics. It's 48km (30mi) long and 15km (9mi) wide, with 189km (117mi) of coastline. Minorca has a rich past and is dotted with prehistoric remains unique to the island and believed to be part of the ancient Talayot culture. The island was under British rule during much of the 18th century and the British influence, particularly in some of the architecture, is still much in evidence. Minorca is the least developed and quietest of the three main islands. Almost half of the island's land is protected. It's noted for its rugged coastline, rolling green landscape and sandy beaches, although the general topography is rather monotonous. Minorca has over 120 beaches, most in secluded coves, regarded by many as the best in the Balearics. It has a slow, relaxed pace of life and isn't for those who want to rave all night (try Ibiza).

Advantages & Disadvantages

Minorca's tranquillity compared with Ibiza and Majorca can be an advantage or a disadvantage depending on your requirements, as even in the high season most of the island is quiet. Minorca boasts some attractive towns and villages, and some of the Balearics' best beaches. Disadvantages include the almost constant strong winds, the lack of things to do outside the high season (and after midnight throughout the year) and poor communications during the winter.

Major Towns & Places of Interest

Mahon: The island's capital (Maó in Catalan) lies on the east coast. It's an attractive city with a port situated on one of the world's largest natural harbours and considered to be one of the most beautiful in the Mediterranean. The city has several notable monuments and some fine Georgian architecture. Amenities are generally good and include Minorca's best shopping.

Ciudadela: The ancient former capital (Ciutadella in Catalan) lies at the opposite end of the island to Mahon. It's an attractive harbour town with several palaces in the old quarter and an interesting cathedral. Ciudadela has a range of amenities and is famous for its Saint John festivities in June, which include jousting tournaments. South of the town lie the resorts of **Los Delfines**, the nearest Minorca comes to a package holiday resort (its brash, noisy atmosphere seems out of place on this tranquil island), **Cala en Blanes** and **Torre del Ram**. These three resorts are probably the island's most developed and have the widest choice of amenities.

South Coast: Most of Minorca's resorts are situated on the south coast, which is characterised by deep gorges and towering cliffs. To the south of Mahon lies **Es Castell** (known as Georgetown by the British), Spain's most easterly town and a popular resort. There are also a number of relatively new resorts on the south and east coasts, including **Binibeca Vell,** with its attractive village and villa developments, **Cala en Porter**, one of Minorca's oldest resorts, which perches high on the cliffs, **Punta Prima**, one of the fastest-developing areas on the island, **Cala Gardana**, which is home to one of the island's most beautiful bays, and **S'Algar**. Because of the terrain along the south coast, resorts tend to be isolated from each other.

North Coast: The northern part of the island is mainly rocky and dotted with pine trees. It is virtually undeveloped, except for a few small resorts. These include the popular **Arenall d'en Castell** and **Fornells** (famous for its lobster dishes)**,** an attractive village in a sheltered bay that has managed to preserve much of its original character in spite of its development into an upmarket resort, and **Port Addaia**, which has an attractive marina and a small villa development. The main inland towns include **Alayor**, which dates from medieval times and is famous for its cheese industry, **Ferreries** and **Mercadal**.

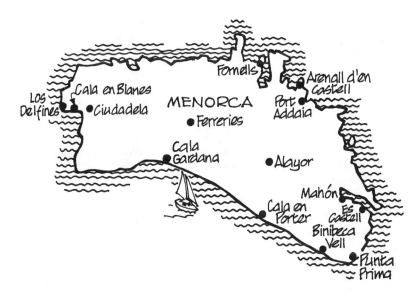

Population

Minorca's population is around 71,000, of which some 2,000 are official foreign residents (mainly German and British), although unofficial figures are higher.

Climate

Minorca has a generally pleasant climate, although it's famous for its almost permanent wind, which is strongest and coldest from October to April. The wind helps to temper the heat in summer, although it can make beach conditions unpleasant. Indeed, locals choose which beach to visit depending on which direction the wind is blowing that day. Average temperatures are 10°C (50°F) in January and 24°C (75°F) in July. Rainfall is concentrated in the autumn and winter months, particular October and November.

Crime Rate & Security

The island generally has a low crime rate and, unlike Ibiza and Majorca, doesn't suffer from 'lager lout' violence.

Amenities

Sports: As is the case throughout the Balearics, water-sports reign supreme on Minorca, which has several marinas with sailing clubs. Other water-sports include windsurfing, which is particularly good on the east and north coasts, and scuba diving off the island's many isolated coves and cliffs. Horse riding is popular and there are several private sports clubs. Minorca has only one golf course, at Son Parc on the north coast, which has nine holes but is being extended to 18.

Leisure: Mahon and Ciudadela have year-round cultural programmes, including classical music recitals and concerts, theatre productions and operas in the Teatro Principal in Mahon. The resorts also have a variety of entertainment, although unlike Ibiza and Majorca, practically everything closes at midnight and little is offered outside high season. Walking and hiking are also popular on Minorca. The island's only theme park is a water-park at Los Delfines on the west coast.

English-language Cinema & Theatre: None, except for the occasional visiting theatre group.

Shopping Centres & Markets: The best shops are in Mahon, which has a wide choice of chain stores and boutiques. Shopping is also good in Ciudadela. Most of the resorts have a selection of supermarkets and small shops, although many shut out of season. Markets are held twice a week at Mahon, Ciudadela, Es Castell and Ferreries.

Foreign Food & Products: Minorca offers a fair range of foreign produce, mainly British and German, available from supermarkets and small shops around the island. Mahon has an English lending library.

Restaurants & Bars: The larger resorts and main towns have a fair selection of restaurants and bars, although in the resorts these may close out of season. Throughout the island, bars tend to close by midnight and live entertainment is limited.

Services

International & Private Schools: There's a British school in Mahon. Private schools in Minorca are 'maintained' and offer a Spanish curriculum, and there are also several private nursery schools.

Hospitals & Clinics: Minorca has only one hospital, at Verge del Toro just outside the capital. There are no private hospitals. There are public health centres in the main towns and also several private clinics, mainly in Mahon and Ciudadela.

Doctors & Dentists: Most medical professionals on the island speak English.

Tradesmen: A limited number of foreign workers serve the expatriate population.

English-language Radio: None.

English-language Press: *Roqueta*, a monthly magazine, is available from bookshops in Mahon, price €1.50.

Consulates: Only Germany has consular representation on Minorca. A number of other countries are represented on Majorca (see page 41).

Churches: An Anglican church in Es Castell has weekly services in English.

Clubs: There's a lively expatriate club scene on the island, based mainly in Mahon and to a lesser extent in Ciudadela. It includes Minorca Cricket Club and the International Rotary Club.

Property

Minorca is popular with the British, who have traditionally been the main foreign homebuyers, although in recent years it has also become popular with Germans. With the exception of a few eyesores, the island is largely unspoilt and there are few high-rise buildings, with low-level, Moorish-style architecture predominating. The sheltered south coast is primarily given over to purpose-built holiday homes and isn't well suited to permanent residence.

Of the four main Balearic islands, Minorca has the cheapest property, although prices in the Mahon area (where the most expensive property is found) are on a par with Majorca. The cheapest property is situated around the resorts of Los Delfines and Cala en Blanes on the west side of the island. Property on Minorca is generally considered to be a good investment.

Typical Homes: Old houses in Mahon and Ciudadela often have an abundance of character and are much prized by foreign buyers. The island's traditional Mediterranean architecture has a Georgian influence (it was ruled by the British for part of the 18th century), reflected in houses without balconies, and the prevalence of sash windows, doorknockers and latches. Traditional properties in need of extensive restoration are available from €125,000, while houses in a good state of repair start at €575,000. Bear in mind that, although property in need of extensive refurbishment may appear cheap, restoration costs are high and will substantially increase the price.

Cost of Housing: The following prices are intended only as a guide and were current in mid-2002.

- **Mahon area**
  Two-bedroom apartment: from €140,000;
  Three-bedroom apartment: from €190,000;
  Villa: from €400,000.

- **South coast**
  Two-bedroom apartment: from €130,000;
  Villa: from €240,000.

- **Ciudadela & west coast**
  Two-bedroom apartment: from €100,000;
  Three-bedroom apartment: from €180,000;
  Villa: from €210,000.

Land: Land is available on Minorca, although as is the case on Ibiza and Majorca, there are strict building restrictions and you should ensure that any plot you're interested in has a building licence (or that one will be obtained) before committing yourself to a purchase. Plots of around 1,000m² are available from around €30,000 and plots with an approved building project cost from €280,000 (including the building).

Rental Accommodation: There's an abundance of holiday and short-term rental accommodation on Minorca, and although long-term rentals are more difficult to obtain, you can find reasonable winter rates. Rents tend to be high, monthly rates for a one-bedroom apartment starting at €750, two-bedroom apartments at €1,100 and villas at €1,800. Short-term and holiday rates are considerably higher, particularly during the summer.

Communications

Air: Minorca has a small international airport (5km/3mi south of Mahon), which receives around 3 million passengers per year. There are charter flights from several European capitals, although these are concentrated in the high season, and in winter there may be no direct flights to some destinations. Flights to mainland Spain are also available, although fares are high.

Sea: Ferries run from Mahon to the mainland (11 hours to Barcelona, 15 hours to Valencia with an overnight service available) and there are also services to Palma and Alcudia on Majorca, but not to Ibiza. Crossings during winter are often suspended on account of bad weather or high winds.

Public Transport: There's a regular bus service from Mahon to Ciudadela, and from both towns to nearby resorts. Services to other parts of the island are infrequent or non-existent and all services are reduced outside the high season. Private transport is often essential.

Roads: The island's roads are generally of good quality, the main route running through the centre of the island between Mahon and Ciudadela with others branching off it to the island's main towns and resorts. A journey across the island typically takes around 45 minutes (the island's speed limit is 90kph/56mph), although local roads are considerably slower. Roads in remoter areas are sometimes little more than tracks, suitable only for four-wheel drive vehicles. Petrol stations are few and far between outside the main towns, and petrol is expensive.

Planned Developments

The ambitious 'Territorial Plan for Minorca' will be implemented by the authorities over the coming years and places great importance on the conservation of the island's coastline, natural parks, agricultural land and rural villages. Minorca also plans to increase the size of its national parks and marine reserves, and to strictly limit future immigration. There are also advanced plans to improve the island's road network and to invest in public transport.

Employment Prospects

Employment prospects are good during the high season, although you need to arrive early to be sure of securing a job and opportunities are limited to the tourist sector. Outside the high season, there isn't much available.

Further Information

Useful Publications

- *AA Essential Menorca*, T. Kelly (AA Publishing)
- *Landscapes of Menorca*, R. Ansell (Sunflower Books)
- *Mini Rough Guide to Menorca*, P. Lee (Rough Guides)

Useful Websites

⌨ www.menorcadigital.com (mainly holiday information)

IBIZA

Ibiza is located 83km (52mi) off the Spanish east coast and 40km (25mi) south-west of Majorca. It covers an area of 572km² (220mi²) and has 179km (105mi) of coastline. Ibiza is a beautiful island, almost Greek in appearance, with a coastline of fine beaches, interspersed with steep cliffs and barely accessible coves. Inland, there's unspoilt countryside and fields of olives, almonds, carob groves, melons and vines. The island is noted for its unique quality of light and its rural architecture.

Ibiza was discovered by artists and the international jet set in the early 1960s, since when it has never looked back. Mass tourism arrived in the mid-1960s, although the over-development which ran riot on Majorca and the mainland *costas* was mostly avoided thanks to strict planning controls. The island still has its share of high-rise eye-sores, however, particularly around San Antonio.

Ibiza isn't simply the trendiest of the Balearics, but one of Europe's 'hottest' destinations. Summer attracts hordes of young Europeans (mainly British and German), in search of all-night parties and discos. The island boasts excellent restaurants and vibrant nightlife and is home to Europe's largest and boldest dance clubs (it's the spiritual home of the 'Euro-raver'). The island's visitors and foreign residents are noted for their love of excess, and 'tolerance' is the watchword if you plan to live here: the island has a large gay population and nude sunbathing is commonplace. Hippies are also a feature of the summer crowd. Winter is quieter, although parts of the island are still busy.

Advantages & Disadvantages

Ibiza's beauty and mild climate are strong attractions, although many people are also drawn to its unique nightlife. The fact that much of the island remains undeveloped means that you can have the best of both worlds: the tranquillity of a deserted beach or an almond grove by day and the exuberance of the club scene by night. Disadvantages include the pressures of mass tourism during the summer (when most resort areas are over-flowing), high property prices and limited amenities in some areas. Also bear in mind that rural life on the island can be lonely and that the local population is sometimes reluctant to embrace outsiders, especially foreigners.

Major Towns & Places of Interest

Ibiza Town is the island's capital and most residents live either there or in the compact suburbs to the east and west of the town, such as **Figueretas** and **Playa d'en Bossa**, both of which are busy resorts. Ibiza Town enjoys a stunning location and is a well-preserved, attractive, old walled town with narrow cobbled streets and one of Europe's oldest medieval fortresses. The island's jet set moor their yachts at its luxurious marina and patronise the world-famous casino. Most of the island's best night clubs are in or near the capital.

San Antonio is on the west of the island and is the second busiest resort, its attractive beaches lined with high-rise apartment blocks. The marina (Portus Magnus) is one of the Mediterranean's oldest ports. San Antonio is popular with young tourists and has an unfortunate reputation for 'lager louts', who are lured by the resort's vibrant night-life.

To the east of Ibiza Town lie several of the island's main resort areas. Although busy, they're generally quieter than either the capital or San Antonio, and Ibiza's authorities promote them as upmarket family resorts. This area includes attractive **Cala Llonga**, until recently accessible only by boat but now a thriving resort, and nearby **Santa Eulalia del Río**, Ibiza's third-largest resort and the island's cultural and gastronomic centre. Although Santa Eulalia des Río has undergone extensive development over recent years, it has managed to retain much of its original character. It's situated at the mouth of the island's only river and boasts a marina as well as good beaches. **Es Cana**, further to the east, is also an attractive, popular resort. In the north-east corner of the island, in one of its most picturesque regions, lies **Portinatx**, a small but rapidly developing resort.

Population

Ibiza's population is around 87,000, a figure that increases dramatically during the summer. There are officially some 6,000 resident foreigners, mainly Germans and British, although unofficial figures are much higher.

Climate

Ibiza is regarded as having the best climate in the islands, with mild, sunny winters (although snow isn't completely unknown) and pleasant summers. Average temperatures are 12°C (54°F) in January and 25°C (77°F) in July. The island suffers from a chronic shortage of water.

Crime Rate & Security

Crime on Ibiza has risen sharply in recent years, and petty crime such as pick pocketing is particularly common during the summer in the resorts. 'Lager lout' violence in San Antonio reached epidemic proportions in the summer of 2001, forcing the local authorities to take action. Drug-related crime is also a problem, particularly in San Antonio and around the night clubs. An increased police presence and stricter licensing laws are expected to help reduce crime levels. In more remote areas and inland the crime rate is very low.

Amenities

Sports: Sports facilities on Ibiza are of good quality and are dominated by water-sports, which are offered at several marinas. If you prefer dry land, there's a race course which has night horse-racing during the summer. There are also numerous tennis clubs and riding centres. At present, there's only one golf course on Ibiza, located at Roca Llisa just north of Cala Llonga, although there are plans for another at San Antonio.

Leisure: Ibiza has a lively cultural scene, with a year-round programme of concerts, plays and recitals, mainly held in Ibiza Town and Santa Eulalia. In the summer months, Ibiza is the party capital of the world and the seven main clubs offer among the wildest and most extravagant nightlife available anywhere. Walking and hiking in the island's spectacular scenery are popular, as is rural tourism in the inland villages. Ibiza has two water-parks, at Ibiza Town and Playa d'en Bossa, and there's an aquarium at San Antonio.

English-language Cinema & Theatre: There's no English-language cinema on Ibiza. Local theatre groups, such as the Theatre Trust, stage regular plays and shows for the expatriate population.

Shopping Centres & Markets: All resort areas have good shopping facilities, although these may be reduced outside the high season. Ibiza Town has an excellent range of shops, particularly fashion boutiques. Ibiza is famous for its 'hippy' markets, held weekly at various locations around the island, including Es Cana, which has the largest and most famous.

Foreign Food & Products: Supermarkets on Ibiza stock a fair range of foreign produce, mainly British and German. There are also some specialist shops, including a British butcher.

Restaurants & Bars: Ibiza offers a wealth of bars and restaurants, concentrated mainly around the resorts. The most exclusive are found in the Ibiza Town marina and the old quarter. Fast food is prevalent in the resorts, although some restaurants specialise in local cuisine.

Services

International & Private Schools: Ibiza has one international school offering a British curriculum (at Santa Eulalia) and there's also a German school. There are few private schools on Ibiza, which are limited to the capital.

Hospitals & Clinics: Ibiza has just one public hospital, located at Can Misses, where waiting lists for treatment are among the longest in Spain. There are no private hospitals on the island. Ibiza has public health centres in the main towns and resorts, and one private clinic in the capital.

Doctors & Dentists: Most medical professionals on the island speak English.

Tradesmen: A limited number of foreign workers serve the expatriate population.

English-language Radio: None.

English-language Press: *The Ibiza Sun* (no relation to the British *Sun*) is published weekly and distributed free at points around the island.

Consulates: Only Germany and the Netherlands have consular representation on Ibiza. A number of other countries are represented on Majorca (see page 41).

Churches: Services on Ibiza are limited to Catholic services in Spanish.

Clubs: Ibiza has a lively expatriate club scene, including theatre groups, sports clubs (including women's netball!) and charities such as Age Concern. See the local press and local notice boards for details.

Property

The property market on Ibiza is buoyant and prices have been rising steadily over the last decade. This trend is expected to continue, especially as stricter controls and quotas on new construction are introduced. Property is generally more expensive on Ibiza than on the other Balearic islands and there are many 'millionaire' villas. The coast between Ibiza Town and Santa Eulalia is particularly exclusive. Like Majorca, Ibiza has become increasingly popular with Germans, who are the main property buyers.

Typical Homes: Typical Ibizan architecture is quite unlike much property on Majorca and Minorca. Ibizan houses have a distinctly Moorish influence, with a cuboid shape, white-washed walls and flat roofs. Most houses have small windows to help reduce the summer heat.

Cost of Housing: Property on Ibiza is expensive and prices are similar across the island, although apartments are slightly cheaper in San Antonio than in other parts of the island. Two-bedroom apartments cost from €200,000 (from €150,000 in San Antonio), while three-bedroom apartments start at €250,000 and villas at €500,000.

Cost of Land: Land is very expensive on Ibiza and, because of the strict controls and quotas imposed by the authorities, it's becoming increasingly difficult to find anywhere to build. **You shouldn't buy land that doesn't already have a building permit.**

Rental Accommodation: As in most popular tourist areas, there's an abundance of holiday and short-term rental accommodation on Ibiza. Choice is wide, ranging from small studio apartments to palatial mansions. Long-term rentals are, however, more difficult to obtain and rents are high. Monthly rents start at around €800 for a one-bedroom apartment, €1,100 for a two-bedroom apartment and €1,800 for a villa. Short-term and holiday rates are considerably higher, particularly during the summer.

Communications

Air: Ibiza's small international airport receives around 4.4 million passengers a year, mainly via summer charter flights from Britain and Germany. Flight frequency is much reduced in the winter and options are often limited to flights via the mainland airports of Barcelona and Valencia. Note that domestic flights are expensive.

Sea: Ferries connect Ibiza Town with Barcelona (ten hours), Denia (under three hours) and Valencia (around three hours) on the mainland and with Palma and Formentera. Formentera is just 7km (4.3mi) from Ibiza, although it's a one-hour ferry or 20-minute catamaran trip because of the strong currents (take your seasickness pills). Ferries also run from San Antonio to Denia. Water taxis operate during the high season between the main towns and resorts and are a good way of getting around.

Public Transport: Ibiza has a good bus service between the resorts and main towns, although services to other parts of the island are infrequent or non-existent. If you live inland, private transport is essential. Special buses run at night during the summer to and from the resorts and the main clubs. Taxis are plentiful and prices are generally reasonable, although you should agree the price before starting a journey, as taxis don't have meters.

Roads: Ibiza has good roads (many of those connecting the main resorts with the capital were rebuilt in the mid-1980s). Traffic congestion is a problem during the summer months, particularly around Ibiza Town, although it's hoped that a new inner ring road will help to reduce the problem. Roads in remoter parts of the island tend to be poor and may be unsuitable for anything other than four-wheel drive vehicles. Petrol on Ibiza is more expensive than on the two other main islands and considerably more expensive than in mainland Spain.

Planned Developments

Strict building controls mean that future development on Ibiza will be confined to essential infrastructure improvements, such as an extension to the airport and the construction of desalination plants to lessen water shortages. A large auditorium is also planned and will be built either in Ibiza Town or at Santa Eulalia.

Employment Prospects

Job prospects are good during the high season, although you need to arrive early to be sure of securing a job and work is generally limited to the tourist sector. Outside the high season, there's isn't much work available.

Further Information

Useful Publications

- *AA Essential Ibiza and Formentera*, R. Sale (AA Publishing)
- *Ibiza Insight Pocket Guide* (Insight Guides)
- *Seagulls in My Soup*, T. Jones (Adlard Coles Nautical)

Useful Websites

- www.ibiza-spotlight.com (a useful website for tourists and residents)
- www-ibizaholidays.com (a website for tourists)

Puerto del Carmen

3.

THE CANARY ISLANDS

The Canary Islands (or Canaries) are one of the world's top tourist destinations (particularly in winter) and attract almost 10 million visitors per year. They're situated in the Atlantic, 95km (60mi) off the north-west coast of Africa and 1,150km (700mi) from Spain. There are seven inhabited Canaries: (in order of size) Tenerife, Fuerteventura, Gran

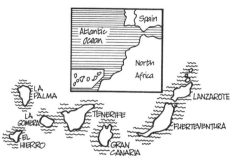

Canaria, Lanzarote, La Palma, Gomera and Hierro, with a total area of 7,272km² (2,808mi²).

The islands are divided into eastern and western administrative provinces: the greener western province of Santa Cruz de Tenerife includes the islands of Tenerife, La Palma, Gomera and Hierro, while the more arid eastern province of Las Palmas de Gran Canaria encompasses Gran Canaria, Fuerteventura and Lanzarote. Volcanic in origin, the Canaries are among the world's most dramatic islands, with imposing geological formations and spectacular vegetation. They were colonised by Spain in the 15th century, before which their inhabitants (the Guanches) were said to have been living in the 'Stone Age'.

The Canaries attract a potpourri of foreign residents, although Germans and British predominate and the islands' *lingua franca* is English. Tourism is the main industry, although fishing and farming (bananas and wine grapes) are also important. One of the Canaries' attractions is that they aren't incorporated into the European Union's tax system and enjoy lower taxes than the mainland. They also offer tax incentives for investors and offshore companies.

For the purposes of this book, the Canary Islands have been divided into five areas: Gran Canaria, Tenerife, Lanzarote, Fuerteventura, and the less-visited La Gomera, El Hierro and La Palma combined as one. Each area is described in detail after the following general comments. Map of islands here.

Advantages & Disadvantages

The Canaries' principal strength is the climate, which is warm and pleasant year-round and generally considered to be one of the world's best (see below). The islands' natural beauty is another attraction, particularly that of the less visited islands. Communications are generally good and the islands are easily reached by air from most parts of the world; inter-island communication is also reasonable. The Canaries have a favourable tax regime, including a lower

VAT rate than the rest of Spain and incentives for investors and offshore companies, including the Special Canary Islands Zone (*ZEC*) scheme.

Disadvantages include the vast influx of tourists, particularly in the high season, which runs from November to February, which causes some parts of the islands to become very crowded. Certain parts of the Canaries, e.g. Tenerife's south coast and Gran Canaria's resort of Maspalomas, are in danger of becoming over-developed, and even traditionally quieter islands such as Lanzarote have seen extensive construction in recent years. Island life can also seem claustrophobic and parochial to some people. The popularity of the islands, however, suggests that the benefits of living on the Canaries far outweigh the drawbacks. Note also that it's difficult to generalise: the diversity of the islands and their differences in population, size and amenities mean that advantages and disadvantages vary considerably from island to island (see island profiles beginning on page 69).

Population

The Canaries have a total population of around 1.7 million, including approximately 130,000 official foreign residents, half of whom are from the EU (mainly Britain and Germany). The unofficial figure, however, is substantially higher, because many foreigners, particularly Britons, aren't official residents, even though they spend much of the year on the Canaries, and the Canaries' population is growing rapidly. Most Canary Islanders live on Gran Canaria and Tenerife.

Climate

One of the Canaries' main attractions is the climate, described as 'eternal spring' (the Romans called them the 'Fortunate Islands'). Winters are mild or warm, summers are temperate and daytime temperatures range between 20°C and 27°C (68°F and 81°F) throughout the year. The inland region of Tenerife experiences around 3,400 hours of sunshine per year, the highest in Spain. Rainfall (mostly between November and February) is low and ranges from less than 100mm (4in) per year on Fuerteventura and Lanzarote to 750mm (30in) on inland Gran Canaria and Tenerife. The 'best climate in the world' is reportedly found 91m (300ft) above sea level on the south of Gran Canaria (Fuerteventura and Lanzarote have similar conditions). Unsurprisingly, the islands – particularly Fuerteventura and Lanzarote – have a shortage of natural drinking water, much of which is provided by desalination plants. The islands occasionally suffer sandstorms from the Sahara desert and thick clouds of suspended, fine sand (known as *calima*), which can descend for several days at a time, causing respiratory problems.

Cost of Living

The cost of living on the Canaries is similar to that in other popular Spanish tourist resorts, although property is among Spain's most expensive. Some imported items such as food and construction materials are expensive, although local produce (of which there's an abundance) is cheap.

Crime Rate & Security

The Canaries generally have an average crime rate for Spain, although it's higher in the main tourist resorts, where pick pocketing and petty theft are rife and theft from hire cars is common. In rural areas, on the other hand, crime is virtually unheard of. You're advised never to leave valuables in your car, always to lock your property when you aren't there (even if you just pop to the swimming pool) and to watch your belongings when you're in crowded places.

Amenities

Sports: There are many opportunities to practise a wealth of sports on the Canaries, particularly water-sports such as sailing, windsurfing, surfing (the islands have some of the best windsurfing and surfing in the world) and scuba diving. On land, most large municipalities have a sports centre, usually with extensive facilities including an indoor pool, where activities and membership are often subsidised. There are also numerous private sports centres and an abundance of gymnasiums and tennis and riding clubs.

While golf isn't as popular as in other parts of Spain (such as the Costa del Sol), the Canaries have several courses, located mainly on Gran Canaria and Tenerife. The courses' lush greens provide a dramatic contrast with the arid landscape of southern Tenerife. Most courses offer a 'pay and play' facility and a round costs from €35. The less populated islands tend to have far fewer sports facilities and have no golf courses.

Leisure: Leisure facilities have improved in recent years, although they're somewhat limited because of the islands' isolation from mainland Spain. The cultural scene includes international music and opera festivals, dance and plays, on both Gran Canaria and Tenerife, mainly in the respective capitals. The Canaries' dramatic, varied landscapes, which include tropical forests and volcanic craters, lend themselves to numerous leisure activities, such as hiking, climbing, and bird-watching. 'Rural tourism' is a growing industry and increasingly popular with residents at weekends. The islands also have numerous villages where traditional Canary life and culture have been preserved.

Theme parks include Loro Parque on Tenerife and Palmitos Park and Sioux City on Gran Canaria, as well as several water-parks on both islands. There are also many recreational and natural parks on the Canaries.

English-language Cinema & Theatre: Although there are several cinema complexes in the large towns and cities, no films are shown in English, with the exception of the occasional screening at a film club. Theatre also tends to be in Spanish, unless there's a visiting play from abroad.

Shopping Centres & Markets: Per head of population, the Canaries have far more shopping facilities than mainland Spain and there's a surprising number of hypermarkets and shopping centres, including large DIY and furniture stores. There are also many bazaar-type shops selling cheap electrical goods and jewellery in all main towns and cities. There's a wide range of smaller shops in most of the large residential areas. On the less populated islands, however, shopping facilities are limited. Weekly markets are popular, particularly in tourist resorts, and there are also daily indoor markets where you can buy fresh produce.

Foreign Food & Products: Almost all supermarkets on the Canaries offer a selection of foreign produce, with particular emphasis on goods from Britain (native Canary islanders are particularly fond of British biscuits and butter!) and Germany. There are also a few foreign stores selling foreign produce, such as Marks & Spencer and the British frozen food company, Iceland. Note, however, that prices of foreign produce are high. The availability of foreign produce on the less populated islands is limited.

Restaurants & Bars: Every popular area of the islands has a plethora of restaurants and bars, offering cuisines ranging from fast food to Thai as well as each island's specialities. For further details, see the area surveys below.

Services

International & Private Schools: Gran Canaria has two British schools as well as American, French, German and Norwegian schools. Lanzarote has two British schools and Tenerife has three. A British curriculum is taught at the British schools, where there's sometimes a parallel Spanish curriculum. All schools are co-educational and most provide education for children aged from 3 or 4 to 16 or 18. Fees are generally high. For further information, consult the European Council of International Schools (⌨ www.ecis.org). There are also Spanish private schools, where fees are high although generally lower than those of the international schools. These are co-educational, except those with a religious affinity.

Language Schools: Most main areas have language schools which teach Spanish, English and German for foreigners. In major tourist areas, the local council sometimes provides subsidised Spanish lessons for foreign residents. The University of La Laguna on Tenerife also offers an extensive range of courses for foreign students, and private lessons are available. English and German are widely spoken throughout the Canaries.

Hospitals & Clinics: All the islands have at least one public hospital (with the exception of Fuerteventura, where one is under construction), although locals generally consider this to be insufficient for the growing population. The University Hospital at La Laguna on Tenerife has an excellent reputation. There are also several private hospitals, including the international Hospital on Tenerife, specifically for foreigners. Most areas have at least one public health centre where you can see a general practitioner, and some larger centres provide emergency treatment, x-rays, and family planning and physiotherapy services. There are also many private clinics, some of which cater for a specific nationality, although the vast majority of doctors and medical staff in the Canaries speak English.

Doctors & Dentists: There's a wide range of English-speaking doctors and dentists in the Canaries.

Retirement Homes: There are few nursing or residential care homes in the Canaries.

Tradesmen: The foreign population on the main islands is well served by expatriates offering a vast range of services, from satellite installation to website design. Many advertise in the local English-language press (see below). While most are hard-working professionals, there are inevitably a few 'cowboys', so you should make sure that you employ someone with references or recommendations. Needless to say, local tradesmen also generally offer an excellent service and may speak some English. For jobs requiring local knowledge Spanish services are often a better choice.

English-language Radio: In recent years, English-language radio services have expanded and there are now several stations, although they can generally be received only on Gran Canaria and Tenerife. See area surveys below for details.

English-language Press: English-language newspapers are available daily at newsagents in main towns and resorts. Some newspapers, such as those printed in the USA, arrive the day after publication. This is the case with all newspapers in more remote parts of the less populated islands. Local English-language publications are also available on some islands. The main local publications are *Island Connections* (fortnightly newspaper, price €1.35), *Island Sun* (fortnightly newspaper) and *Tenerife News* (fortnightly free newspaper).

Consulates: Consulates on Gran Canaria serve Gran Canaria, Fuerteventura and Lanzarote and include those for Austria, Belgium, Britain, Denmark, Finland, France, Germany, Ireland, Italy, Luxembourg, the Netherlands, Norway, South Africa, Switzerland and the USA. Consulates on Tenerife serve Tenerife, La Gomera, El Hierro and La Palma, and include those for Britain, France, Germany, Ireland, South Africa and the USA. La Palma also has a German consulate, which can provide assistance to all EU nationals.

Churches: The main islands have churches representing various denominations, mainly Anglican, German and Swedish, and there are Catholic services in Spanish in churches everywhere. Local press (see above) and notice boards often contain information regarding meetings and services.

Clubs: The abundance of foreign residents in the main resorts ensures a wide variety of clubs and activities, including dining out, Bridge and walking tours. There are political clubs, such as Conservatives Abroad and the Labour Supporters, and clubs representing national groups, such as the American Club. There are also chapters of world-wide social clubs, such as the Lions Club and Rotary International, and charitable and self-help groups, such as Alcoholics Anonymous and Weight Watchers, are also represented. Local press (see above) and notice boards often contain details of clubs. Spanish speakers can also join Spanish clubs, of which there's a wide variety. The local town council will provide information.

Property

The property market on the Canaries, in particular on Gran Canaria and Tenerife, has been booming in recent years and shows no sign of slowing down. There's a wide variety of properties for sale, especially holiday apartments, and property in the Canaries is considered to be a good investment; there's also an excellent rental market. Prices have been rising steadily (in common with the rest of Spain), and property on the islands isn't cheap. Moreover, islands such as Lanzarote have halted new construction and others, such as Tenerife, are expected to follow suit before long, which will lead to a shortage of resale properties and consequently further price increases. There's also a shortage of available building land (owing to strict building regulations), and vast areas are protected or part of national parks.

A wide range of properties is available, from small studios in apartment blocks to large villas on golf courses and typical Canaries farmhouses with their own banana plantations. The cheapest property is to be found in older apartment blocks in resorts such as Las Américas on Tenerife and Playa del Inglés on Gran Canaria; the most expensive is in new developments such as Orotava on Tenerife and Maspalomas on Gran Canaria, as well as near golf courses. Bargains can still be found, especially in rural parts of the less populated islands, where you can buy old houses and land cheaply. Be careful, however, because restoration costs mean that the 'real' price can be considerably higher.

There are many new developments under construction, particularly as building companies are trying to cash in before the authorities halt development. Several new resort areas have sprung up recently, particularly on the south coasts of Gran Canaria and Tenerife and at Playa Blanca on Lanzarote. If you're intending to buy off plan in the Canaries, you should bear in mind that not all new construction is carried out by reputable, professional companies; do some checking before committing yourself to anything. Construction prices for villas range from €700 to €1,000 per m², depending on the quality of the materials used.

Typical Homes: Property on the Canary Islands usually falls into one of three categories: apartment blocks in or near resorts, often with communal gardens and swimming pools; villas on the outskirts of resorts, around golf courses or on luxury developments near the main towns; and typical Canaries properties, comprising either white houses with hardwood balconies or white, cube-shaped houses with flat roofs, usually found in villages. (In view of the lack of rainfall, rainwater is often collected on house roofs, for both domestic and agricultural use.)

Cost of Housing: The price of property varies with the island and the location (see area surveys below) but in general:

One-bedroom apartment: from around €70,000;
Two-bedroom apartment: from €90,000;
Three-bedroom apartment: from €110,000;
Three-bedroom townhouse: from €150,000;
Three-bedroom villa: from €200,000.

Land: There's a shortage of building land on the Canaries, and what is available is generally expensive. In view of strict building regulations, it's essential to take professional advice before committing yourself to a purchase. Many buyers have found themselves with land on which they cannot build or may build a property of a restricted size only. Make sure that you have an official copy of the regulations from the correct authorities and check what types of construction are allowed before you purchase land. Prices vary enormously from island to island and even in different parts of the same island, e.g. from €30 per m² in parts of Lanzarote to over €650 per m² in parts of Gran Canaria. Generally, the minimum plot size is at least 1,000m², although this varies from one locality to another.

Rental Accommodation: As a major tourist destination, the Canaries has a thriving rental market, particularly for short-term (under six months) lets, and many foreign property owners rent their properties profitably. Long-term rentals are generally difficult to find at short notice and you will need to plan ahead. Prices have risen considerably over recent years, in line with the general rise in property prices, although out of season it's possible to find cheap lets on the quieter islands. For rental costs on individual islands, see the surveys below.

Communications

Air: The main islands of Tenerife, Lanzarote and Gran Canaria have international airports and are well served by inexpensive charter flights from the Spanish mainland, Britain, Germany and other European countries. Tenerife's Reina Sofía airport (south) is the archipelago's busiest (in high season planes take off every six minutes). Two companies, Binter and Iberia, operate inter-island flights, with frequent shuttle services between the capitals, although fares can be high unless you book well in advance. The smaller islands all have airports, although services are limited, especially out of season, and tend to be restricted to flights to the other islands. The airports are generally well served by buses to nearby resorts and main towns. Taxis also provide an inexpensive service to and from the airports, and car hire is usually available.

Sea: Ferry services operate from Cadiz in mainland Spain to Tenerife, Gran Canaria (Las Palmas), Lanzarote and Fuerteventura. Cruise ships call at Las Palmas and Santa Cruz (Tenerife). Island-hopping is easy and popular, as inter-island ferry and jetfoil services link all the islands, with frequent and reasonably priced crossings for both car and foot passengers, although services are sometimes interrupted by bad weather. Residents of the Canary Islands are sometimes entitled to discounts on air and sea travel between the islands and mainland Spain.

Public Transport: There are no rail services on the Canaries, although all of the islands have a generally excellent bus service linking the main resorts to each other and the capital. Fares are reasonable and bus companies on some of the islands offer discounted fares of up to 50 per cent if you purchase a discount card (*bono*). The main cities also have good internal bus services.

Taxis are plentiful (and cheap if there are several of you) and are usually the quickest way to travel. Most taxi drivers speak English and they're often good guides. Make sure to choose official taxis (with a green light on the roof) and that the taxi has a working meter, unless you agree the price beforehand.

Roads: In recent years there have been vast improvements to the islands' road networks, particularly on Tenerife, where there are now dual carriageways linking the main resorts. Gran Canaria also has reasonable main roads. However, despite the fact that roads are well maintained, the nature of the terrain on the islands means that they're usually winding and can be narrow, and the many mountain roads can be treacherous for the unwary and inexperienced. On the smaller islands such as El Hierro and La Gomera there are few 'main' roads, and on all the islands access to remote areas may be only via tracks, meaning that you may need a four-wheel drive vehicle. Note that car hire insurance usually excludes any driving on non-tarmac surfaces. Petrol is usually cheap, although on the smaller islands there aren't many petrol stations.

Planned Developments

Both the authorities and residents of the islands agree that the Canaries will soon reach their maximum limit of development, and there's growing support for a moratorium on construction on all the islands and the promotion of 'eco-tourism' and the conservation of the islands' unique scenery. It's therefore likely that there will be little major development in the future, except for the expansion of airports (such as Reina Sofia, where a second runway has been approved) and improvements to essential infrastructure such as roads and hospitals.

Employment Prospects

Unemployment is high on the Canaries (around 13 per cent in early 2002), where the vast influx of illegal immigrants from Africa has contributed to the shortage of jobs. There are, however, many opportunities for expatriates, although jobs are mainly limited to the tourist and services sectors, particularly catering. Being able to speak at least three languages is often an essential requirement. There are also plenty of opportunities for self-employment, although these are also mainly limited to catering. Part-time work in shops and bars is easy to find.

Further Information

The Canary Islands Tourist Board offers a telephone information service in several languages, including English and German (☎ 902-371-372 at local call tariffs). 'Walking Guides to the Canaries', which include detailed maps and walks as well as accommodation and transport information, are available for most of the islands from 🖥 www.walking.demon.co.uk.

Useful Publications

● *Canary Islands* (Thomas Cook Publishing)

Useful Websites

🖥 www.canaries-live.com (a useful general guide)
🖥 www.ecanarias.com (general information)
🖥 www.ic-web.com (an online version of the *Island Connections* newspaper)
🖥 www.tennews.com (an online version of the *Tenerife News* newspaper)

TENERIFE

Tenerife is the largest and best known of the Canaries, covering 2,053 km^2 (2,793mi^2). The population is around 680,000 (islanders are called *Tinerfeños*), including a large number of foreign residents. There's an intense rivalry between Tenerife and Gran Canaria, who have fought over 'leadership' of the islands for centuries. The capital of Tenerife, Santa Cruz de Tenerife, is a smaller, quieter and altogether more pleasant town than Las Palmas (the capital of Gran Canaria), although it isn't much favoured by foreign homeowners. Tenerife is home to the Canaries' university, which is at La Laguna, the former capital.

The island is split in two by mountains, the south being arid with sandy beaches, while the north is lush, with banana trees, a dramatic, rugged coastline, ancient woodlands and black sandy beaches at Taganana in the extreme northeast. Tenerife is noted for its wealth of natural beauty, rich sub-tropical vegetation and extraordinary range of flora and landscape. The Orotava Valley and Las Cañadas National Park are national treasures and include Spain's highest mountain, the snow-capped Pico del Teide (3,718m/12,198ft). The world's third largest volcano, it last erupted in 1909 and is believed to be more or less dormant, the risk of a major eruption being minimal.

The island is highly developed in places, with many vast hotels and apartment complexes. The most popular resorts are along the west coast, including Playa de Las Américas, Puerto de la Cruz, Los Gigantes and Los Cristianos, while Costa del Silencio, Puerto Santiago and Las Galletas are quieter. Tenerife offers a vast range of facilities and everything you could wish for from a popular holiday destination. The island is unsurprisingly popular with holiday homeowners and also has numerous timeshare developments.

Advantages & Disadvantages

Tenerife is the most popular Canary island, mainly because of its excellent climate, spectacular, varied scenery and range of amenities, which are probably the best in the archipelago. It has many lively towns, which offer plenty to do all year round, the island is easy to get to and flights are cheap. Disadvantages include the vast number of tourists in the resorts during the high season, aggressive touting from timeshare sellers and restaurant and discotheque staff, and the monotony of the south's barren, arid landscape.

Major Towns & Places of Interest

In the north, the main residential areas are centred around the capital, **Santa Cruz de Tenerife**, which is a lively, cosmopolitan city with a rich colonial history. It has a wide range of cultural and leisure facilities, and one of Spain's most important ports, used by numerous tourist cruisers, ferries and cargo ships. The city is world famous for its wild Carnival celebrations in February, second in exuberance only to those at Rio de Janeiro. Santa Cruz isn't particularly popular with foreign property buyers, although it's within easy reach of most of the rest of the island and is an excellent shopping and cultural centre.

On the north coast is the city of **Puerto de la Cruz**, a resort favoured by rich Britons and Germans during Victorian times. It remains popular and has excellent hotel and congress facilities, making it busy all year round. The resort's beaches are modest, although there's a man-made swimming pool complex with seven pools, and nearby beaches are good. Inland lies the Orotava Valley, one of Tenerife's natural treasures and an area of stunning natural beauty. The valley was the centre of early tourism on the island and remains popular with foreign residents. Houses there are generally large with balconies and gardens.

On the west coast lies the quiet, pleasant resort of **Los Gigantes**, named after the 'Cliffs of the Giants', towering, sheer cliffs plunging into the ocean. The area is popular with foreign homebuyers for its scenery and tranquillity. Los Gigantes is a well planned, attractive resort, where construction has been in tune with the natural surroundings. Next to Los Gigantes lies Puerto de Santiago, with its fishing port and marina. The nearby Playa de la Arena beach is attractive and well served with amenities. This area's steep terrain makes it unsuitable for older and disabled people.

Further south, but still on the west coast, are the many resorts of the district known as **Costa Adeje**: Playa de San Juan, which is popular with the French and Germans and where a new beach has been created and several construction projects are under way; Callao Salvaje, which is the site of many apartment and townhouse developments; San Eugenio, Fañabe and Playa Del Duque, the last two being rather exclusive residential areas; and San Eugenio and Torviscas, which are essentially satellite resorts of **Las Américas**, Tenerife's largest (and loudest) resort. Las Américas is comparable with Benidorm and Torremolinos on the mainland and has literally hundreds of apartments, bars and discos as well as excellent beaches. Las Américas is primarily a young person's resort and not to everyone's taste. Indeed, many people find the noise and nightlife a deterrent, while the area of Las Verónicas has serious problems with violence among drunken youths.

Further to the south lies Tenerife's second-largest resort, **Los Cristianos**, which was originally a quiet fishing village and is now home to Tenerife's second port, with heavy ferry traffic to the islands to the west.

Round the headland lies the **Costa del Silencio** (the Coast of Silence), which although it has no beach has several pleasant resorts, including Las Galletas and Chafoya, the latter popular with families because of its proximity to international schools. The Costa del Silencio has seen major development over recent years and many new complexes have been built. Inland from the Costa del Silencio lie Golf Amarilla, Tenerife's oldest golf course, with several building complexes and some of the more competitive property prices on the island, and Golf del Sur, a 27-hole golf course surrounded by exclusive complexes. Property in the Golf del Sur is among the most expensive on Tenerife, although its resale potential is excellent. Both golf courses also offer sports clubs, shops and restaurants. A major disadvantage of the Costa del Silencio (and one that wildly contradicts its name) is its proximity to Reina Sofia airport, whose landing flight path lies directly over several of the area's complexes. It's also one of the windiest parts of the island. To the east of the Costa del Silencio lies El Médano, a fashionable water sports village where the strong winds have made it ideal for the surfing championships that are held there.

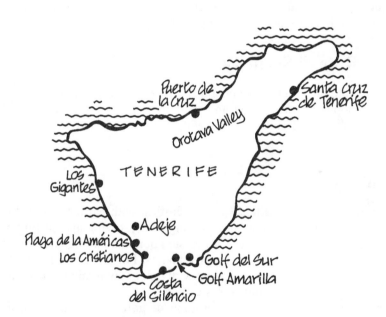

Population

Along with the other islands, Tenerife has a rapidly growing population, owing to the increase in the number of holiday homes and the attraction of associated business opportunities. Official 2001 figures put the number of foreign residents at around 54,000, of whom almost 23,000 are EU nationals, predominantly British and German. Unofficial figures, however, suggest almost 30,000 British residents alone.

Climate

Tenerife enjoys one of the best climates in the Canaries, with year-round warmth. The west coast is generally considered to have the best climate, with gentle sea breezes in the summer to temper the fierce sun. The south-west coast around Punta Roja and the Médano beach are affected by strong winds; not for nothing are major surfing championships held there. These winds also affect play on the two golf courses in the area.

The north of the island tends to be cooler and wetter than the south, although even here rainfall can be scarce. La Laguna is the coolest inhabited spot on Tenerife – the only place, apart from the summit of Mount Teide, where you need a sweater in the winter! The island is occasionally affected by sand storms from the Sahara desert. For those suffering from multiple sclerosis, asthma, arthritis and migraines, the area around Los Cristianos has a unique balance of salt and iodine particles in the air which, together with the sun, are considered to have curative powers.

Crime Rate & Security

The crime rate on Tenerife is generally low, although pickpockets are active in certain popular tourist spots and theft from hire cars is common. Some areas, such as Las Verónicas, suffer with 'lager louts', and violent fights are common.

Amenities

Sports: Tenerife has excellent sports facilities, with particular emphasis on golf and water-sports. Of the latter, sailing, scuba-diving and surfing are the most popular, and the island has six pleasure ports, including large marinas at Los Cristianos and Santa Cruz. Los Cristianos, Puerto de la Cruz and Santa Cruz all have municipal sports centres with indoor swimming pools and most resorts have private gyms and sports centres.

Tenerife has the highest concentration of golf courses in the Canaries. There are six of them, mostly 18-hole, although Golf del Sur has 27 holes. Amarilla Golf and Golf del Sur are both championship courses, the latter famous for its black sand bunkers and lush tropical vegetation. Most courses have surrounding residential complexes and those in the south have added some welcome, refreshing greenery to the otherwise arid surroundings. The strong breezes in the south add to the challenge of the courses!

For football fans, Santa Cruz football club has been in the first division of the Spanish league (although they were relegated in the 2001/2002 season) and has an enthusiastic following throughout the Canaries.

Leisure: Tenerife has an extensive cultural scene, particularly in the capital, home to the nationally famous Symphonic Orchestra of Tenerife and host to the prestigious annual Canary Island Festival of Music. The capital also has several theatres and holds numerous art exhibitions, as well as spectacular carnival celebrations in February. Puerto de la Cruz has an annual season of classical music concerts and the island also has several museums, three casinos and an almost infinite variety of nightclubs and restaurants.

Loro Parque in Puerto de la Cruz is Tenerife's principal theme park and offers a wide selection of birds and an aquarium. The Eagle Parque in Aguilas del Teide has a bobsleigh that runs around the park's enclosures and an assault course set in a wooded area. There are also several water-parks on the island.

English-language Cinema & Theatre: There are several cinema complexes on the island, although English-language films are shown only during the summer, at the Los Cristianos complex.

Shopping Centres & Markets: There are several large shopping centres on Tenerife, including two near the capital, and the furniture shop IKEA and DIY giant Leroy Merlin also have branches. In late 2001, a huge El Corte Inglés department store opened in Santa Cruz. There are smaller shopping centres in resort areas and most residential areas have reasonable shopping facilities.

Weekly street markets are popular on Tenerife, particularly in the resorts and are held in Alcalá on Mondays, Playa San Juan on Wednesdays, in

Torviscas on Thursdays and Sundays, and in Los Cristianos on Sundays. Some 70,000 people reportedly visit these markets weekly, so go early to avoid the crowds! There's also a popular craft fair in the main square at Puerto de Santiago on the second Sunday of every month. Most towns have daily indoor markets selling fresh produce, including the famous African market at Santa Cruz, where there are over 300 stalls.

Foreign Food & Products: Supermarkets in the resorts stock an extensive selection of foreign food, particularly British and German, although prices can be high. There are also specialist shops catering for specific nationalities. Puerto de la Cruz has an English lending library and an English second-hand book shop.

Restaurants & Bars: Most of Tenerife's busier areas have a huge variety of restaurants and bars, serving a wide range of food. Particularly cosmopolitan are the capital and Puerto de la Cruz, while resorts tend to offer mainly British and fast food.

Services

International & Private Schools: There are three British schools on Tenerife, at Cabo Blanco, Golf del Sur and Puerto de la Cruz. There's also a German school. The main private school is Spanish, in the south of the island, and there are several others in the capital. Places are usually in short supply.

Hospitals & Clinics: There are currently three public hospitals on Tenerife, at La Orotava, La Laguna and Santa Cruz, and new hospitals are being built at Los Cristianos and Bueno Paso, expected to open in late 2002. There are private hospitals specifically for foreigners at Puerto de la Cruz (two), Las Américas and Santa Cruz. Most areas have a health centre where emergency treatment may be available. There are numerous private clinics on Tenerife, mainly concentrated in the capital, in Las Américas and the surrounding area, and in Puerto de la Cruz. Many clinics are aimed at foreigners and practically all have English-speaking staff.

Doctors & Dentists: English-speaking doctors and dentists are easy to find on Tenerife.

Tradesmen: Tenerife has many foreign companies and tradesmen serving just about every possible need, especially in the southern resorts.

English-language Radio: Four English-language radio stations broadcast on Tenerife: Radio Oasis, Gold FM, Power FM and Waves FM, programmes concentrating on music and local news and information.

English-language Press: *The Horizon Guide to Property in Tenerife*, a useful quarterly publication offering advice and information about property on Tenerife from The Horizon Property Group, one of the island's main estate agents (see advert above); *Island Connections*, published fortnightly, price €1.35. Although the newspaper includes news from Gran Canaria, the majority is dedicated to Tenerife; *Island Sun*, a fortnightly free paper; *The Paper*, also a fortnightly free paper and a sister publication of the British *News of the World*; *Tenerife News*, published fortnightly and distributed free; *Western Sun*, free paper covering the Los Gigantes area.

Consulates: British (☎ 922-286-863), German (☎ 922-284-812), Irish (☎ 922-245-671), South African (☎ 922-226-004) and USA (☎ 922-222-552).

Churches: Several foreign religious denominations are represented, including the Church of England, Christian Fellowship and the Swedish Church in Los Cristianos, and there are Anglican, German and Swedish churches in Puerto de la Cruz.

Property

Property prices on Tenerife have risen over the last few years and are now among the most expensive in the Canaries. Despite a massive amount of recent construction, there's a shortage of resale properties in the most popular areas of the south, i.e. around the resorts of Los Cristianos and at Playa de Las Américas. This tendency looks set to continue, and property on Tenerife is generally considered to be an excellent investment, particularly if you're seeking rental income.

Typical Homes: Like Gran Canaria, Tenerife has some typical Canaries buildings, which in inland rural areas tend to be cube-shaped with flat roofs. Most have little or no garden because of the shortage (and cost) of water, although some have extensive tracts of land devoted to fruit trees and farming.

Cost of Housing: The following prices are intended only as a guide and were current in mid-2002.

- **Callao Salvaje**
  One-bedroom apartment: from €85,000;
  Two-bedroom apartment: from €100,000;
  Three-bedroom villa (on a 500m^2 plot): around €300,000.

- **Costa del Silencio**
  One-bedroom apartment: from €70,000 to €110,000;
  Two-bedroom apartment: from €85,000 to €150,000;
  Three-bedroom villa (on a 500m^2 plot): from €200,000.

- **Las Américas**
  One-bedroom apartment: from €85,000;
  Three-bedroom apartment: from €110,000.

- **Los Cristianos**
  One-bedroom apartment: from €85,000 (up to €150,000 if beachfront);
  Two-bedroom apartment: from €130,000 upwards.

- **Costa Adeje**
  Two-bedroom apartment: from €110,000;
  Three-bedroom villa (on a small plot): from €200,000 in a small resort and up to €275,000 in San Eugenio.

- **Golf del Sur**
  One-bedroom apartment: from €100,000 to €150,000;
  Two-bedroom apartment/small villa: from €175,000;
  Three-bedroom villa (on a 500m² plot): from €275,000.

- **Amarilla Golf**
  One-bedroom apartment: from €70,000;
  Two-bedroom apartment: from €95,000 to €215,000.

- **La Orotava:** Two-bedroom villa (on a 500m² plot): from €260,000;
  Three-bedroom villa (on a larger plot): from €300,000;

Rural properties in Tenerife are available from €75,000, depending on the size of the plot and the condition of the building.

Land: Land is in short supply on Tenerife and there are strict building regulations. Plots are usually over 1,000m² and prices per square metre start at €150 in rural or less popular areas and at €225 close to the resorts. Before you commit yourself to the purchase of land, you should double-check that you will be able to obtain permission to build on it. The authorities have called a halt to the construction of hotel and tourist complexes for the foreseeable future.

Rental Accommodation: Holiday and short-term lets, are readily available in all parts of Tenerife. Long-term lets (longer than six months) may be difficult to find and should be looked for well in advance. Typical monthly rentals are from €480 for a one-bedroom apartment, from €720 for a two-bedroom apartment and from €900 for a townhouse.

Communications

Air: Tenerife has two airports, Reina Sofía (☎ 922-759-200), which is in the south near the Costa del Silencio, and Los Rodeos (☎ 922-635-998), in the north near the capital, which was recently refurbished and has a new terminal. Reina Sofía is by far the busier, with an abundance of charter flights, mainly to and from Britain and Germany, and plans have been approved for a second runway. Los Rodeos mainly handles domestic and inter-island flights.

Sea: Along with Gran Canaria, Tenerife is the shipping hub of the Canaries and a popular cruise destination: cruise ships bring nearly 100,000 visitors to Santa Cruz every year. Ferry services (passenger and car) are run by Fred Olsen, Trasmed and Jet Foil, which between them operate a vast network of services between Tenerife and the other islands. Express services run twice daily between Tenerife and Gran Canaria and take one hour. Normal services take just over two hours.

Public Transport: A comprehensive bus service linking all major centres is operated mainly by Titsa, plus a few smaller companies. Services are frequent and fares reasonable, and Titsa also offers up to 50 per cent discount on fares if you purchase a discount card (*bono*) valid for up to a year. Santa Cruz and Puerto de la Cruz also have good urban bus services. Taxis are common and are a quick and relatively inexpensive way to travel.

Roads: The building of new roads has vastly improved communications over recent years, particularly in the north, where many places are now easily accessible by car. Tenerife also has motorways (which have only two lanes) running from the capital along the south coast to the resorts, and from Santa Cruz to La Orotava. There are also advanced plans for a motorway extension in the north to Los Realejos, although local opposition (mainly for environmental reasons) has halted proceedings. Tenerife's roads are generally good, but bear in mind that many secondary roads are winding and narrow, making driving hazardous.

Planned Developments

These include a second runway at Reina Sofia airport, a continuation of the motorway in the north of the island and the construction of several four and five-star hotels on the Costa Adeje. Several cinema complexes are also currently under construction in the south and a second Loro Parque will be built, also in the south. Several more golf courses are also planned, as well as a large marina at Amarilla Golf.

Employment Prospects

Employment prospects on Tenerife are good, although limited mainly to the tourist and service sectors. Speaking at least three languages (including English and German) is often an essential requirement. There are also many opportunities for self-employment, again mainly in the tourist industry.

Further Information

Useful Publications

- *Landscapes of Tenerife*, N. Rochford (Sunflower Books)
- *Mini Rough Guide to Tenerife and La Gomera*, C. Williams (Rough Guides)
- *Tenerife Insight Pocket Guide* (Insight Guides)

Useful Websites

⌨ www.horizonpropertygroup.com (one of Tenerife's main estate agents)
⌨ www.tennews.com (Tenerife's English-language newspaper online)
⌨ www.tenerifeowners.com (a site designed for property owners, with general information about Tenerife)

FUERTEVENTURA

The oldest island in the Canaries, the closest to Africa and the second-largest after Tenerife, covering an area of 1,688km² (652mi²). Puerto del Rosario, the island's capital and major port, has a lively fishing industry and is home to the Spanish foreign legion. Fuerteventura is tranquil and unspoilt, with long, white sandy beaches (the best in the Canaries, some say the world), and is noted for fishing, windmills, camels, surfing and windsurfing. It has almost no rainfall and little vegetation, and the arid terrain is reminiscent of the desert landscapes of north-west Africa, especially the Sahara-like sand dunes. Over a quarter of the island's territory is protected under the Canaries' national park legislation. It is virtually undiscovered by tourists and is ideal for a relaxing holiday away from it all, although some resorts have become built-up in recent years.

Advantages & Disadvantages

Fuerteventura's main advantage is its tranquillity and excellent beaches. Disadvantages include the intense summer heat and limited leisure facilities.

Major Towns & Places of Interest

Puerto del Rosario, the capital, is the largest and liveliest town. Most tourist resorts are situated along the 25km (16mi) of beaches south of the capital and nearby airport, including Caleta de Fuste, which is popular with British tourists, although it is on the airport's approach path and can be noisy. Corralejo in the north (a fishing port with superb, long sandy beaches) has recently become a popular resort, with good amenities and plenty to do. The Jandía peninsula in the south is gaining in popularity and has several resorts around the small town of Morro del Jable. The peninsula boasts the island's best beaches with fine, white sand, including Barlovento beach, which stretches for over 20km (12.5mi). Betancuria, the old capital, lies in the centre of the island, and is an attractive, beautifully preserved town with traditional architecture. The coastal resorts of Corralejo, Caleta de Fuste and Morro del Jable are the most popular for foreign property buyers and contain most of Fuerteventura's holiday home developments.

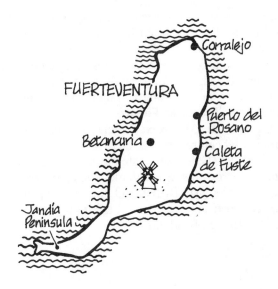

Population

The population of Fuerteventura is around 53,900, of which official figures state that some 7,600 are foreigners, nearly 3,700 of them from the EU, mainly Britain and Germany. Actual foreign resident figures are undoubtedly higher.

Climate

Along with the rest of the Canaries, Fuerteventura generally has a pleasant climate all year round. It's the sunniest island, can be very hot in the summer and receives little rainfall. As a result of this, much of the island has an arid appearance, with little vegetation. The west coast can be very windy.

Crime Rate & Security

The crime rate is generally low, although theft from hire cars can be a problem.

Amenities

Sports: Water-sports are Fuerteventura's prime sporting attraction: the island's north coasts offer some of Europe's best windsurfing and surfing. Sailing and big game fishing are also popular and Fuerteventura is a scuba-diver's Mecca, with numerous attractive diving locations around the island. Tennis is also popular. Fuerteventura has no golf courses, although two are currently under construction, at Caleta de Fuste and Corralejo.

Leisure: Fuerteventura's main attraction is its beaches, which are some of the finest in Europe. The unique landscapes and scenery offer many opportunities for hiking, horse-riding and mountain-biking.

English-language Cinema & Theatre: None.

Shopping Centres & Markets: Caleta de Fuste and Corralejo have reasonable commercial centres with a range of shops, and the capital also has good shopping facilities. Caleta de Fuste has a street market on Saturdays.

Foreign Food & Products: Supermarkets in resort areas are well stocked with foreign food, particularly British, although it's expensive.

Restaurants & Bars: The resorts offer a fair range of bars and restaurants, catering mainly for foreign residents.

Services

International & Private Schools: There are no international schools or private schools on Fuerteventura, although there's a wide choice of state schools in the main towns.

Hospitals & Clinics: There are currently no hospitals on the island, although the Canary Island government has advanced plans for one at Puerto del Rosario. The main towns have public health centres and there are several private clinics, mainly in Puerto del Rosario.

Doctors & Dentists: There are several English-speaking doctors and dentists on the island, mainly in the capital.

Tradesmen: In view of Fuerteventura's small foreign population, English-speaking tradesmen aren't always easy to find.

English-language Radio: None.

English-language Press: See page 64.

Consulates: There are no consulates on Fuerteventura and you should consult your country's representation on Gran Canaria or Tenerife (see pages 86 and 75).

Property

The property market on Fuerteventura is booming and currently growing by around 20 per cent per year. Demand for resale and new properties is high and there's a lot of new construction. Although prices are rising, they aren't on a par with other islands and property on Fuerteventura is generally considered to be a good investment.

Cost of Housing: The following prices are intended only as a guide and were current in mid-2002.

Two-bedroom apartment: from €100,000;
Three-bedroom apartment: from €110,000;
Three-bedroom townhouse: from €150,000;
Three-bedroom villa with private garden: from €200,000.

Land: There's a wide choice of building plots on Fuerteventura, where prices begin at €35 per m². Minimum plot size is usually 1,000m².

Rental Accommodation: The demand for rental accommodation is growing, particularly for holiday lets. There's currently a shortage of accommodation for rent, with long-term lets being in the shortest supply, although this is expected to improve over the next few years. Monthly rentals for a two-bedroom apartment start at €400 and for a three-bedroom apartment at €500.

Communications

Air: Fuerteventura has an international airport (☎ 928-860-500) to the south of the capital. During the high season, it's well served by charter flights and there are regular flights from Madrid and Barcelona. Out of season, the flight schedule is greatly reduced.

Sea: A regular ferry service connects Puerto del Rosario with Las Palmas on Gran Canaria.

Public Transport: Public transport is limited on Fuerteventura, although bus services operated by Maxorata Bus link the capital with most of the main towns and villages, and prices are reasonable. Taxis are also available and are generally reliable. More remote villages and parts of the islands have no public transport, making a car essential.

Roads: The roads around the capital are good and include a stretch of motorway running south to the resorts. From the capital there are also reasonable roads to the main towns on the rest of the island, although Fuerteventura's other roads aren't always well maintained and can be narrow and winding. The roads generally have little traffic and, except on the motorway, the speed limit is 90kph (56mph). There's a shortage of petrol stations, particularly in remote areas.

Planned Developments

The construction of a hospital at Puerto del Rosario and the completion of road improvements, particularly on the Jandía Peninsula.

Employment Prospects

These are limited, with fewer opportunities in the tourist sector than on the busier islands, although Fuerteventura is developing quickly and employment opportunities will increase.

Further Information

Useful Publications

- *AA Essential Lanzarote and Fuerteventura*, A. Sanger (AA Publishing)
- *Landscapes of Fuerteventura*, N. Rochford (Sunflower Books)

Useful Websites

- 💻 www.cabildofuer.es (the island's official website, with some tourist information)
- 💻 www.lanzarote-fuerte.com (general information about Fuerteventura and Lanzarote)

GRAN CANARIA

Despite its name, Gran Canaria is only the third-largest of the Canary Islands, it has an area of 1,532km² (592mi²), but it is very often referred to as that of a 'miniature continent' because of its dramatically varied scenery. Las Palmas, the capital of Gran Canaria (population 350,000), is the largest town in the Canaries (with the largest port in Europe) and is the region's capital and seat of government. The north (the most beautiful part of the island) and west coasts are rugged and remote with tall cliffs, while the south is noted for excellent long beaches, such as Playa del Inglés, Playa Canteras, San Agustin and Maspalomas, which are interspersed with traditional fishing villages. Unfortunately the south coast is generally dominated by large modern resorts, most of them ugly, unappealing and lacking in charm, although the resorts to the west are considerably more attractive and quieter. Inland, the island has stark mountains, ravines and tranquil valleys cultivated with sugar cane, banana plantations (in the north), papaya and mango trees. Gran Canaria is also famous for its magnificent sand dunes, which are prevalent along the south coast.

Advantages & Disadvantages

Gran Canaria's climate is the principal reason why many foreigners choose to visit or live on the island. The south-west is regarded as having 'therapeutic' weather conditions, and some doctors recommend a visit for those suffering from arthritis and rheumatism. The spectacular, contrasting scenery is another of Gran Canaria's strengths and the island is also easy to travel to and from. Drawbacks include the effects of mass tourism during the high season. This is more of a problem in the south, although it's relatively easy to escape from the crowds and the excessive development in the resorts, which has done much to spoil the island's natural beauty.

Major Towns & Places of Interest: The capital, Las Palmas, has an interesting old quarter and a 7km (4mi) coastline and was the first resort on the island; 40 years ago it was highly fashionable with the world's 'jet set'. It's no longer as popular as a resort but has become a bustling, cosmopolitan town with a large foreign population.

The south coast of the island, centred around Maspalomas and Playa del Inglés, is Spain's fourth most popular tourist destination and attracts foreign property owners and businesses. Maspalomas, Playa del Inglés and San Agustín are reminiscent of mainland Spain's crowded resorts of Benidorm and Torremolinos. The area has many amenities and a thriving nightlife, an attraction for some, although a deterrent for those in search of tranquillity. If you travel just a few kilometres away from the centre of the resorts you can find quieter residential areas. Maspalomas has the best beach on the island, while Vecindario, a town 15km (9mi) east of Playa del Inglés, has become extremely popular with foreign residents in the last few years, partly because of its excellent shopping centre.

To the west of Maspalomas lie the quieter, more exclusive resorts of Puerto Rico, where development has been intense in recent years, Arguineguín, Patalavaca and Puerto de Mogán. Puerto Rico has a wide choice of property (apartments, bungalows and luxury villas) and is well served by amenities, including two shopping centres, numerous bars and restaurants, and the island's largest marina. Puerto de Mogán, known as 'little Venice', is an exceptionally attractive development built around a fishing port and marina. Property here is mainly low level apartments and villas built around the mostly pedestrianised streets. Inland from Maspalomas are several developments, such as Sonnenland (as its name suggests, popular with Germans) and Bellavista.

The north of the island is essentially untouched by mass tourism, and one of its highlights is the town of Arucas with its traditional Canary Island architecture.

Population

Gran Canaria has one of the fastest growing, youngest populations in Spain. The total is around 745,000, of which almost 45,000 are officially foreign residents. EU nationals, mainly from Britain and Germany, officially account for just over 12,000 of these, although the unofficial figure is thought to be considerably higher.

Climate

Gran Canaria's west coast is reputed to have the world's 'best' climate, the high temperatures tempered by refreshing sea breezes. The rest of the island also enjoys excellent conditions, although the south-east coast can be very hot in summer and inland areas can be humid. The east and south of the island are occasionally engulfed by a deep, sandy fog that can last for several days, as happened in December 2001, when many elderly people and young children had to be treated for respiratory problems. Tap water, although safe to drink, has a saline taste and most people prefer bottled water. Water on the island is scarce, so mains water is very expensive.

Crime Rate & Security

Gran Canaria has an average (for Spain) level of crime, although petty theft (especially pickpockets) and theft from hire cars are growing problems. Never leave anything of value in your hire car (even in a locked boot) and take extra care of your belongings in crowded places. Handbags and camera equipment are particularly attractive to petty thieves.

Amenities

Sports: In common with the other Canary islands, Gran Canaria's principal sporting activities are centred on the sea, although the emphasis in Gran Canaria is on sailing. There are five marinas in the south and two in the north, and the island hosts the annual 'Atlantic Rally for Cruisers' (from Gran Canaria to Barbados), as well as numerous other regattas. The largest marina is at Puerto Rico, from where you can go deep-sea fishing and scuba diving. Las Palmas' port, Puerto de la Luz, is Europe's largest and a popular cruise and pleasure yacht destination.

Most towns and resorts have a good range of sporting facilities, often including a municipal sports pavilion and a choice of private gyms and sports centres. Popular sports include tennis, horse riding, trekking and mountaineering. Golf is also popular on Gran Canaria, which has five courses (two near Las Palmas, the others in the south near the resorts) and several more are under construction. The Real Club de Las Palmas course is one of the world's most spectacular, located on an extinct volcanic crater. Most of the island's courses have a 'pay and play' facility.

Leisure: Las Palmas has a lively cultural scene and the city holds prestigious annual festivals of classical music, opera, theatre and dance (in the autumn), and cinema and jazz (during the summer). The city has an auditorium and several theatres, as well as two casinos. There's also usually plenty to do in the island's resorts, which offer a range of nightclubs and discos, particularly in high season, when the area around Maspalomas parties 24 hours a day. For those in search of the quieter life, the island's beautiful scenery lends itself to rural tourism, sightseeing in the northern villages and walking and climbing in the mountains.

Gran Canaria's theme parks include Palmitos Park, which has an excellent selection of flora and fauna, Sioux City (an adventure park based on a Wild West theme) and several water-parks, mainly in the southern resorts.

English-language Cinema & Theatre: The island has several cinema complexes, in the capital and in Vecindario. Films, however, are shown only in Spanish, although there are plans for English-language screenings.

Shopping Centres & Markets: Gran Canaria has a wealth of shopping facilities, including large department stores such as the Spanish flagship store, El Corte Inglés, and several shopping centres, such as Las Arenas, La Ballena and Siete Palmas. The area of Triana has many exclusive boutiques. There are also several large furniture and DIY stores near the capital. The southern resorts are extremely well-equipped with shopping facilities, including large supermarkets, and there's an abundance of well designed shopping centres in Vecindario, Faro II and Varadero, offering boutiques, chain stores, multi-screen cinemas and hypermarkets. In rural areas, shops may be few and far between and the range of produce available limited.

Foreign Food & Products: Supermarkets in resort areas stock a wide selection of foreign food, particularly British and German, although prices can be high. There are specialist shops in the resorts catering for specific nationalities, for example the British frozen food company, Iceland. Las Palmas also has a Marks & Spencer store.

Restaurants & Bars: Las Palmas has a cosmopolitan selection of bars and restaurants, including those offering typical Gran Canarian cuisine (where bananas make an appearance in more than just the desserts!). Resort areas are well provided with hundreds of bars and restaurants (often foreign-owned), with a preponderance of British and fast food establishments.

Services

International & Private Schools: There are two British schools on the island as well as American, French, German and Norwegian schools, most of them in or near the capital. The capital also has several private schools, all with a Spanish curriculum.

Hospitals & Clinics: Las Palmas has several public hospitals, including a children's hospital, and a number of private hospitals also serve the capital, among them a British hospital. There are numerous private clinics on Gran Canaria, mainly concentrated in the capital and the resorts. Many provide services specifically for foreigners and practically all have English-speaking staff.

Doctors & Dentists: There are many English-speaking doctors on Gran Canaria, particularly in the capital and the resorts. There are also several English-speaking dental clinics. Many doctors and clinic staff also speak other European languages.

Tradesmen: The resorts are home to many foreign workers, who often advertise on local notice boards and in the local press.

English-language Radio: None, although there are plans for a service in the near future.

English-language Press: See page 64.

Consulates: Many countries have consulates in Las Palmas, including Britain (☎ 928-262-658), Germany (☎ 928-491-880), Ireland (☎ 928-297-728), South Africa (☎ 928-226-004) and the USA (☎ 928-222-552).

Property

The property market has been rather static in the south in recent years: many properties have been put on the market at high prices, despite the fact that this has made them slow or impossible to sell. In fact, low levels of sales have forced many estate agents to close. This means that prices have stabilised recently and it's forecast that future price rises will be slight. Nevertheless, property is expensive on Gran Canaria and it's difficult to find a two-bedroom property in the south below €120,000. The shortage of beach-front properties means that you can expect to pay a large premium for them. Many areas are undergoing massive construction projects, especially the resorts of Vecindario and Puerto Rico, which has nudged prices up. The most expensive property on the island is found at Maspalomas, Playa del Inglés and San Agustín, while the cheapest is in the residential area of San Fernando.

Typical Homes: Gran Canaria is famous for its fine white houses with beautiful wooden balconies on the facades. Larger houses have interior patios bedecked with tropical plants, overlooked by wooden balconies or galleries along the sides of the patio. The old quarter of Las Palmas has some particularly fine examples of this style of architecture. In inland rural areas, houses tend to be cube-shaped with flat roofs. Most properties on the island have little or no garden because of the shortage (and cost) of water.

Cost of Housing: The following prices are intended only as a guide and were current in mid-2002.

- **Maspalomas**
  Three-bedroom villa: from €480,000 (Maspalomas has few apartments).

- **Puerto Rico**
  Two-bedroom apartment: from €200,000;
  Three-bedroom apartment: from €400,000.

- **Puerto de Mogán**
  Two-bedroom apartment: from €100,000;
  Three-bedroom apartment: from €160,000;
  Three-bedroom villa: from €400,000.

- **Playa del Inglés**
  Two-bedroom apartment: from €145,000;
  Three-bedroom apartment: from €180,000;
  Three-bedroom villa: from €360,000.

Land: Land in the south of the island is now in short supply and it's increasingly difficult to obtain permission to build, although the authorities are still permitting some residential construction, especially individual homes. Available land tends to be outside the main resorts and expensive, e.g. over €200,000 for a plot of 300m² (or over €650 per m²), although inland plots can be had for around €300 per m². The minimum plot size usually 500m². Before committing yourself to the purchase of land, it's vital to ensure that the plot either already has a building licence or that one will be obtainable. Construction costs start at €700 per m².

Rental Accommodation: Rental accommodation, particularly for holiday and short-term lets, is readily available in all parts of Gran Canaria. Long-term lets (over six months) can be difficult to find and you must plan well in advance. Typical monthly rentals are expensive, from €600 for a one-bedroom apartment, from €900 for a two-bedroom apartment and from €1,500 for a villa. Rented accommodation in Las Palmas is slightly cheaper than in the resorts.

Communications

Air: Gran Canaria's airport, on the east coast at Gando (☎ 928-579-000), is one of the busiest in Spain, receiving over 5 million visitors per year. Charter flights from mainland Spain and Europe (mainly Britain and Germany) are widely available and cheap during most of the year. The airport is well connected with the north and south of the island, and there are frequent bus services to the capital and southern resorts. Taxis are plentiful, as are hire cars.

    Sea: Puerto de la Luz in the capital is the most important mid-Atlantic port and is visited by hundreds of ships every year. Ferries from the port offer daily services to neighbouring islands and mainland Spain.

    Public Transport: Gran Canaria has a good, inexpensive bus service, run by two main companies, SALCAI in the south and UTINSA in the centre and north, and all but the remotest parts of the island are connected by bus. SALCAI runs a direct service linking the southern resorts as far as Mogán. Several towns and resorts, such as Telde, Maspalomas and Playa del Inglés in the south and Arucas and Gáldar in the north, have their own bus services, which sometimes extend to neighbouring areas. Bear in mind that bus services to inland and more remote areas may be infrequent and slow, owing to the mountainous terrain. Taxis also provide a comprehensive service around the island.

    Roads: Like its western neighbour, Tenerife, Gran Canaria has motorways connecting the north and south, via the east coast. The motorways (two-lane only) run from Las Palmas west to Trasmontana, inland to Tafira Alta (these two stretches are very short) and south along the entire east coast to the southern resort of Arguineguín, with a connection inland to the town of Telde. Other population centres are connected by generally reasonable roads, although many roads are tortuous because of the mountain terrain, and driving can be dangerous for the unwary and inexperienced. Certain parts of the island, particularly the west coast, have few paved roads, and remote areas can be reached only by four-wheel drive vehicles.

Planned Developments

The island's authorities have called a halt to the construction of all tourist complexes and currently allow only the building of individual residences. Future developments include the completion of several golf courses and shopping centres, mainly in the south. Disney also has plans to build a theme park on the island, although these are still on the drawing board.

Employment Prospects

Employment prospects for foreigners who speak at least two languages are generally reasonable on Gran Canaria, although limited to the tourist and service industries, e.g. estate agency. Self-employment, usually running bars and shops, is a popular option in the resorts.

Further Information

Useful Publications

- *AA Essential Gran Canaria*, G. MacPhedran (AA Publishing)
- *Gran Canaria*, C. Turner (Landmark Publishing Ltd)
- *Landscapes of Gran Canaria*, N. Rochford (Sunflower Books)

Useful websites

- www.spain-grancanaria.com (useful for general tourist information)
- www.gran-canaria-info.com (general information)

LANZAROTE

Lanzarote is the fourth-largest island, covering an area of 813km^2 (314mi^2). Arrecife, the capital and main port, is a run-down, unattractive, modern town. The old capital of Teguise, which lies 11km (7mi) inland, is more interesting and there are also a number of unspoilt inland villages. Lanzarote has a unique character and is noted for whitewashed houses with bright green doors and shutters, its profusion of exotic flowers, vineyards, palm trees, camels and fine white (as well as black) beaches (some say that Playa Famara is the best beach in the Canaries). Lanzarote is also famous for its spectacular 'Fire Mountains', lunar landscapes, stark volcanic rocks and over 300 extinct volcanoes, which form the Timanfaya National Park (covering around a third of the island, which has been a Biosphere Reserve since 1993).

Unlike Tenerife and Gran Canaria, Lanzarote isn't overdeveloped, mainly because of the efforts of César Manrique, one of Spain's most famous artists and sculptors, who dedicated much of the latter part of his life to preserving the island and ensuring that new construction adhered to traditional architectural styles. His trust, La Fundación de César Manrique, continues to be active on the island, although Lanzarote has grown hugely in popularity over the last decade and there are a number of massive new coastal developments, particularly at Playa Blanca. Locals are strongly against further construction, however, and it seems likely that the authorities will limit future building.

Advantages & Disadvantages

Lanzarote's spectacular, unique scenery is its main attraction, closely followed by the pleasant climate and beautiful beaches. Disadvantages include a limited range of leisure options and the impact of mass tourism around the resorts. Some people regard the desert-like, practically treeless landscape as monotonous, others find it starkly beautiful.

Major Towns & Places of Interest

The main resorts are clustered around or near the capital in the south of the island, where the best beaches are. Arrecife, home to over half the island's population, is popular with locals, although less so with foreigners, who prefer the nearby resort of Puerto del Carmen and its extension, Matagorda. It's a modern, thriving resort with excellent beaches, calm waters, good shopping facilities and lively (i.e. noisy) nightlife. Further east is the quieter resort of Costa Teguise, with good beaches and amenities. Costa Teguise is essentially a man-made resort and is often accused of lacking character.

Inland is the typical Lanzarote town of Tías, which has preserved a more traditional way of life.

In the south-west of the island is the resort of Playa Blanca, which has seen massive hotel and apartment development over recent years, although most of the construction has tried to follow traditional architectural styles. Playa Blanca has good shopping and restaurants, and the resort is best known for its beautiful beaches, particularly those at Papagayo, a short distance to the east. Berrugo, Lanzarote's first marina, is currently under construction at Playa Blanca. In the north and east of the island, there are other small villages, which tend to be quiet and are favoured by those wanting to get away from it all.

Population

Lanzarote has a population of around 65,000, and official figures put the number of foreign residents at around 12,000, of whom 5,600 are EU nationals, the majority British and German. Unofficial figures are slightly higher.

Climate

Lanzarote enjoys the same pleasant climate as the rest of the Canaries and, in the summer, refreshing breezes help to moderate temperatures. Note, however, that these breezes can be strong on the north and west sides of the island.

Crime Rate & Security

Lanzarote has a low crime rate; it has reduced over recent years because of an increased police presence. In crowded resorts, however, pickpockets and theft from hire cars are common.

Amenities

Sports: Numerous water-sports are available on Lanzarote, including surfing off the northern beaches and scuba diving all around the island. Hang gliding and parascending are also popular, as are deep-sea fishing trips. The island also plays host to an 'Iron-man' triathlon every summer. A sports complex is planned at Playa Blanca, which when completed in around 2007 will be one of the largest in the world, including an athletics track, a velodrome, swimming pools and numerous other facilities. Lanzarote has only one golf course, an 18-hole course at Costa Teguise (€48 per round), although two more are being built, at Puerto del Carmen and Yaiza.

Leisure: Lanzarote's leisure activities include hiking and walking in the spectacular countryside, and visiting the island's more remote villages. Puerto del Carmen has a casino and, along with Arrecife, offers lively nightlife with a wide choice of bars, discotheques and nightclubs. There are frequent concerts and recitals at Puerto del Carmen and, less frequently, at Tías. Lanzarote's one theme park, Guinate Tropical Park, is in the north of the island and offers a wide variety of flora and fauna. The Timanfaya National Park can be visited only on an official coach tour.

English-language Cinema & Theatre: There are three multi-screen cinemas on Lanzarote, although films are shown only in Spanish. There are no theatres.

Shopping Centres & Markets: Given its modest size and population, Lanzarote has more than its fair share of shopping centres, including four in and around Arrecife and the Deiland shopping centre and cinema further to the north. Most of these centres have a hypermarket. The main resorts also have good shopping, with many bazaar-type establishments selling a vast range of electrical goods and other items. There are weekly markets in the main resorts.

Foreign Food & Products: A variety of foreign produce is available at the island's supermarkets and hypermarkets, although prices tend to be high.

Restaurants & Bars: Lanzarote's resorts offer many different types of restaurant, with a preponderance of fast-food and Chinese establishments. The island also has several good restaurants serving local cuisine and there are numerous bars, many run by expatriates. As Lanzarote has no particularly 'low' tourist season, bars and restaurants tend to be open all year round.

Services

International & Private Schools: There are two British schools on Lanzarote, at Tahiche and Teguise, including the British school of Lanzarote, which caters for children aged 4 to 16. A few private schools operate on the island, mostly with a religious affiliation.

Hospitals & Clinics: There are two public hospitals in Arrecife, including a geriatric hospital, but these are overstretched and many locals think that the island needs more hospitals. There's also one private hospital, catering specifically for foreigners, at Tías. There are numerous public health centres in the island's towns and also several private clinics, mainly in Puerto del Carmen.

Doctors & Dentists: There are several English-speaking doctors and dentists on Lanzarote, mostly in the resorts.

Tradesmen: In view of the small foreign population on Lanzarote, English-speaking tradesmen aren't always easy to find, although this is changing as the island develops.

English-language Radio: None.

English-language Press: See page 64.

Consulates: There are no consulates on Lanzarote and you should refer to your country's representation on Gran Canaria or Tenerife (see pages 86 and 75).

Churches: The Anglican, Baptist and Evangelical churches hold regular services and meetings either in Arrecife or Puerto del Carmen.

Property

Lanzarote's property market is booming and much construction is under way. Local opinion, however, is turning against further building, which will probably be halted soon. Property should therefore be a good investment.

Cost of Housing: The following prices are intended only as a guide and were current in mid-2002.

- **Costa Teguise**
  One-bedroom apartment: from €70,000 to €85,000;
  Two-bedroom apartment: from €115,000;
  Townhouse: from €175,000 to €205,000;
  Three-bedroom villa: from €300,000 to €400,000.

- **Puerto del Carmen**
  One-bedroom apartment: from €85,000;
  Two-bedroom apartment: from €102,000;
  Townhouse: around €180,000;
  Three-bedroom villa: from €300,000.

Land: There's a reasonable choice of building plots, with prices varying according to location. For large rural plots of over 5,000m², prices start at €30 per m². Smaller coastal plots (around 1,000m² is generally the minimum) cost from around €50 to €100 per m².

Rental Accommodation: The holiday rental market on the island is thriving, although long-term lets (over six months) can be difficult to find and prices are high. Monthly rentals for a two-bedroom apartment range from around €500 to €900 and for a three-bedroom apartment they start at €750.

Communications

Air: Lanzarote's international airport, Guacimeta (☎ 928-811-450), is just outside the capital and has daily flights to other islands, mainland Spain and several European destinations, mainly in Britain and Germany. It's among Spain's busiest, with over 5 million passengers per year.

Sea: Ferries (monohulls, hydrofoils and catamarans) connect Lanzarote with other islands, and services are generally reliable, sometimes including the opportunity to make day trips. Boats leave mainly from Arrecife. The small island of Graciosa off the north coast of Lanzarote is connected to it by boat from Orzola.

Public Transport: Lanzarote's bus services are generally inexpensive and reliable, with routes connecting the main resorts. Arrecife Bus is the main company, with services from Arrecife to Costa Teguise, Puerto del Carmen and Playa Blanca (journey time 90 minutes). As is the case on other islands, taxis also provide a relatively inexpensive service, including guided tours of the island.

Roads: Lanzarote's roads are generally good, although the signposting leaves a lot to be desired. There are sections of dual carriageway from Arrecife to San Bartolomé and to the airport and Tías, although they're short. Roads inland can be winding and slow, and in more remote areas there are no petrol stations.

Planned Developments

Local opinion on Lanzarote is now very much against further major construction on the island, and plans for more golf courses and marinas have been shelved to avoid further destruction of the island's natural environment. The authorities are keen to move away from the mass tourist market and to attract more eco-tourism. It's therefore likely that future development will be strictly limited to small projects which are in harmony with the natural surroundings.

Employment Prospects

These are limited and there aren't as many opportunities in the tourist sector as on the larger islands.

Further Information

Useful Publications

● *AA Essential Lanzarote and Fuerteventura*, A. Sanger (AA Publishing)

Useful Websites

⌨ www.lanzarote.com (general information about the island)
⌨ www.lanzaroteisland.com (a comprehensive, informative website)

LA PALMA, LA GOMERA, EL HIERRO

La Palma is the fifth-largest and most westerly of the Canary Islands (20 minutes by air from Tenerife), covering an area of 728km^2 (281mi^2), with a population of around 80,500. The island is a distinctive, triangular shape and is the greenest of the Canaries, often referred to the 'Green Pearl of the Atlantic'. It also has the most varied landscape and is renowned for its majestic mountains (reaching 2,426m/7,959ft at Roque de los Muchachos, site of one of Europe's most important observatories), lush woodlands (including Los Tilos, a unique laurel tree forest), terraced hillsides (where crops are grown), a beautiful coastline of black sandy bays, and a huge volcanic crater (one of the world's largest, at 9km/5.5mi in diameter and nearly 1.5km/1mi deep), the Caldera de Taburiente, which is a national park. The south of the island is home to the active volcano Teneguía, which last erupted in 1971. This was a fairly tame affair and had no ill effects on any towns or villages, which are situated in the north of the island. The capital is Santa Cruz de la Palma, an attractive, unspoilt town noted for its colonial architecture. La Palma was a latecomer to package tourism because of its thriving, self-supporting agricultural industry and even now, although tourism has grown in importance, agriculture is still the island's main source of income.

La Gomera is the second-smallest inhabited island in the Canaries, covering 535km^2 (207mi^2) and with a population of 18,000. The island is almost totally unspoilt, with stunning valleys and mountains. Mount Garajonay in the Garajonay National Park reaches a height of 1,487m

(4,879ft). The island is noted for its tall cliffs, extraordinary rock formations, lush valleys, lichen-covered rain forests, terraces, date palms, fertile red soil and the natives' strange whistling language, which is used to communicate over long distances. San Sebastian de Gomera, on the eastern side of the island, is the capital and an attractive, historic town from where Christopher Columbus set out across the Atlantic in 1492. The island is becoming more popular with those foreign residents who are looking for a quieter life than is available on Tenerife, and many small apartment blocks are under construction.

El Hierro is the smallest of the inhabited islands (and was until 1492 the farthest westerly point known to Europeans), with an area of 278km² (107mi²) and just 6,000 inhabitants. The main town is Valverde, the only Canary Island capital situated inland, while the island's beaches are located along the southern, virtually inaccessible coastline (El Julan). El Hierro's dramatic landscape is wild and remote, including a massive crater, and the island is almost totally undeveloped and rarely visited by tourists. It was declared a Biosphere Reserve in 2000 and some 60 per cent of its territory is protected, including the area around the port of La Restringa in the south, which has been a marine reserve since 1996. Livestock farming and agriculture (bananas, pineapples and almonds) are the mainstays of the local economy and the island produces wine (considered among the best in the islands). Tourism is very much a secondary activity.

Advantages & Disadvantages

Their balmy climate and spectacular scenery are the main advantages of the three smaller inhabited islands, as is the fact that they've been relatively unaffected by tourism, unlike the other Canaries. All three offer the chance really to get away from it all, and the local inhabitants are renowned for their friendliness and hospitality. Disadvantages include the lack of amenities and infrastructure, the limited range of leisure activities and the islands' relative inaccessibility. Some people may find their small size claustrophobic: both La Gomera and El Hierro can be toured in a day.

Major Towns & Places of Interest

La Palma: Unlike the other Canary islands, La Palma isn't known for its beaches, although the island does have several interesting towns. Santa Cruz de la Palma was once one of the most important ports in the Spanish empire and, although it's no longer so significant, it has retained a colonial air and is an attractive, quiet, well-preserved city, housing many colourfully painted buildings, with typical Canarian wooden balconies. To the south lies Los

Cancajos, a quiet beach resort within easy reach of the capital, offering a wide range of accommodation. In the south of the island, near the Teneguía volcano, lies the lively town of Fuencaliente de la Palma. On the western side of the island are the resorts of Puerto de Tazacorte, a largish town with a fishing port, and Puerto Naos, a purpose-built resort with little character, although it does have one of the island's best beaches. Inland from Puerto de Tazacorte is the island's second-largest town, Los Llanos, and the small town of El Paso. Resident foreigners

on the island tend to live in the Valley of Aridane inland from the west coast, and in the area between El Time and Garafía in the north-west.

La Gomera: San Sebastian de Gomera, situated on the eastern side of the island, is the capital and an attractive, historic town where Christopher Columbus stopped on his way to discover the New World. The town has many interesting monuments and is the island's main port. Valle Gran Rey, on the opposite side of the island, is favoured by foreigners attracted to the town's unique position on the sides of a steep valley. Tourism is a major activity in Valle Gran Rey, which as a result

has grown substantially in recent years. Other places of interest include Vallehermoso and Agulo in the north, and Alajero in the south.

El Hierro: Valverde is the tiny capital (its population is around 4,000), where there are no buildings higher than three storeys and no traffic lights! Despite its small size, Valverde has good amenities, including a hospital, cinema and theatre. Other main towns include Mocanal in the north, Frontera inland and La Restringa in the south. The island's best beaches are to be found at Timijiraque and Hoya del Verdoval on the eastern side.

Population

La Palma: There are around 9,000 official foreign residents on La Palma, of whom nearly 4,000 are EU nationals, the majority are German.

La Gomera: The official foreign population is around 1,600, of which some 900 are EU nationals, mainly German.

El Hierro: Like La Gomera, El Hierro has a small foreign resident population, nearly 1,400, of whom a mere 450 are EU nationals, mainly German.

Climate

La Palma: La Palma is one of the cooler, wetter islands, although rainfall is generally limited to the autumn and winter, peaking in November. While the island's central peak is often covered in dark cloud, the coastal areas are often clear and sunny. During the summer, the island is occasionally affected by clouds of fine dust, which descend for several days at a time.

La Gomera: The island has a mild climate for most of the year, temperatures rarely rising above 25°C/77°F in the summer or falling below 12°C/54°F in winter. Conditions can, however, change quickly and it can be very windy. The centre of the island is significantly cooler and wetter than the rest. January is the wettest month and is when the island is susceptible to storms.

El Hierro: The main climatic characteristics of El Hierro are the strong wind that blows practically all year round and the thick mist that covers parts of the north of the island, often for days at a time. The west of the island is affected by Atlantic storms, which are often strong.

Crime Rate & Security

La Palma: The close community ensures that there's a low incidence of crime on the island.

La Gomera: The island is one of the few remaining places in Spain where you can leave the key in your front door safe in the knowledge that no one will rob you! The island's inhabitants all know each other and respect people's property. Consequently, crime is practically unknown on La Gomera.

El Hierro: Like La Gomera, the island has an extremely low crime rate.

Amenities

Sports & Leisure: The islands' towns offer a limited range of indoor sports facilities. None of the three islands has a golf course, although there are plans to construct one on La Palma. La Palma has an interesting zoo, Maroparque, near the capital, with a range of animals, birds and marine life. Cultural Park, also on La Palma, is dedicated to the traditional Canary Island way of life, and is set in an avocado grove.

La Palma's leading leisure activities take advantage of its spectacular scenery, with walking and trekking extremely popular. Note that the mountainous terrain can be dangerous for the inexperienced and the use of a guide is recommended. Caving and pot-holing are also popular, as is scuba diving, the island having spectacular underwater fauna. Although small, La Palma has more than its fair share of local fiestas, including carnival in February and the internationally-famous procession of the Virgin of the Snow, which is held once every five years.

La Gomera's main sporting activities are sailing along the island's magnificent coastal scenery, windsurfing, scuba diving and fishing (including deep-sea). Walking and hiking around the island are also enjoyed by both locals and tourists, while riding and cycling are also popular.

Water and adventure sports are widely practised on **El Hierro**, where scuba diving (particularly in the south), windsurfing and hang-gliding are especially popular, as is sailing along the island's spectacular coastline. Valverde has a cinema and a theatre, although films and plays are only in Spanish, and two discotheques. Otherwise, leisure opportunities are somewhat limited.

English-language Cinema & Theatre: There are multi-screen cinemas in Santa Cruz de La Palma and at Los Llanos, although screenings are only in Spanish. La Gomera has one cinema and films are also screened outdoors in the summer, although films are shown only in Spanish. Theatre groups occasionally visit the island. There's a cinema on El Hierro, although films are shown only in Spanish.

Shopping Centres & Markets: Although there are no shopping centres on **La Palma**, the island has a reasonable selection of supermarkets, which stock a wide variety of products, including imported produce. La Palma is well known for its excellent fresh produce, particularly fruit and vegetables, which are generally available all year round. There are covered markets at Santa Cruz and Los Llanos selling fresh produce daily and farmers' markets at Mazo and Barlovento at weekends.

La Gomera has numerous supermarkets (over 30 in Valle Gran Rey alone!) and there are also many other shops, such as specialist food stores and boutiques. Fresh produce is excellent and there are indoor markets in the main towns.

There's a selection of supermarkets and small shops on **El Hierro**, mainly concentrated around Valverde and Frontera.

Foreign Food & Products: Imported produce, particularly German and, to a lesser extent, British, can be found at most large supermarkets on the islands.

Restaurants & Bars: Santa Cruz de **La Palma** has several excellent restaurants serving typical Canaries food, plus a selection of other restaurants, such as Italian and Chinese. Outside the capital, options are more limited, although Los Llanos has a few restaurants. **La Gomera** has a wide variety of restaurants and bars, mainly concentrated around Valle Gran Rey, and many serve typical local food. Valverde on **El Hierro** has a few restaurants and bars, and a limited number can be found in other small towns.

Services

International & Private Schools: None, except a Waldorf school at Los Llanos on La Palma.

Hospitals & Clinics: La Palma has a new hospital at Breña Alta. The main towns each have a health centre. Some, e.g. the one at Los Llanos, treat emergency cases. There are also a few foreign medical and dental clinics.

San Sebastian on **La Gomera** has one hospital and there are advanced plans for a large private hospital in Valle Gran Rey. The main towns each have a public health centre and there are also several private clinics, some of them specialist.

Valverde on **El Hierro** currently has two hospitals, one of them incorporating a heliport to provide quicker emergency transfers to hospitals on Tenerife. The island has one public health centre and limited private facilities.

Doctors & Dentists: Doctors and dentists on the islands generally speak English.

Tradesmen: On account of the small foreign population on the islands, English-speaking companies and workers aren't always easy to find.

English-language Radio: No English-language radio stations broadcast from the islands, although along some parts of the east coast of La Gomera you can receive the English-language stations broadcasting from Tenerife (see page 74). The German radio station on La Gomera occasionally broadcasts a programme in English.

English-language Press: *Infomagazin* is a monthly magazine published locally in English, German and Spanish, and also available online 🖥 www.lapalma-magazin.com.

Consulates: There's a German consulate on La Palma, which helps other EU nationals (☎ 922-420-689).

Property

Resale property tends to be scarce and new construction is limited by the Canary Islands' moratorium on building. There are, however, plans to exclude the three smaller islands from this moratorium in order to allow development, although it's expected that any construction will be carried out in such a way as to protect the environment. The three islands are aware that their success will depend on their ability to offer exclusive eco-tourism rather than the mass package tourism found on the other islands. Demand for property is high on all three islands and prices, in particular the price of land, have risen in recent years, although they've yet to reach Tenerife levels. Prices are expected to continue to rise over the next few years.

Cost of Housing: The following prices are intended only as a guide and were current in mid-2002.

- **La Gomera**
  Two-bedroom apartment: from €110,000 to €140,000;
  Three-bedroom apartment: from €130,000 to €160,000;
  Three-bedroom villa with a garden: from €160,000 to €400,000;
  House in the countryside with a large plot: from €200,000 to €400,000.

- **El Hierro**
  Two-bedroom apartment: from €80,000;
  Three-bedroom apartment: from €100,000.

- **La Palma:** Two-bedroom apartment: from €70,000;
  Three-bedroom apartment: from €90,000;
  Three-bedroom villa with a garden: from €160,000;
  House in the countryside with a large plot: from €250,000.

Land: There's a shortage of available building land on **La Palma**, where securing approval for building licences can be a lengthy process. Much of the island's land is classified as rural or agricultural, making it essential to ensure that building permission will be granted before you commit to the purchase of any land. Prices start at around €50 per m². Land prices on **La Gomera** vary greatly. Foreign buyers tend to prefer the more expensive areas, where land costs from €120 to €150 per m². There's little land available for construction on **El Hierro**.

Rental Accommodation: Rented apartments are generally easy to find on **La Palma**, although rented houses are in short supply. Monthly rates for a small apartment (one or two bedrooms) start at €300 and for a house with garden at €750. Long-term rentals are difficult to find on **La Gomera** and **El Hierro**, as property owners prefer the higher returns from short holiday lets. Monthly rates for a small apartment (one bedroom) range from €360 to €450, for a two-bedroom apartment from €450 to €540 and for a house with a garden from €600 to €780.

Communications

Air: La Palma has a small airport situated to the south of the capital, from where there are daily flights to Tenerife Los Rodeos (20 minutes) and to Gran Canaria (40 minutes). Regular flights are also available from Madrid,

Amsterdam and several German airports, but generally not from Britain, from where you need to fly via Tenerife or Gran Canaria. As only small aircraft can land at La Palma's airport, seats are in short supply and you should book as early as possible.

La Gomera's modest airport was finally finished in 1999 and, although it has provided a welcome alternative to the ferry, only small aircraft can use the short landing strip and flights link the island only with Tenerife Los Rodeos and Gran Canaria. As these services are often out of sync with international flights, which usually leave from Tenerife Reina Sofia, many tourists continue to use the ferry (see below).

El Hierro's airport was built in 1972 and is situated to the east of Valverde. It's a small airport and is currently served only by flights to and from other Canary Islands: there are three daily flights from Tenerife Los Rodeos, two weekly flights from Gran Canaria and a weekly flight in the summer only to La Palma.

Sea: Daily ferry services connect **La Palma** with Santa Cruz de Tenerife (journey time 7 hours) and Gran Canaria. **La Gomera** can be reached by ferry from Tenerife, La Palma and El Hierro, and a fast catamaran service was recently introduced from Los Cristianos (Tenerife). Ferry (car and passenger) services are limited to one per day between **El Hierro**'s Puerto de la Estaca (situated a few kilometres to the south-east of Valverde) and Tenerife's Los Cristianos port.

Public transport: La Palma has a reasonable bus service, linking most main centres, and discounted fares are available. **La Gomera** has a good bus service linking the main areas, although services are limited and private transport is sometimes the only option. Public transport on **El Hierro** is limited to a daily bus service between the capital and the other towns. Taxis are readily available and offer an inexpensive way of getting around, although private transport is sometimes the only option.

Roads: In view of the small size of the **La Palma**, the road network is excellent and the quality of roads good. Future bridge and tunnel construction will further improve communications. **La Gomera** has one good main road, resurfaced in 2000, which crosses the island via the National Park, and several secondary roads, all of which follow the natural contours of the central mountain. All roads are narrow and progress is slow. **El Hierro**'s roads are mainly minor and, in view of the mountainous terrain, winding and narrow. A major engineering project has begun to link Valverde with Frontera directly by road, including a 25km (15mi) tunnel, and is expected to be finished by 2004. This will vastly improve communications between the two towns. Bear in mind that petrol stations are often few and far between on the islands.

Planned Developments

La Palma: Bridges are currently being built to improve communications between the main towns and a tunnel is under construction from Breña Alta to El Paso. Two new marinas are being built at Tazacorte and Santa Cruz, and there are plans for a golf course at Los Llanos, although the project has yet to be officially approved.

La Gomera: Building work will commence in 2002 on the marina at Valle Gran Rey, an ambitious project which will greatly improve the island's nautical facilities. A golf course is also planned for Playa de Santiago, although work has yet to start.

El Hierro: The project to link Valverde with Frontera directly by road (see above) is expected to be finished by 2004.

Employment Prospects

These are limited, with fewer opportunities in the tourist sector than on the larger islands. Seasonal work can sometimes be found in agriculture.

Further Information

Useful Publications

● *Landscapes of La Palma and El Hierro*, N. Rochford (Sunflower Books)

Useful Websites

⌨ www.isladelapalma.com (useful general information about La Palma)
⌨ www.lapalma.com (useful tourist information about La Palma)
⌨ www.gomera-island.com (La Gomera's official website)
⌨ www.gomera.net (tourist information about La Gomera)
⌨ www.gomera.org.uk (a useful website about walking on Gomera, with other information about the island)
⌨ www.el-hierro.org (El Hierro's official website)

Cervantes Monument & Edificio de España, Madrid

4.

CITIES

Yﾟou may choose or need to live in or near a major city rather than a resort or rural area. This chapter deals with five of Spain's largest and most attractive cities: Barcelona and Valencia on the east coast, Granada and Seville near the south coast, and the capital, Madrid, in the very centre of Spain. Other cities are considered in the chapters dealing with the relevant areas (e.g. Alicante in Chapter 5 and Malaga in Chapter 6).

BARCELONA

Barcelona is one of Europe's liveliest cities, famous for its avant-garde culture and cosmopolitan atmosphere, apparent at every turn. Gothic and Art Nouveau buildings grace the city and Gaudi's modernist architectural projects, e.g. the still unfinished cathedral, the *Sagrada Familia*, provide an extraordinary backdrop to the tree-lined boulevards of the centre. The city has one of Europe's largest ports and is Spain's most prosperous commercial centre. Barcelona hosted the Olympics in 1992, an event which left a rich architectural legacy. The city also offers some impressive museums (the Picasso museum is of particular note) and a wealth of other cultural and leisure attractions.

Advantages & Disadvantages

Barcelona's main attraction is that it's a lively, cosmopolitan city, in which it's easy for foreigners to become integrated. The city itself is stylish and also has the benefits of its Mediterranean backdrop and a generally pleasant climate. There's a wealth of things to do and Barcelona offers one of the richest cultural scenes in Europe, if not the world. Public transport is generally reasonable, as are communications in and out of the city. Drawbacks include chronic traffic congestion, lack of parking, high property prices in popular residential areas and high noise levels.

Major Areas & Places of Interest

Foreign residents tend to favour the areas of Pedralbes, Sarriá and Tres Torres to the north of the city, where there are extensive residential areas and spectacular views of the city centre and Mediterranean. Sant Just and Cuidad

Diagonal to the north-west are also favoured, their townhouses and villas being some of the most expensive property in the area. Les Corts in the west is also popular, as is the city centre, known as *Eixample,* where there are lots of apartments, and the Vila Olímpica on the seafront near the Olympic port, where there are many new apartment blocks. Popular commuter destinations outside Barcelona include Sant Cugat to the north and Castelldefels and Sitges on the coast (see **Costa Brava** on page 226).

Much of the centre of Barcelona is on the tourist route, including the Gothic Old Town, Las Ramblas, the various Gaudi monuments and the Montjuic area. The city is perennially popular with tourists, whose numbers have increased dramatically in recent years.

Population

The total population of the city is around 1.5 million, of which almost 24,000 are official foreign residents (the actual figure is much higher). The largest European groups are British, French, German and Italian, although the vast majority of foreigners originate from Africa and South America.

Catalan Language

Catalan is one of Spain's four official languages and is Europe's seventh most spoken language, used by around 7 million people in Spain and parts of France and Italy. It's related to Spanish and French but is also quite different from them. Spanish and Catalan are the official languages of Catalonia and the vast majority of inhabitants are bi-lingual, with instruction in Catalan compulsory in schools. The people of Catalonia regard it as a nation within a nation (although within Catalonia, Barcelona is probably the least 'nationalistic' area) and in many areas the Catalan language predominates. Although everyone speaks Spanish, integration into Catalan society and culture is probably easier and quicker if you speak Catalan too. There are several Catalan newspapers and television channels.

Climate

Barcelona has a broadly Mediterranean climate, with cool winters and hot summers, when temperatures can be high. As is the case in other Spanish Mediterranean regions, Barcelona sometimes suffers from the 'cold drop' (*gota fría*) phenomenon in early autumn, when hot air rising from the sea hits colder layers, causing violent storms and torrential rain. Average temperatures are 13°C (56°F) in January and 28°C (83°F) in July.

Cost of Living

Barcelona's cost of living is among the highest in Spain, although it's still one of Europe's cheapest cities.

Crime Rate & Security

While the general level of crime is low in Barcelona and violent crime less common than in many large cities, petty crimes such as bag-snatching and pick pocketing are serious problems and reached 'epidemic' levels in 2000. A recently increased police presence has helped to reduce them, although there are still many areas of Barcelona (e.g. popular tourist spots, the metro and the beaches) where thieves are active. You're advised always to take care of your belongings, especially in crowded places.

Amenities

Sports: The Olympic centres are now Barcelona's sporting showpieces, although the city offers many other excellent sporting venues. You can practise practically any sport in Barcelona, where water-sports are particularly popular. There are many municipal sports centres, indoor swimming pools and private sports clubs, and Barcelona Royal Tennis Club is particularly prestigious. Football is incredibly popular and FC Barcelona (known as *Barça*) isn't simply one of Europe's top clubs but also a source of Catalan pride and identity. Barcelona has two golf courses, one 9-hole and one 18-hole, and there are several more on the nearby Costa Brava (see page 226).

Leisure: One of Barcelona's main attractions is its cultural and leisure scene; the city is packed with museums, exhibitions, cinemas, theatres and leisure complexes. It hosts several important festivals every year, including the prestigious jazz festival in November, and the recently restored Liceu theatre has an extensive opera and ballet programme.

The Tibidabo hill overlooking the city has an amusement park with several rides. Barcelona's Aquarium is the largest in Europe and has an excellent variety of Mediterranean sea-life. The well-maintained zoo includes the world-famous albino gorilla, 'Snowflake'. Port Aventura, located an hour and a half to the south, is one of Europe's largest theme parks, with the latest, scariest rides and attractions set in five themed areas.

The area around the port was extensively remodelled for the Olympics and is popular with residents, offering a range of walks, cafes and restaurants, many of which are housed in the vast Maremagnum complex. Heron City, a vast leisure facility just outside the city centre which opened in 2001, offers a range of shopping, dining, cinemas, concerts, games and activities for all ages and tastes. Barcelona also has several parks and green areas where you can get away from the bustle. Escaping the city is easy and the surrounding countryside and coastal areas have plenty to recommend them. Andorra and France are within easy reach, as are ski resorts in the Pyrenees.

English-language Cinema & Theatre: Some of the city's many cinemas show films in their original language, including English, and there are several small annual foreign film festivals at art and cultural centres. Details can be found in the '*Cines V.O.*' section of the local press.

Shopping Centres & Markets: Several large shopping centres have sprung up in and around the city in recent years, offering an excellent range of shops and leisure activities. The city itself also has excellent shopping facilities and there are over 40 covered food markets, including the world famous Boqueria in Las Ramblas, as well as numerous other specialist markets, such as the weekend flea market on Port Vell.

Foreign Food & Products: Some of the larger supermarkets and department stores stock a selection of foreign foods, although the choice may be limited and prices high. There are two English bookshops in Barcelona, and the British Council has an extensive lending library of British books and publications.

Restaurants & Bars: Barcelona has a seemingly unlimited choice of restaurants and bars, offering a rich variety of cuisines from around the world. Catalan cooking is widely recognised as one of Spain's best and at the forefront of *nouvelle cuisine*, and there are many specialist restaurants around the city.

Services

International & Private Schools: Barcelona has several international schools, including one British, one American, three French and one German. To the north, Castelldefels also has a British school. There are numerous private schools, mainly in the city itself, where instruction is in Spanish; many have a religious affiliation. Fees are high, although not as high as for some of the international schools.

Language Schools: Barcelona has a large number of language schools offering Spanish and Catalan classes to foreigners, and the university also provides a good range of courses. Private classes are widely available.

Hospitals & Clinics: Barcelona is reputed to have some of the best health care in the country. There are a number of public hospitals and several private hospitals, some nationally prestigious. There are also many private clinics, several run by foreigners, and many have English-speaking staff.

Doctors & Dentists: Barcelona has many private medical and dental practices, run by English speakers.

Tradesmen: Many foreign professionals and tradesmen work in Barcelona and between them offer just about every service you could want, from relocation to mobile hairdressing and from satellite installation to insurance. Many advertise in the local English-language press (see below).

English-language Radio: There are no English-language radio stations in Barcelona.

English-language Press: The main English newspapers are printed in Madrid and are available on the morning of publication at international newsagents in Barcelona. Other English and foreign-language newspapers may arrive later in the day or, in the case of some US newspapers, the following day. The main local English-language publication is *Barcelona Metropolitan*, a free monthly paper with news and views about the city and an extensive classified advertisements section.

Consulates: Many countries have consular representation in Barcelona, including Australia, Britain, Canada, Ireland, New Zealand and the USA. For addresses and telephone numbers consult the white or yellow pages under '*Consulados*'.

Churches: Several churches in Barcelona hold meetings and services in English, including Anglican and Catholic churches. The city is home to important Jewish and Muslim populations, served by synagogues and mosques. French and German churches are also represented and the city has a unique, non-denominational International Church. Information about meetings, service times and locations can be found in the English-language press (see above) and at consulates (see above).

Clubs: There are numerous clubs for foreigners in Barcelona, with activities ranging from country dancing to theatre and bridge, and sports such as cycling, football and skiing, as well as political groups such as Conservatives Abroad and Democrats Abroad, and national groups such as the American Club and the Dutch Association. There are also chapters of world-wide social clubs such as the Rotary Club and charitable/self-help organisations such as Alcoholics Anonymous and Lux Mundi. For further details, consult the English-language press (see above) and embassy notice boards.

Property

Property prices in Barcelona are among the highest in Spain, although lower than Madrid's, and there are huge variations between districts. The most expensive property is found in the residential areas to the north and west of the city, the least expensive in the old quarter. Property in the centre tends to be limited to apartments (loft conversions are increasingly popular), while townhouses and villas are located mainly to the west and north on the higher ground overlooking the city. Property is expensive, particularly in the main residential areas, although in the old quarter you can still find cheap properties.

Cost of Housing: The following prices are intended only as a guide and were current in mid-2002.

- **North of the city (Pedralbes, Tres Torres)**
  Two-bedroom apartment: from €190,000;
  Three-bedroom apartment: from €210,000;
  Large apartment: from €550,000;
  Townhouse with a small garden: from €650,000.

- **L'Eixample and Vila Olímpica**
  Two-bedroom apartment: from €230,000;
  Three-bedroom apartment: from €270,000.
  Note that property prices in this area vary enormously according to their orientation, views and condition.

- **Ciutat Vella**
  Two-bedroom apartment: from €150,000;
  Three-bedroom apartment: from €200,000.

Rental Accommodation: As in all large cities, rental accommodation in Barcelona is in short supply, and what's available is among the most expensive in Spain. Most accommodation is let unfurnished and monthly rentals start at €1,200 for a two-bedroom apartment and at €1,500 for a three-bedroom apartment, although prices can be much higher if the apartment is in a desirable location, offers panoramic views or has recently been refurbished.

Communications

Air: Barcelona's Aeroport del Prat is 12km (7mi) south of the city, one of Spain's busiest airports. Most major European airlines have daily scheduled flights to the city and there are daily services to Madrid and the Balearic Islands. The airport is easily reached by train and bus from the centre. Airport information can be obtained from ☎ 932-983-838 or 🖥 www.aena.es/ae/bcn.

Sea: Barcelona is one of the main ports for connections to the Balearics and there are frequent services to and from the three main islands, increased during the summer. There's also a thrice-weekly ferry between Barcelona and Genoa.

Public Transport: Barcelona has a comprehensive public transport system, including a metro (underground railway) with five lines, an overground rail network covering the suburbs, and a good urban bus service. Although these services are operated by different companies, they're well integrated and transport is cheap. Barcelona has two mainline railway stations: Barcelona-Sants (just outside the city, but with metro and bus connections) and Estació de França, with connections to France, the east coast of Spain and Madrid. The *AVE* high-speed train is due to connect Barcelona with the capital in 2004. A funicular and cable car also operate in Montjuic, although these mainly for tourists.

Roads: Barcelona is served by an excellent motorway network running from the city in all directions, although several of the motorways are toll roads. At weekends and on public holidays, roads to and from the city, particularly along the coastal routes, often turn into one long traffic jam. The city itself has a good, easy-to-navigate road system, although as in most large cities it's almost permanently grid-locked and parking is very difficult. Many residents don't use their cars in the city itself, preferring public transport.

Planned Developments

Barcelona's skyline will change dramatically over the next few years with the construction of nine skyscrapers, including the 142m (470ft) Agbar Tower. It's hoped that building will be finished in time for Fòrum 2004, a major international cultural event.

Employment Prospects

Many major international and Spanish companies have head offices in Barcelona, and the city and its suburbs are home to a number of important manufacturing companies. Barcelona, however, can be a difficult place to find well paid work, and many English speakers find their job prospects limited to the tourist sector, translating and English teaching. Speakers of Spanish and Catalan are at a distinct advantage.

Further Information

Useful Addresses

- Cultural Information Office, Palau de la Virreina, La Rambla, 99, Barcelona (☎ 933-017-775)
- Metropolitan Information Service (☎ 010)

Useful Publications

- *Barcelona*, R. Hughes (Panther)
- *La Guía del Ocio*, a weekly magazine listing the city's events, available from newsagents.

- *Homage to Barcelona*, C. Toibin (Picador)
- *Lonely Planet: Barcelona*, D. Simonis (Lonely Planet Publishing)
- *Rough Guide to Barcelona*, J. Brown & B. Catlos (Rough Guides)
- *TimeOut City Guides: Barcelona* (TimeOut Publications/Penguin)

Useful Websites

💻 www.barcelonametropolitan.com (general information about the city)
💻 www.bcn.es/english (the official website for Barcelona City Council)
💻 www.timeout.com/barcelona (up-to-date cultural and leisure information)

GRANADA

Granada is a small city in eastern Andalusia, sitting behind the high mountains of the Sierra Nevada. It lies in a fertile plain in the foothills of these almost permanently snow-covered mountains; agriculture is the surrounding region's main activity. Granada was the last Moorish stronghold in Spain before the country's unification under the Catholic monarchs, and the city's magnificent, internationally famous Moorish palace, the Alhambra, is Spain's most visited monument, receiving several million visitors per year. Granada is one of Spain's major tourist cities, and other popular areas include the Albaicin, the original Moorish quarter, which has many palaces and beautiful houses (known as *carmenes*), and the Sacromonte cave area. Granada is also an important university city and a cosmopolitan place to live.

Advantages/Disadvantages

The attractions of Granada include the beauty of the old part of the city, an excellent cultural scene, some lively nightlife and a cosmopolitan atmosphere. Among its disadvantages are the chronic traffic congestion in the centre (although this has improved in recent years), a lack of investment in the city's infrastructure and the extremes of temperature.

Population

Granada's total population is around 250,000, with few official foreign residents. The city, however, has a large itinerant foreign population and is particularly popular with British and Americans.

Climate

Granada has a typical continental climate, with cold, dry winters and hot summers. The proximity of the snow-covered Sierra Nevada means that night temperatures are often below freezing in winter and cool even at the height of summer. Average daytime temperatures are 5°C (40°F) in January (with night temperatures below freezing) and 27°C (80°F) in July.

Crime Rate & Security

The crime rate is generally low, although around tourist areas petty crime such as bag snatching is common.

Amenities

Sports: There are a number of municipal sports centres around the city, as well as private centres and gyms. Skiing is the city's main sport and the Sierra Nevada's season is one of the longest in Spain, running from early December to late April. The resort has been extensively modernised (the World Championships were held there in 1993) and has over 60km (37.5mi) of ski runs. Granada has one golf course, at La Gabia to the south-west of the city.

Leisure: Granada has an excellent, varied cultural scene, including the prestigious Festival of Music and Dance in early summer, and theatre and jazz festivals. There's usually a wide choice of plays, concerts, lectures and exhibitions catering for all tastes and ages at the city's many arts venues. Visiting the city's monuments and patronising the numerous bars and restaurants are also popular leisure activities. Granada celebrates many annual fairs and festivals, principally during Easter Week and on Corpus Christi (normally in June). Granada has one of Spain's best science museums, with an excellent planetarium and butterfly park. There are two water-parks on the outskirts of the city, open during the summer.

English-language Cinema & Theatre: Granada has several cinemas and theatres, although films and plays are mostly in Spanish, with the exception of visiting plays during festivals.

Shopping Centres & Markets: Shopping facilities are generally good in Granada, whose centre has a wide selection of small shops and chain stores. A large shopping centre with a hypermarket has opened on the outskirts of the city, a daily indoor market is held in the centre and an ethnic market is held on Saturdays; there's also a Christmas market.

Foreign Food & Products: A limited range of foreign produce is available in the large supermarkets and hypermarkets, and prices are high. In the Albaicín quarter, there are several shops specialising in Moroccan goods.

Restaurants & Bars: Granada has an excellent range of restaurants, mainly specialising in local or Spanish cuisine, although there are also international restaurants. Bars and cafés are plentiful and the city has preserved the traditional custom of serving a free *tapa* with every drink. In the Albaicín area, there are several Arab tea-rooms.

Services

International & Private Schools: There are no international schools in the area. Numerous private schools serve Granada, although most have a religious affiliation and places tend to be in short supply.

Language Schools: Language learning is big business in Granada, where there's a large number of language schools offering Spanish classes to foreigners. Granada university also provides a range of courses, and private classes are readily available.

Hospitals & Clinics: There are several public hospitals in Granada, including the prestigious University Hospital, as well as some private hospitals. Construction of a major new health complex (Campus de la Salud) is due to start in late 2002; this will include facilities for medical research, university teaching and several specialist hospitals. Granada has a wide choice of private clinics, many of which specialise in particular areas of medicine. There are also several public health centres around the city.

Doctors & Dentists: There are few foreign doctors and dentists in Granada, although many of them speak English.

Tradesmen: Very few foreign tradesmen operate in the city, where local artisans are usually excellent.

English-language Radio: None.

English-language Press: Most major English newspapers are printed in Madrid and are available in the city. Other foreign newspapers may arrive later in the day or, in the case of some US newspapers, the following day. Granada has no local English-language publications.

Consulates: Italy and Belgium have consulates in the city, other countries being represented in Malaga (see page 179).

Churches: The city has important Moslem and Jewish communities, but no religious services in English.

Clubs: There are numerous clubs in the city offering a range of activities, including sporting, social and self-help. Most, however, are Spanish.

Property

Granada has a healthy property market and in recent years there has been massive construction around the outskirts and in surrounding villages, catering mainly for young commuters, who account for over a third of house buyers. Within the city itself, resale property is in relatively short supply and prices have risen by more than 20 per cent over the last three years. High demand means that prices are likely to continue to rise. Houses in the Albaicín district are particularly sought-after and fetch premium prices.

Typical Homes: Like most Spanish cities, Granada's property is dominated by apartments. In the Albaicín and Realejo districts, however, there are many small houses with wrought-iron balconies and interior patios. Granada's premium properties (with prices to match) are known as *carmenes*, palatial mansions with gardens and fountains.

Cost of Housing: The following prices are intended only as a guide and were current in mid-2002.

City Centre
Two-bedroom apartment from €110,000;
Three-bedroom apartment from €120,000.

Outskirts
Three-bedroom townhouse from €90,000.

Land: Within the city itself, there's practically no available building land and prices are sky high, although on the outskirts and in nearby villages there's generally a good choice of plots. Prices start at around €30 per m^2.

Rental Accommodation: Since Granada has a large university population, rental accommodation is in short supply and can be difficult to find, particularly at the start of the academic year (i.e. in September and October). Typical monthly rents are from around €400 for a two-bedroom apartment and from €500 for a three-bedroom apartment.

Communications

Air: Granada airport is situated to the west of the city (17km/11mi from the centre) and is served mainly by domestic flights, including a daily service to Madrid. There aren't many international flights, although there are some weekly charters from Britain in the winter months as part of skiing packages. However, Malaga airport (see page 181), which has an extensive range of international flights, is easily accessible, the journey taking around 90 minutes by car. Airport information is available on ☎ 958-245-200.

Public Transport: Granada has good bus services linking the centre with most parts of the city (season tickets are available) and mini-buses provide transport from the centre to the Alhambra and the Albaicín areas. A new bus station has recently been opened in the north of the city. Bus services to surrounding towns and villages and to Madrid and Andalusia's other major cities are generally reasonable and frequent. Granada has a train service to Malaga and Madrid, although both services are notoriously slow and many people prefer to drive or take a bus. The high-speed train network isn't projected to extend to Granada in the foreseeable future.

Roads: Granada is easily reached by fast dual-carriageway from the Costa del Sol, Madrid and Seville. Road links with the Granadan coast, the eastern part of the province and Almería aren't as good, with dual carriageways yet to be finished. Roads to nearby towns and villages are generally good. Within the city itself, traffic congestion is chronic, although the local authorities have done much to improve noise and pollution levels in the centre by prohibiting or restricting vehicle access. Parking in the centre is practically impossible, despite the presence of several large car parks.

Planned Developments

These include the completion of dual carriageways to the coast and to Almería, and the construction of a second ring road around the city.

Employment Prospects

Employment prospects for foreigners in Granada are generally limited to the tourist sector and to the teaching of English as a foreign language.

Further Information

Useful Publications

- *Spain: Granada, Seville and Cordoba*, D. Facaros & M. Pauls (Cadogan Guides)
- *Lorca's Granada*, I. Gibson (Faber & Faber)

Useful Websites

- 💻 www.granada.org (the official website)
- 💻 http://granadainfo.com (a comprehensive tourist guide, including accommodation and small ads)

MADRID

Madrid, which sits almost in the middle of Spain, has been its capital since the 16th century. It's Europe's highest capital city (600m/2,000ft above sea level) and the third-largest city in the European Union (after London and Paris). Madrid is a sprawling metropolis of 3 million inhabitants (known as *Madrileños*) and has the highest population density in Spain. It's a major manufacturing centre with Spain's highest per capita GDP, and foreign investment in the capital has risen spectacularly in recent years, in 2001 accounting for 70 per cent of the total foreign investment in Spain.

Madrid is one of Europe's great cities, with its wealth of museums and art galleries (the Prado houses one of the world's finest collections), magnificent parks and gardens, striking architecture, lively theatres, fine restaurants and fashionable night-spots. It's also a friendly, free-wheeling city and has been dubbed the capital of joy and contentment. *Madrileños* have a reputation as (late) night-birds, and a *siesta* is essential if you wish to keep up.

Advantages & Disadvantages

Madrid's main advantage is its seemingly endless range of leisure and cultural activities. It also enjoys Spain's best services and amenities. The public transport system is generally efficient and inexpensive, and there's an abundance of employment opportunities. Drawbacks include the extreme climate and the usual large city phenomenon of continuous traffic congestion, noise (Madrid is reckoned to be the world's third-noisiest city), pollution and high property prices.

Major Areas & Places of Interest

Within the city, neighbourhoods (known as *barrios*) popular with foreign residents include: the historic area around the Plaza Mayor; Martínez Campos and Salamanca (both in the centre); Chamartín, Mirasierra and the exclusive La Moraleja development to the north; Hortaleza and Arturo Soria to the east. Madrid's main tourist areas are around the Puerta del Sol and the Plaza Mayor.

There's also a number of 'dormitory' towns on Madrid's periphery. To the north are the large towns of Tres Cantos (Europe's youngest city), San Sebastián de los Reyes, Colmenar Viejo and Alcobendas. To the west are Las Rozas and Pozuelo de Alarcón (the richest towns in the country), and the luxury development of Majadahonda. In the east are found the busy towns of Arganda del Rey, Coslada, San Fernando de Henares and Torrejón. The suburbs to the south (e.g. Fuenlabrada, Getafe, Leganés and Móstoles) are traditionally working class areas.

Population

Madrid's total foreign resident population is around 285,000 (almost 10 per cent of the total), of which the vast majority are of African and South American origin. There are around 3,000 official British residents and a similar number of Americans.

Climate

Like Granada, Madrid has a typical continental climate, characterised by harsh extremes. Winters can be very cold (skiing is possible in nearby mountains) and foggy, while summers are generally scorching. Average daytime temperatures are 9°C (49°F) in January and 31°C (88°F) in July.

Cost of Living

A Eurostat survey in 2001 reported that Madrid was the second-cheapest capital city in the EU, after Lisbon, and the cheapest for clothing, food, dining out and public transport. Only for health services was Madrid considerably more expensive than other EU capitals. Within Spain, however, Madrid is one of the most expensive cities, with particularly high property prices.

Crime Rate & Security

Madrid generally has a low crime rate, although there are certain areas of the city, e.g. some streets around the Gran Vía and parts of the old quarter, that are best avoided at night. Bag snatching and pick pocketing are commonplace in popular tourist spots and on public transport, and you should take particular care of your belongings in crowded places.

Amenities

Sports: There are numerous sports centres, both municipal and private, in the capital, which has some of Spain's best sporting facilities. Madrid is also a football city, with several clubs, including the world-famous Real Madrid, arguably the world's most glamorous team. Skiing in the nearby mountains is popular, and Madrid and its surroundings have some 14 golf courses, among them Golf La Dehesa to the west of the city, one of Spain's finest courses. Some of the clubs are private, others have pay-and-play facilities.

Leisure: Madrid vies with Barcelona as Spain's cultural Mecca, and the city offers a wide range of cultural activities, including plays, concerts, operas, dance, exhibitions and one of the world's best selections of art galleries.

Madrid zoo is one of Spain's best, with a wide variety of animals, and spring 2002 saw the opening of Faunia, a park where visitors can see animals in their natural habitats. (It includes an Antarctic area, where the temperature is -5°C (23°F), which should prove attractive to visitors during the heat of August). Soto de Viñuelas is a vast area to the north of the city, which the authorities plan to keep as a nature and wildlife reserve open to the public. The Madrid amusement park is an old favourite in the capital and can be reached by cable car. There are three water-parks on the outskirts of the city, open during the summer, and one of the largest theme parks in Europe, Warner Brothers Movieworld, opened in spring 2002 at a huge site south of Madrid. In Alcobendas to the north, there's an interesting science museum with a planetarium.

English-language Cinema & Theatre: Several small cinemas in Madrid show films in their original language, often English. Details are listed in the local press under '*Cines V.O.*'. Some of the city's film festivals also screen films in their original language, including English.

Shopping Centres & Markets: Madrid is one of Europe's shopping capitals, with a wide range of shops to suit all budgets. Most boutiques are centred around Serrano street, although there are shops practically everywhere, and the El Corte Inglés department store has numerous branches in the city. Shopping centres have sprung up all over Madrid and its outskirts in recent years, and several more are being built. Supermarkets and hypermarkets are popular, although Madrid has also retained many of its small food shops, and most neighbourhoods have a good selection, some open until late. The capital has several indoor markets, selling fresh produce every day except Sundays. One of Spain's largest flea markets, El Rastro, is held every Sunday morning in the streets around Ribera de Curtidores.

Foreign Food & Products: Foreign foods aren't easy to obtain in Madrid, especially since the closure of Marks & Spencer's stores. The delicatessen counters of large stores such as El Corte Inglés and some hypermarkets may stock a limited selection, although prices are usually high. Madrid is served by a number of international and second-hand bookshops.

Restaurants & Bars: The number and variety of Madrid's restaurants is overwhelming. The capital is home to several of the Spain's best restaurants as well as to establishments serving food from just about every country in the world, including Cuba, Kurdistan and the Philippines. Prices range from reasonable to outrageous, although most of the good restaurants are more expensive than those in the rest of Spain. Fast food outlets are common, as are bars, which can be found on virtually every corner in the city. *Tapas* are a particular favourite with *Madrileños*, especially in the bars around the Plaza Mayor.

Services

International & Private Schools: Madrid has numerous international schools, a few of them nationally renowned. There are several British schools, mostly catering for children aged 4 to 18, although there are also British nursery and primary schools. The city also has an American School, a Spanish-Irish school and schools catering for other nationalities, including French (with five schools) and German (two schools). Note that some of the larger schools are situated on the outskirts of Madrid (mostly to the north) and are therefore a bus ride from the centre. Fees tend to be high. Madrid also has numerous private schools, many with a religious affiliation, where instruction is in Spanish. Fees are high, although not as high as at some of the international schools, and private schools tend to be located in the city itself.

Language Schools: Madrid has a large number of language schools offering Spanish classes to foreigners, and private classes are also available.

Hospitals & Clinics: Madrid's public hospitals are among the best in Spain and include the prestigious Hospital de la Paz and the Hospital Doce de Octubre. There are also numerous private hospitals. Most districts have a public health centre, often with facilities for dealing with emergencies. There's also a wide range of private clinics, many specialising in particular areas of medicine.

Doctors & Dentists: Madrid has many English-speaking medical professionals, some of them native speakers, and many Spanish doctors and dentists have a good command of English.

Tradesmen: Numerous native English-speaking professionals operate in Madrid and between them offer just about every service, from relocation to mobile hairdressing, satellite installation and insurance. Many advertise in the local English-language press (see below).

English-language Radio: Madrid's only English-language radio programme is broadcast on Thursday evenings by Radio Círculo (100.4FM). The half-hour programme includes news about Madrid, music and interviews.

English-language Press: Most English newspapers are printed in Madrid and are available at international newsagents. Other English and foreign newspapers may arrive later in the day or in the case of some US newspapers, the following day. Madrid is also served by two local English-language publications: *The Broadsheet*, published monthly, offers information about Spain in general, with particular emphasis on Madrid, and is distributed free at points around the capital; *Guidepost*, the official magazine of the English-speaking community and American Club in Madrid, is published monthly and distributed free at tourist offices and hotels around Madrid.

Consulates & Embassies: Numerous countries have diplomatic representation in Madrid. For a list of addresses and telephone numbers look under '*Embajadas*' or '*Consulados*' in the white or yellow pages.

Churches: Several Christian denominations are represented in Madrid, including Anglican, Baptist, Methodist and Presbyterian, and some services are held in English. Catholic services in English are also held and the city has synagogues and mosques for its Jewish and Muslim populations. Information about service times and locations can be obtained from the English-language press and from consulates and embassies (see above).

Clubs: Madrid has a vast range of clubs catering for foreigners, including toastmasters' organisations, theatrical groups, bridge clubs, sports clubs (cycling, cricket and skiing, among many others), political organisations such as the Conservatives Abroad and the Democrats Abroad, and national groups such as the American Club and the British Ladies' Association. There are also chapters of world-wide social clubs such as the Rotary Club and charitable and self-help organisations such as Alcoholics Anonymous and Lux Mundi. For further details, consult the English-language press and embassy notice boards (see above).

Property

Madrid's property prices are the highest in Spain and have increased over recent years after hitting a low during the recession of the early 1990s. There's a good choice available and new construction, mainly in the suburbs, continues.

Typical Homes: Many residential buildings in Madrid are made from red brick and most accommodation within the city is in the form of apartment blocks, often high-rise. In the suburbs, terraced houses or townhouses are increasingly popular, often located around communal gardens with a swimming pool.

Cost of Housing: Prices vary greatly according to the location and the age of a property, as follows:

Two-bedroom apartment: from €150,000 to €500,000;
Three-bedroom apartment: from €200,000 to €500,000;
Three-bedroom townhouse: from €270,000;
Three-bedroom house with a garden: from €350,000 to over €2 million in exclusive areas.

Land: Within the city itself, building land is in short supply and virtually unobtainable. Outside the city there's also a shortage and prices vary from around €140 to over €500 per m².

Rental Accommodation: Rental accommodation is in short supply in Madrid and costs are generally high in all areas. Monthly rentals start at around €900 for a small apartment, at €1,150 for a three-bedroom apartment, at €1,800 for a townhouse and at €2,500 for a villa with its own pool.

Communications

Madrid is at the centre of mainland Spain's road, rail and air networks, and communications are generally excellent.

Air: Madrid's Barajas airport (16km/10mi east of the centre) is Spain's busiest, with an annual volume of some 34 million passengers. Flights are available to world-wide and domestic destinations, and there's a daily service to Barcelona, as well as other major cities. Barajas has seen massive extension in recent years, with the completion of a third runway and terminal, and further extension is planned. The airport can be reached by bus or taxi from the city centre and also by the new metro line. Airport information is available from ☎ 913-058-343 or 🖥 www.aena.es/madrid-barajas.

Public Transport: Madrid has a comprehensive public transport system, including an extensive network of buses linking practically all areas of the city with the centre, an underground metro with 11 lines and a local train network with ten lines, travelling mainly to the northern and southern suburbs. All modes of transport are inexpensive and you can buy season tickets and ten-journey tickets for use on both the buses and metro (€5 for ten journeys in early 2002).

Roads: There's an extensive road network around Madrid, including the M-30 and M-40 ring roads, both of which circle the city; a further ring road, the M-50, is under construction. Spain's main motorways begin at Madrid and branch out in most directions. There are good roads, often dual-carriageways, to the main suburbs and towns outside the city. Within the capital driving is little short of nightmarish, with chronic traffic congestion nearly everywhere. Needless to say, parking is all but impossible. Travel by car is particularly stressful and time-consuming at the start and end of weekends and during holidays, when *Madrileños* depart *en masse* for the countryside and the coasts, and mile-long traffic jams are commonplace.

Planned Developments

Madrid has several major plans for the future, including a bid for the 2012 Olympics and the construction of the M-50 ring road, which will improve connections to the airport and the eastern suburbs.

Employment Prospects

The vast majority of multi-national companies in Spain are based in Madrid, and employment prospects in the capital are generally good. The ability to speak Spanish is a distinct advantage. Teaching English as a foreign language is a popular source of employment for foreigners.

Further Information

Useful Addresses

- International Newcomers' Club of Madrid (☎ 913-764-469, ✉ 101606. 2001@compuserve.com). A club open to all English-speaking people in Madrid, with monthly meetings and a wide range of activities in and around the city. It has around 250 members and there's an annual membership fee.

Useful Publications

- *Broadsheet* (free monthly magazine about Spain but focused on Madrid, where it's published)
- *Lonely Planet: Madrid*, D. Simonis (Lonely Planet Publishing)
- *Madrid*, E. Nash & M. Jacobs (Signal Books)
- *Madrid: The Rough Guide*, S. Baskett (Rough Guides)
- *Time Out: Madrid Guide* (Penguin Books)

Useful Websites

- 🖥 www.munimadrid.es (the official Madrid website)
- 🖥 www.madridman.com (a comprehensive website about the city, run by an American expatriate)
- 🖥 www.gomadrid.com (useful, mainly tourist information)
- 🖥 www.timeout.com/madrid (particularly good for current listings and events)

SEVILLE

Seville (Sevilla in Spanish), in western Andalusia, is one of Spain's most historic and most visited cities. In fact, for many people, Seville is the quintessential Spanish city (it was the setting for great works of literature, such as Quevedo's Don Juan, and e.g Bizet's Carmen and Mozart's The Marriage of Figaro). The old quarter around Santa Cruz and the cathedral is Seville's prime tourist area, followed by Torre de Oro (Golden Tower) on the river and the Maria Luisa park.

The Guadalquivir River divides the city in two: to the north is the historic centre, with the Giralda spire and cathedral (the largest Gothic church in the world) and the old Jewish quarter, Santa Cruz, famous for its beautiful narrow streets lined with white houses, and now the city's main commercial centre;

to the south of the river lie the working class districts of Triana and Los Remedios, the latter now Seville's most popular residential area.

Advantages & Disadvantages

Seville's attractions include the city's beauty and wealth of monuments, and its extensive range of leisure and cultural activities. It also has good communications with the rest of Spain. Disadvantages include the climate, with overwhelming summer heat, and the noise and pollution levels. Traffic congestion is also a problem.

Population

Seville's total population is around 700,000, with few official foreign residents. The city has a large itinerant foreign population, however, and Seville is particularly popular with British and Americans.

Climate

Seville has an extreme climate, with practically only two seasons, summer and winter. Summer starts early (around April) and the city experiences some of the highest temperatures in Europe, with an average of around 35°C (95°F) at the height of the summer and frequent days of over 40°C (104°F). Seville becomes a virtual ghost town in July and August, when many of its inhabitants escape to the coast. Winters are mild, with average temperatures of around 15°C (59°F), although often with persistent rain. Rainfall is mostly confined to the early winter months.

Crime Rate & Security

Seville has an above average crime rate for Spain, particularly for petty crime and car theft; bag snatching is also common. The recently increased police presence in the city has helped to reduce the problem, although thieves are still active in many popular tourist spots, especially the narrow streets in the Santa Cruz district. You're advised to take particular care of your belongings in crowded places. Some suburbs of Seville have a particularly high incidence of crime, mainly drug-based, and the suburb known as the 3000 Viviendas has become a no-go area even for the police.

Amenities

Sports: Seville has some of the best sports facilities in the region and of particular note is the Athletics Stadium at Cartuja, where the 2000 World Athletics Championships were held. There are numerous sports centres around the city and water-sports facilities on the river, particularly for rowing. The city is home to two football clubs, Sevilla and Betis, whose followers are fanatical rivals. Both teams have been up and down between the first and second divisions in recent seasons. There are three golf courses within easy reach of the city.

Leisure: Seville offers a wide range of cultural activities, including an extensive opera and theatre programme at the city's Maestranza Theatre. There are also several other theatres and numerous art exhibitions in the city. Seville is world-famous for its two festivals (when the whole city grinds to a standstill for several days and for which it spends the rest of the year preparing!), during Easter week and at the April Fair. Isla Mágica on Cartuja Island is one of Andulusia's main theme parks, with a range of attractions and shows based on life and Spain and the New World in the 16th century. The park is closed during the winter.

English-language Cinema & Theatre: None.

Shopping Centres & Markets: Seville has excellent shopping facilities centred around Calle Sierpes, including several branches of the El Corte Inglés department store. There's also a wide range of foreign and national chain stores, as well as numerous boutiques. On the outskirts of the city there are several shopping centres, most with a hypermarket and multi-screen cinema.

Foreign Food & Products: A limited range of foreign produce is available in the large supermarkets and hypermarkets, and prices are high.

Restaurants & Bars: Seville has a vast selection of restaurants and bars, with particular emphasis on *tapas* and fried fish.

Services

International & Private Schools: There are no international schools but numerous private schools in Seville, all offering a Spanish curriculum. Most have a religious affiliation and places tend to be in short supply.

Language Schools: Spanish classes for foreigners are popular in Seville, particularly with British and American students, and there's a large number of language schools offering Spanish classes. Private classes are also available.

Hospitals & Clinics: There are several public hospitals in Seville, as well as private ones. Seville also has a wide choice of private clinics, many of which specialise in certain areas of medicine. There are several public health centres around the city and in the outlying districts.

Doctors & Dentists: Doctors and dentists in Seville are mainly Spanish, although some speak English.

Tradesmen: Few foreign services are available in the city, although local expertise is good.

English-language Radio: None.

English-language Press: Most English newspapers are printed in Madrid and are available at international newsagents in Seville. Other English and foreign newspapers may arrive later in the day or in the case of some US newspapers, the following day. Seville has no local English-language publications.

Consulates: Several countries have consular representation in Seville, including Australia, Austria, France, Germany, Italy, the Netherlands, Portugal and the USA. The British consulate in Seville was temporarily closed in early 2002, when the nearest representation was in Malaga.

Churches: No church services are held in English.

Clubs: Numerous clubs operate in the city, offering a range of activities including sporting, social and self-help. Most, however, are Spanish.

Property

Property in Seville is generally cheap, although prices have risen over recent years. A lot of new construction has taken place, both in the city centre and on the outskirts; it has become fashionable to live in one of the many residential areas outside the city. The most expensive property is found along the river, where a new apartment can cost more than twice as much as one elsewhere.

Typical Homes: Like most Spanish cities, property in Seville is mainly apartments. In the centre and Santa Cruz districts, however, there are many small houses with wrought-iron balconies and beautiful interior patios, as well as some large, palatial residences.

Cost of Housing: The following prices are intended only as a guide and were current in mid-2002.

Two-bedroom apartment: from €100,000;
Three-bedroom apartment: from €110,000;
Three-bedroom house (on the outskirts of the city): from €230,000.

Land: Within the city, there's practically no available building land and prices are sky high, although on the outskirts and in nearby villages there's generally a good choice of plots. Prices start at around €40 per m².

Rental Accommodation: There's an abundance of rental property, both short and long-term, although accommodation can be difficult to find at Easter and during the April Fair. Monthly rentals start at around €200 for a small two-bedroom apartment in the centre.

Communications

When Seville hosted the international exhibition 'Expo 92' in 1992, the city's infrastructure was vastly improved and it now has some of the best road and rail connections in the south of Spain.

Air: Seville's San Pablo airport (12km/7.5mi from the city centre) is small and serves mainly domestic flights, with few international connections. Airport information is available on ☎ 954-449-023.

Public Transport: Seville has an excellent urban bus network, with routes serving all parts of the city, and there are advanced plans for a metro. There are train services to other cities in Andalusia, and Seville is connected to Madrid by high-speed train (*AVE*), with a journey time of under two and a half hours.

Roads: Seville has excellent road connections to other cities in Andalusia, as well as to Madrid and western Spain. There's a dual-carriageway ring road, which provides easy access to most parts of the city and its suburbs. Within the city itself, traffic congestion is chronic, particularly around the old quarter (and also on the ring road during rush hours). Needless to say, parking is virtually impossible, except in underground car parks.

Planned Developments

The construction of the underground metro is one of the largest current projects, and further development of the technological park on Cartuja Island is also planned.

Employment Prospects

Employment prospects in Seville are generally limited to the tourist sector and to the teaching of English as a foreign language.

Further Information

Useful Publications

- *Eyewitness Travel Guide to Seville and Andalusia*, D. Bown (DK Publishing)
- *Spain: Granada, Seville and Cordoba*, D. Facaros & M. Pauls (Cadogan Guides)

Useful Websites

⌨ www.sevilla.org (the official Seville website)
⌨ www.sol.com/seville (tourist information)

VALENCIA

Valencia lies almost exactly halfway down Spain's east coast and is the country's third-largest city, with a rich, colourful history. Although Valencia doesn't have the cultural heritage or the vitality of either Barcelona or Madrid, it's vibrant and cosmopolitan and enjoys a Mediterranean setting. Over recent years, the city has undergone a transformation and many parts have been restored, including the port. Valencia is famous for its San José celebrations in mid-March (see below), and the city is an international exhibition and congress destination throughout the year. The city centre is a major tourist attraction, especially since the opening of the City of Arts and Sciences, and in property terms Valencia is one of Spain's up-and-coming cities.

To the south of Valencia lies the Albufera, a vast freshwater lagoon and wildlife sanctuary surrounded by rice fields. The countryside around Valencia is planted with extensive citrus orchards.

Advantages & Disadvantages

Advantages include the city's vitality, its range of leisure activities and the pleasant climate. Disadvantages are the pollution and noise: Valencia has the dubious honour of being one of the world's noisiest cities.

Population

Valencia has a population of around 753,500, of which only a small number (around 3,300) are official residents from other EU countries, mainly Britain and Germany.

Language

Valenciano, a dialect of Catalan, is widely spoken in the city, and many inhabitants are bi-lingual, with instruction in Catalan compulsory in all schools. The Valencianos are strong 'nationalists' and in many areas the Valenciano language predominates. Although everyone speaks Spanish, integration into Valencian society and culture is probably easier and quicker if you speak Valenciano too.

Climate

One of Valencia's main attractions is its climate, which provides over 320 days of sunshine per year. Temperatures are mild all year round, with an average of 16°C (61°F) in January and 32°C (90°F) in July. Rainfall is usually sparse (often limited to torrential autumn downpours) and the region suffers from frequent droughts.

Cost of Living

The cost of living in Valencia is average for Spain, although the city offers some cheap property, particularly on the outskirts.

Crime Rate & Security

Valencia currently has one of the highest crime rates in Spain; it rose by an alarming 25 per cent in 2001. Petty crime, car theft, car burning and drug-related crimes are the most common. You should avoid certain areas of the city at night, e.g. the district around the port, and take care of your belongings in crowded places.

Amenities

Sports: The city offers a wide choice of sporting activities, with several municipal sports centres and many private ones, as well as a velodrome and an athletics stadium. There are several marinas within easy reach of the city, in addition to the large one in the port. There are four golf courses near the city.

Leisure: Valencia has a wealth of leisure activities, including many theatres, which have an extensive programme of opera and ballet as well as plays throughout the year. The avant-garde City of Arts and Sciences, with its acclaimed waterside architecture, is the latest Valencian cultural offering. Valencia also has a museum, an underwater city (L'Oceanografic) and an IMAX cinema. The city has excellent beaches and a long promenade, which is a popular recreational area. Valencia is also famous for its fiestas, particularly that held in honour of San José (believed to have been Jesus' father) in March, when huge cardboard and papier-mâché effigies (*fallas*) of famous (or infamous) people are burned in the streets and hundreds of fireworks are set off. Terra Mítica, near Benidorm, is the city's main theme park.

English-language Cinema & Theatre: Valencia has two cinemas showing films in their original languages, including English, with Spanish subtitles. Information about films and times is given in local press under '*Cines V.O.*'. Occasionally, visiting theatre groups perform in English.

Shopping Centres & Markets: Valencia offers excellent shopping facilities, with several large shopping centres around the city and on the outskirts, where you can find most national chain stores and often a hypermarket. The El Corte Inglés department store has several branches in the city, and international boutiques are also represented. Street markets are held every day and there's a popular antiques and flea market on Sundays.

Foreign Food & Products: Foreign foods and goods aren't easy to find in Valencia, although some hypermarkets have a small selection and El Corte Inglés stock a limited supply. You will, however, find copious supplies on the nearby Costa Blanca (see page 136).

Restaurants & Bars: Valencia has a wide range of restaurants and bars, with particular emphasis on those offering local cuisine based on rice, in particular *paella*, which was invented in the area.

Services

International & Private Schools: Valencia has a number of international schools, including several British schools, situated both within the city and on the outskirts. There's a number of private schools, all offering a Spanish curriculum, many with a religious affiliation.

Language Schools: There are a large number of language schools offering Spanish and Catalan classes to foreigners. Private classes are also available.

Hospitals & Clinics: The city is well served by both public and private hospitals. There are several public health centres within the city, generally one in each district, and numerous private clinics.

Doctors & Dentists: Although there aren't many native English-speaking medical professionals in the city, there are plenty on the nearby Costa Blanca (see page 136). Many Spanish professionals speak English.

Tradesmen: It may be difficult to find English-speaking workers and services in Valencia, and those working on the Costa Blanca may either be reluctant to travel to the city or charge extra for doing so. The city has excellent Spanish professionals, however, and if you have a basic knowledge of Spanish you should have no difficulty finding somebody to undertake repairs and installation work.

English-language Radio: None, although the Costa Blanca radio stations can be received (see page 141).

English-language Press: Most English newspapers are printed in Madrid and are available at international newsagents in Valencia. Other English and foreign newspapers may arrive later in the day or in the case of some US newspapers, the following day. For local English-language publications, see Costa Blanca on page 141.

Consulates: Several countries have consular representation in Valencia, including Belgium, France, Germany, the Netherlands and the USA. The nearest British consulate is in Alicante.

Churches: There are no English-language services in the city, although you may consider travelling to the nearby Costa Blanca (see page 136).

Clubs: Clubs within the city tend to be Spanish, although there are several expatriate clubs on the nearby Costa Blanca (see page 136).

Property

There's an abundance of property on the market in the city, and in recent years there has been an increased demand for beach properties in nearby resorts, both to the south towards the Costa Blanca, and to the north towards the Costa del Azahar. Within the city itself, most of the available property is apartments; if you want to buy a house, you'll need to look outside the city, where they can be surprisingly cheap. In recent years, there's been an increased demand for older restored property in the city, which is often sold at premium prices.

Typical Homes: Valencia's architecture is almost exclusively baroque, and elaborately decorated façades line the streets of much of the city centre.

Cost of Housing: The following prices are intended only as a guide and were current in mid-2002.

Two-bedroom apartment: from €70,000;
Three-bedroom apartment: from €80,000;
Three-bedroom house: from €80,000.

Land: Virtually no land is available for building within the city, although there are plots to be bought on the nearby Costa Azahar and Costa Blanca (see page 136).

Rental Accommodation: Rental property is readily available in the city, although it can be difficult to find at the beginning of term, when university students return. Monthly rates for a two-bedroom apartment are from €600 and for a three-bedroom apartment from €700.

Communications

Air: Manises airport, situated 8.5km/5mi from the city centre, is one of Spain's smaller airports and receives around 2.3 million passengers per year. There's a limited service to Valencia from London, Brussels, Paris and a few other European capitals, in addition to extensive domestic services. Some charter flights use the airport in the summer.

Sea: The port of Valencia is increasingly popular as a stop for cruise ships, and ferries run to the Balearics throughout the year.

Public Transport: Valencia is on a main train line from Madrid and by 2006 will be connected to the capital by high-speed train (*AVE*), cutting the journey time by more than half. Trains also run to Alicante and Murcia, and coaches travel to and from the city to most major destinations in the region. Within the city, public transport is good, with an extensive network of buses and a metro with three lines.

Roads: Valencia is connected by the N-III to Madrid and by the A-7 motorway both to Barcelona in the north and the Costa Blanca in the south, although there are tolls on all sections of the A-7. Both have good access roads to the city. Within Valencia, traffic congestion is chronic and parking practically impossible.

Planned Developments

Among Valencia's many projects is the completion of the Arts Palace by 2003, whose huge auditorium will put the city on the international cultural map. Restoration of the port will also be completed.

Employment Prospects

The prospects of finding work in Valencia are reasonable, provided you have a good command of Spanish.

Further Information

Useful Publications

● *Valencia and the Costa Blanca*, M. Roddis (Lonely Planet Publications)

Useful Websites

⌨ www.turisvalencia.es (the official Valencia website)

Altea Harbour

5.

COSTA BLANCA

The Costa Blanca (White Coast) stretches for 100km (63mi) along Spain's east coast, between the cities of Valencia in the north and Alicante in the south, most of it within the province of Alicante (Gandía is in Valencia). It's so-called because of the clear light and bright sands that are characteristic of this part of Spain's coast. The main industry is tourism, although agriculture is also important, with fruit, vegetables and rice the major crops. The Costa Blanca is one of Europe's top retirement areas and has a large number of foreign residents.

Geographically, the Costa Blanca has two clearly defined sections. The northern part enjoys a dramatic backdrop of high mountains, such as the Montgó at Denia and Puig Campana at Benidorm. There are cliffs and sandy coves along the coast, while inland, mountain valleys are filled with almond, orange and lemon groves, vineyards and pines. The southern coast comprises lowlands, with flat salt plains backing long sandy beaches.

For the purposes of this book, however, the Costa Blanca has been divided into five areas: **Marina Alta** in the north, including the towns of Calpe, Denia, Gandía, Jávea and Moraira; **Marina Baja**, centred around Benidorm, Altea and Villajoyosa; **Alicante** city; the **southern Costa Blanca**, including Guardamar, Torrevieja and Orihuela; and the **Mar Menor** area. Note that, although the Mar Menor area is officially part of the Costa Cálida (the Warm Coast), for the purposes of this book it has been included in the Costa Blanca.

There follows an overview of the Costa Blanca, followed by a directory for each area.

Advantages & Disadvantages

The Costa Blanca's main advantages are its pleasant year-round climate (the principal reason many foreigners choose the area), its attractive scenery, excellent sandy beaches, good communications and amenities in most areas, and attractive property prices. Drawbacks include the impact of mass tourism in the summer months, when many resorts are impossibly crowded, the roads jammed and the beaches packed. The N-332 road becomes particularly congested, especially at places such as Orihuela, Guardamar del Segura, Villajoyosa and Altea, where the road passes near or through the towns themselves, causing long queues. There has been massive development in recent years and many areas are no longer as tranquil as they once were.

Major Towns & Places of Interest

The most popular coastal resorts with foreigners are in Alicante province, including Altea, Calpe (with its famous 'Rock of Ifach'), Denia (named after the goddess Diana), Gandía, Jávea (which has one of the largest expatriate communities), Moraira and Torrevieja. Inland, there are many picturesque villages with panoramic views of the surrounding orange, lemon and almond groves, including Benitachell (an attractive inland village north of Moraira with many nearby residential developments), Orba, Orbeta and Tormos, with others in the Jalon Valley (a conservation area where building is strictly controlled). Benidorm (meaning 'good sleep') is infamous for its ugly, high-rise apartment blocks and hotels, a prime example of coastal development at its worst. Despite this, it's a popular resort, both in the summer and the winter, when northern Europe's retirees flock there. At the southern end of the coast lies the Mar Menor, one of Spain's top tourist destinations.

Population

The Costa Blanca is one of Spain's fastest growing regions and the population is currently around 750,000. There are around 52,000 official foreign residents, the majority British (accounting for nearly 30 per cent of the total), although unofficial figures are considerably higher.

Climate

One of the Costa Blanca's main attractions is its pleasant climate, with over 320 days of sunshine per year. Temperatures are mild year-round, with an average of 16°C (61°F) in January and 32°C (90°F) in July. Rainfall is usually scarce and the area suffers from frequent droughts, although the mountainous north has considerably more rainfall than the south. In the autumn, torrential rain often results from the *gota fría* ('cold drop'), when cold fronts form because of a combination of warm winds, seawater and cold air. In 2001, there were major floods in Alicante and extensive damage to coastal areas such as Calpe, where a large part of the sea front promenade was swept away. Despite such occasional extremes, the Costa Blanca's climate has been described by the World Health Organisation (WHO) as among the healthiest in the world.

Cost of Living

The cost of living on the Costa Blanca is generally low and the area has some of the cheapest property on Spain's coasts, although prices have risen in recent years, particularly in the northern part of the area.

Language

Most of the Costa Blanca lies within the Valencian community, where Spanish and Valenciano share official status as languages. Valenciano is a dialect of Catalan, which is Europe's seventh most widely-spoken language and one of Spain's four official languages. Most inhabitants are bi-lingual and the Valencian authorities have an official policy of promoting the use of Valenciano, although its use is more common in the northern part of the region. Valenciano names of towns and cities are often used in preference to their Spanish equivalents, for example Xabia and Alacant instead of Jávea and Alicante. Like the Catalans, many inhabitants of the Costa Blanca are 'nationalistic', and you may find integration into the local community easier if you make the effort to learn at least some Valenciano, particularly if you choose to live inland in a rural community.

Crime Rate & Security

In general, the crime rate on the Costa Blanca is on a par with the rest of Spain, i.e. low by western European standards. However, levels of crime have increased sharply in Alicante and the Vega Baja area, especially Torrevieja, causing concern among locals. The authorities are taking the matter seriously and there's an increased police presence in the area. Petty crime is common throughout the region during the summer.

Amenities

Sports: The Costa Blanca offers a wide range of sporting activities, primarily water-sports, but with a reasonable variety of 'dry' sports too. There are around 21 marinas along the coast, many of which have sailing and scuba diving clubs and organise year-round activities, including the famous 200-mile regatta held at Altea. Most large towns have municipal sports centres and there's a wide range of private sports centres and gyms along the coast. Riding is also popular, and there are many riding clubs and stables. One of the Costa Blanca's main attractions is its golf courses, and the climate allows play all year round. The coast has around 14 courses, including two near Alicante and three in Orihuela, and several more are planned. Prices for a round start at €21 for a 9-hole course and €30 for an 18-hole course.

Leisure: There's a wealth of cultural activity on the Costa Blanca, with particular emphasis on music, which reaches its height in the August Festival at Alicante. Benidorm is home to the International Song Festival (where Julio Iglesias first made a name for himself) and Torrevieja hosts the Cuban Habaneras festival. The theatre is popular and there's an annual contemporary theatre festival in Alicante and a medieval theatre festival in Elx. L'Alfas del Pi, Elx and Orihuela all hold cinema festivals.

Most resort areas have excellent nightlife, with a wide variety of venues to suit all ages and tastes. Choice is at its widest during the summer, although most places stay open all year round. As is the case in the rest of Spain, the Costa Blanca has fairs and festivities all year round and of particular note are the Alicante fair and the Moors and Christians 'battle' in Alcoy. Valencia is world famous for its San José celebrations held around 19th March every year, when huge effigies of (in)famous people are burned around the city (see page 130). The Levante region of Spain (of which the Costa Blanca is part) is known throughout the world for its pyrotechnic skills and no local festival is complete without a spectacular display of fireworks.

The Costa Blanca's major theme park is Terra Mítica, situated near Benidorm, which opened in 2000 and received over 2 million visitors in its first year. It's based around a mythological theme, with fairground attractions, restaurants and souvenir shops. The region also has several water-parks, open during the summer months. A new aquarium, Seaworld near Benidorm, is the region's latest attraction.

English-language Cinema & Theatre: Several cinemas on the Costa Blanca show films in English, English-language videos can be hired from most video stores. The English-language theatre scene is lively and several towns have active theatre groups. See individual listings below or the local press for further details.

Shopping Centres & Markets: Shopping facilities are generally good on the Costa Blanca, and larger towns such as Alicante, Benidorm, Denia, Gandía and Valencia have a wide range of shops. There are several shopping centres, usually situated on the outskirts of towns and including a hypermarket. Every locality on the Costa Blanca has at least one weekly market and many have indoor markets selling fresh produce daily. Antique and flea markets and car boot sales are also popular and held regularly in several places.

Foreign Food & Products: Virtually every supermarket on the Costa Blanca (with the exception of those in Alicante) has a selection of foreign produce from a variety of countries, mainly Britain, Germany and Norway. There are also a few stores dedicated to foreign produce, such as the British company, Iceland. Most areas also have speciality shops, such as British butchers and German delicatessens. Note, however, that despite the wide availability of these goods, prices are often high.

Restaurants & Bars: The cosmopolitan nature of the coast is reflected in its variety of restaurants and bars, offering just about every sort of food. Many specialise in local cuisine, based on fresh fish, seafood and rice, inevitably including *paella*, which was invented in Valencia.

Services

International & Private Schools: Along with the Costa del Sol, the Costa Blanca probably has the best choice of international schools in Spain. There are several in the region, including British (the majority), American and French. Valencia also has five international schools offering a British curriculum and one German school. Fees tend to be high and places are often difficult to obtain. For further information on accredited international schools with a British curriculum, consult the ECIS website (💻 www.ecis.org) or the National Association of British Schools in Spain (NABSS) website (💻 www.nabss.org). Private schools are found in many of the main towns and cities, especially Alicante, Benidorm and Valencia. All teach a Spanish curriculum, although some offer tuition in other languages. Fees are high, although somewhat lower than those at international schools, and places are often in short supply.

Language Schools: There are numerous language schools on the coast and most local town councils offer courses in Spanish for foreigners. The University of Alicante also runs an extensive programme for all levels of Spanish and private lessons are available in many places. English is widely spoken on the Costa Blanca, although it's rarer inland and in Alicante city.

Hospitals & Clinics: The region is well provided with hospital services, both public and private. Public hospitals are found in Alicante, Benidorm, Denia, Elche, Gandía and Orihuela, and the city of Valencia has excellent hospitals, some of them specialised. Most areas have a private hospital. All of the main towns on the Costa Blanca have a public health centre, where GPs and primary medical services are available, as well as emergency treatment, x-rays, family planning advice and physiotherapy. There are also numerous private clinics, ranging from general medical practices to those specialising in everything from homeopathy to cosmetic surgery. Clinics are sometimes aimed at specific nationalities, although English is spoken at most.

Doctors & Dentists: The Costa Blanca has many doctors, covering the various medical fields, many of whom have excellent reputations. Most speak English and some cater for specific nationalities. There are also many English-speaking dentists.

Retirement Homes: Retirement complexes are as yet virtually unknown on the Costa Blanca and at present the only retirement village is at Calpe, although two more are currently under construction, in Moraira and in the Calpe area. There are several private nursing homes in the region.

Tradesmen: The foreign population on the Costa Blanca is well served by expatriates offering a vast range of services, from plumbing to decorating and electrical work to satellite installation. Many advertise in the local English-language press, particularly the *Costa Blanca News*. While most are hard-working professionals, the Costa Blanca isn't without its 'cowboys' and you should be cautious before using services or parting with large sums of money without having seen credentials or references.

English-language Radio: There are two English-language radio stations on the Costa Blanca: Onda Cero International Costa Blanca, which broadcasts all day, and Radio Altea, which broadcasts on Fridays for an hour.

English-language Press: Most English newspapers are printed in Madrid and are available at international newsagents on the Costa Blanca. Other English and foreign newspapers may arrive later in the day or, in the case of some US newspapers, the following day. There's also a thriving local English-language press on the coast, where many publications are distributed free at supermarkets and large cafés. The main publications are: *Costa Blanca News*, published weekly on Fridays, price €1.35; *The Euro Weekly News/The Entertainer* published weekly on Thursdays; *Female Focus*, published monthly, free; *Valencia Life*, a quarterly magazine, price €3; *Views Magazine*, published monthly, free; *The Weekly Post*, published on Sunday, price €1.20.

Consulates: Alicante has consulates representing Belgium, Britain, Denmark, France, Germany, Italy, Luxembourg, Morocco, the Netherlands, Norway and Sweden. Benidorm has consulates for Finland, Iceland, the Netherlands and Sweden, and there's a Norwegian consulate in Torrevieja.

Churches: There's a range of foreign churches on the Costa Blanca, including Anglican, Baptist, Christian Fellowship, Evangelical, Jewish, Dutch and Norwegian. Catholic services are also held in English at several places. For further information, see area surveys below.

Clubs: The cosmopolitan nature of the Costa Blanca society has spawned a wide variety of clubs, covering interests ranging from bridge to square dancing, as well as a selection of sports and political clubs, the latter represented by groups such as Conservatives Abroad and Labour Supporters. There are also branches of world-wide social clubs such as the Lions Club and Rotary International. Charitable and self-help organisations such as Alcoholics Anonymous, Lucha contra el Cáncer (cancer care) and animal protection groups also operate. For further details of the region's clubs, see the local press (*Costa Blanca News* in particular) and local notice boards. Spanish speakers have the option of joining the many Spanish clubs. Local town halls can provide further information.

Property

The Costa Blanca's property market is buoyant, prices have risen sharply in recent years (around 15 per cent annually) and this trend looks set to continue, at least in the near future. Demand is high and most property buyers are British, who are looking for either retirement homes or holiday residences.

A wide choice of property is available on the Costa Blanca, ranging from small studios in apartment blocks to palatial mansions on private estates. Generally, prices are cheaper in the south of the region and at their cheapest in the older apartment blocks in central Torrevieja and Benidorm, where the quality of construction and finish is, at best, average. The Costa Blanca's most expensive property is in the north, around Altea, Moraira and Javea. There's a shortage of good three-bedroom villas throughout the Costa Blanca.

Recent years have seen a rash of new developments, although many town councils are now calling a halt to construction, particularly those in the north of the region. Construction, however, continues unabated in some areas of the south, particularly in Torrevieja. Those intending to buy off plan on the Costa Blanca should be aware that not all new construction is carried out by reputable, professional companies, and that the resale market for new property is slow, despite what the promoter may tell you! New development is expected to slow in the near future because of a lack of available building land. Construction prices for villas range from €1,000 to €1,200 per m^2, depending on the quality of materials. Villas take at least a year to complete.

As a result of the property boom, a surfeit of estate agents and so-called 'middle men' has emerged on the Costa Blanca, many of them not professionals. Before you commit yourself to an agent, check that he's registered with the GIPE and, if possible, choose a well-established agent. A reputable agent won't pressurise you into a sale, will offer you objective advice and should insist that you're aided by an independent lawyer in your purchase. Note that property prices may vary widely from one agent to another – the higher the price, the greater the commission for the agent. You can sometimes save yourself at least 5 per cent of the price by buying privately (look at the classified advertisements in the local press), although this is more time-consuming than with an agent and carries risks.

Typical Homes: In the southern part of the region, apartment blocks built around communal gardens and a swimming pool are the most common type of construction. In the north, villas are more common. The region's traditional architecture is known as *riu-rau*, a popular type of house with an arcaded front. Many of the area's villas are built in this style.

Land: As is the case in all of Spain's popular residential and tourist areas, available building land on the Costa Blanca is now in short supply. Many town councils, particularly those in the north of the region, are putting curbs on further construction. Prices of plots start at around €90 per m^2.

Rental Accommodation: Not surprisingly, the Costa Blanca has a thriving rental market, almost exclusively for holiday and short-term lets of under six months. Alicante city centre, however, has a shortage of all types of rented accommodation. Long-term lets are available on the Costa Blanca, although difficult to come by, as returns for owners are lower than with short-term rentals and Spanish rental laws favour the tenant rather than the owner. In some parts of the Costa Blanca, it's virtually impossible to find rental accommodation for longer than a couple of months. Rental costs have risen in recent years, in line with the general rise in property prices, although it's still possible to find reasonably cheap winter lets. For specific rental costs in individual areas, see the surveys below.

Communications

The Costa Blanca has good communications. Unusually for Spain, it's served by an extensive road network and no fewer than three airports.

Air: The Costa Blanca's main airport and the international gateway to the Costa Blanca is El Altet, 11km (7mi) from Alicante city centre, which receives over 6 million passengers per year and is one of Spain's busiest airports. It has regular flights (mostly charter) to some 22 countries, most often Britain and Germany, as well as a range of domestic flights, including several every day to Barcelona and Madrid.

The Costa Blanca's second airport is at Manisses, 8km (5miles) from the centre of Valencia, which handles regular flights to many Spanish destinations, as well as several scheduled flights to European airports. San Javier Murcia Airport is 30km (19.5mi) south of the border of Alicante province and therefore convenient for the southern part of the Costa Blanca. It handles only charter flights from British and German airports and from Dublin, as well as domestic flights. Further information is obtainable from Alicante airport (☎ 966-919-000), Valencia airport ☎ (961-598-500), and San Javier Murcia airport (☎ 968-172-000, 🖳 www.aena.es/ae/mjv).

Sea: There's a regular boat service from Alicante Port to the Balearic Islands and Oran (Algeria), and from Denia to Palma de Majorca and Ibiza. Services are increased during the busy summer months.

Public Transport: Public transport is generally good on the Costa Blanca, with a choice of modes of transport. Two RENFE train lines run from Madrid to Alicante and Alicante to Murcia, and there's a narrow-gauge train line run by the Generalitat Valenciana (known as 'Trenet'), which connects Alicante and Denia. The line runs near to the coast and stops at most places on the way, including Teulada, Benissa, Calpe, Altea, L'Alfas del Pi, Benidorm and Villajoyosa. Although the journey is long, the route takes in some beautiful scenery and services are frequent and inexpensive.

Bus routes connect the region's main centres, although services tend to be irregular. An exception is the good service between Alicante and Valencia, which stops at main towns en route. Most large towns also have an urban bus service.

Roads: The Costa Blanca has two main arterial roads: the N-332, which runs parallel to the coast, and the A-7 toll motorway, which has exits to several main resort areas and extends as far as the French border. Both have links to the airport and to main roads to Murcia, Madrid and Almería. Like all Spanish toll-roads, the A-7's fees are high, although discounted season tickets are available.

The N-332 isn't a dual-carriageway throughout its length and it's notorious for tail-backs, particularly during the summer and at certain places, where it runs close to towns (such as Guardamar del Segura, Torrevieja and along the Orihuela coast) or through towns (e.g. Villajoyosa and Altea). The tail-backs are regularly several kilometres long in the high season at these points. There are plans to ease traffic congestion with bypasses and roundabouts, with work starting on the Villajoyosa bypass in late 2002. The region's other roads are generally reasonable, although most aren't dual-carriageways and hold-ups are frequent during the summer and on market days.

Planned Developments

The road network will be improved with the construction of bypasses around towns on the N-332 (see above) and new roads in the Jávea area. New golf courses are also planned, as well as several hotel complexes.

Employment Prospects

Unemployment is generally low on the Costa Blanca and there are many employment opportunities for expatriates (particularly those who speak more than one language). Jobs, however, tend to be limited to the service sector, particularly catering and property. A working knowledge of Spanish isn't always necessary, although definitely an advantage, and a good knowledge of German is sometimes required.

Further Information

Useful Addresses

● British Consulate, Plaza Calvo Sotelo 1, Alicante (☎ 965-216-022 or 965-216-190)

Useful Publications

- *AA Essential Costa Blanca*, S. Roy (AA Publishing)
- *Costa Blanca Insight Pocket Guide* (Insight Guides)
- *Costa Blanca Mountain Walks*, B. Stansfield (Cicerone Press)
- *Lonely Planet: Valencia and the Costa Blanca*, M. Roddis (Lonely Planet Publications)

Useful Websites

- 🖥 www.comunidad-valenciana.com (the official tourist website for the area, also available in English and German)
- 🖥 www.costablanca.org (the official Costa Blanca tourism website, with a wealth of useful information in several languages)
- 🖥 www.costablanca-news.com (the website for the English-language newspaper)

MARINA ALTA

The Marina Alta area comprises the northernmost part of the Costa Blanca, including the towns of Calpe, Denia, Gandía, Jávea and Moraira.

Advantages & Disadvantages

This part of the Costa Blanca is scenically the most attractive and many of its towns and villages have retained much of their original character. The towns of Moraira and Jávea have the distinct advantage of not being on any major roads and are therefore relatively quiet. The area also has a good range of amenities and services, and the summers aren't as hot as on the southern Costa Blanca. Disadvantages include the impact of mass tourism during the summer, road congestion and the most expensive property on the Costa Blanca.

Major Towns & Places of Interest

Calpe is an attractive town which sits on a sandy bay. The famous Peñón de Ifach (a 330m/1,100ft high rock) lies at its northern end and is one of the Costa Blanca's symbols. Calpe is one of the liveliest towns on the coast.

Denia is backed by the Montgó mountain and boasts almost 20km (12.5mi) of coastline, with long sandy beaches to the north of the town and small rocky coves to its south. Denia is the 'capital' of the Marina Alta area and offers an extensive range of facilities and services. Inland from the town

(32km/20mi), lies the village of **Gandía**, in the province of Valencia. A large town, it sits at the foot of the dramatic Safor mountain range and has several important monuments, a fishermen's quarter and port at Grau, and an excellent beach.

Jávea is one of the Mediterranean's most attractive sea ports and is known as the 'Pearl of the Costa Blanca'. Like Denia, it's backed by the Montgó mountain. The town is divided into three main areas: the old town lies 2km (1.2mi) inland from the coast and is famous for its beautifully preserved traditional architecture, with arched entrances to the narrow streets and large gothic windows; the old fishermen's quarter (known as Aduanas del Mar) is on the coast near the marina and fishing port; the main beach and resort area is called El Arenal. Jávea offers a choice of beaches, ranging from the busy El Arenal to the quieter Caleta cove, and the islands of Portichol and Descubridor, which may be visited with a special permit, lie just off the coast. In recent years, many villas have been built in the Jávea area.

Moraira is situated almost due south of Jávea. It was once a small fishing town but is now primarily a tourist and residential area, although the fishing port is still active. The town has several villa developments, an excellent sandy beach and many restaurants. The coastline around Moraira includes some spectacular cliffs. Inland lies the attractive town of **Teulada,** set in the hills and overlooking the coast. Terraced vineyards surround the area, which has good sporting facilities.

Orba has a tranquil atmosphere popular with foreign residents, who live mainly in villa developments. The valley around Orba and the attractive nearby villages of **Alcalalí** and **Jalón** are famous for their wines and orange and almond groves.

Population

Calpe: Calpe's foreign population is around 11,670. Germans are the largest group, followed by the British.

Denia: Nearly a fifth of Denia's total population of 34,000 is foreign, the largest group being German.

Gandía: The foreign resident population is around 3,000, the largest group being British.

Jávea: Out of a total population of around 27,500, nearly half are foreign, more than 40 per cent of them British.

Climate

Marina Alta enjoys the same pleasant climate as the rest of the Costa Blanca. Denia, Jávea and Moraira have the best micro-climates, as the Montgo mountain range protects them from excessive cold in the winter and severe heat in the summer.

Crime Rate & Security

This part of the Costa Blanca generally has a low crime rate for Spain, although petty crime, particularly during the summer months, can be a problem.

Amenities

Sports: Calpe has a new marina and yacht club at which you can take part in a range of water-sports. **Denia** is a major centre for water-sports, its marina having over 500 moorings. Windsurfing is popular, as are 'adventure' sports such as hang-gliding and abseiling. La Sella Golf and Country Club has an 18-hole golf course (currently being extended) and there's a well established golfing community in the area.

Gandía has a selection of sports facilities, including a full-size athletics track and an 18-hole golf course. **Jávea** boasts a marina with excellent facilities and, among the many water-sports on offer, scuba diving is especially popular. Jávea Golf Club has a 9-hole course and the town also has a municipal sports centre and several private sports clubs. **Moraira** also has a popular 9-hole golf course, and the Safor mountain range is nationally famous for its climbing. (See also **Planned Developments** on page 150.)

Leisure: The area offers a rich variety of cultural events, including concerts, plays (there are many amateur dramatic groups), recitals and the International Classical Music Festival in Gandía. Most towns in the Marina Alta offer a wealth of nightlife, for example at Las Marinas in Denia and El Arenal in Jávea; it's particularly lively during the summer. Mountain biking is popular, particularly on the Montgó mountain with its panoramic views, as is rural tourism. This part of the Costa Blanca lacks theme parks (which some people would regard as an advantage); the nearest theme parks are in Benidorm (see page 139).

English-language Cinema & Theatre: Three cinemas in the area, at Calpe, Gata and Jávea, have a weekly English film, usually a recent release. There are also several English-language theatre groups, including the Castle Theatre in Denia, the Jávea Ensemble Theatre School, the Jávea Players and the Careline Theatre in Orba. All groups have full annual programmes of plays and social events.

Shopping Centres & Markets: The region has good shopping facilities, particularly larger towns such as Denia, Gandía and Moraira. Weekly markets are held at Calpe on Saturday, Denia on Monday, Jávea on Thursday and

Moraira on Friday. Antique markets are held in Jalón on Saturday and Teulada on Sunday.

Foreign Food & Products: There's plenty of foreign produce in the area's supermarkets, particularly from Britain and Germany. There are also specialist foreign shops.

Restaurants & Bars: This part of the Costa Blanca has restaurants and bars to suit all tastes and pockets, and there's an abundance of restaurants serving local specialities as well as international cuisine.

Services

International & Private Schools: The Marina Alta area has the best choice of international schools on the Costa Blanca, with two British schools in Jávea and another in Alfas del Pi. Gandía has an English nursery school. There are several private schools in the region's towns and Gandía is home to Valencia University's Polytechnic School.

Hospitals & Clinics: Denia and Gandía have small public hospitals. Some cases are referred to Alicante or Valencia, which have larger hospitals offering specialised services. All of the main towns in the Marina Alta area have at least one public health centre and several private clinics, which offer a range of services including GP consultations, dental treatment, chiropody and cosmetic surgery.

Doctors & Dentists: Many foreign doctors and dentists serve the area and most speak English as well as other languages. There are also several Spanish medical practices where staff speak English.

Tradesmen: The area has an abundance of foreign companies and workers serving just about every possible need.

Churches: Several foreign churches are represented in the Marina Alta area, including Anglican churches in Denia, Jávea and Moraira, Baptist and Evangelical churches in Jávea and a Christian Fellowship church in Calpe.

Property

This part of the Costa Blanca is the most popular with foreign buyers and therefore has the coast's most expensive property, especially around Jávea and Moraira. Villas are plentiful and there's currently a further programme of villa construction, particularly just inland from the coast. Villa prices have risen in recent years, and you can pay astronomical sums for a luxury property with a good view. Although there's a lot of new construction, the rate of building is slowing down and the height and density of new developments are strictly controlled. For example, in Moraira buildings may not be higher than five storeys.

Cost of Housing: The following prices are intended only as a guide and were current in mid-2002.

- **Benitachell**
  Two-bedroom apartment: from €100,000;
  Three-bedroom apartment: from €115,000;
  Three-bedroom villa on a 1,000m² plot: from €200,000.

- **Calpe**
  Two-bedroom apartment: from €70,000 (sea-front from €155,000);
  Three-bedroom apartment: from €120,000 (sea-front from €190,000);
  Villa on a small plot: from €170,000.

- **Denia & Jávea**
  Two-bedroom apartment: from €110,000 (from €160,000 near a golf course);
  Three-bedroom apartment: from €130,000;
  Villa on a 1,000m² plot: from €250,000 (from €325,000 to €1.5 million for seafront villas).

- **Gandía**
  Two-bedroom apartment: from €50,000 (from €70,000 on the sea-front);
  Three-bedroom apartment: from €80,000;
  Three/four-bedroom villa on a 1,000m² plot: from €160,000.

- **Moraira**
  Two-bedroom townhouse: from €150,000;
  Villa on a 1,000m² plot: from €240,000.

Land: Plots are available in the area, although they're easier to find inland, coastal plots being in increasingly short supply. Prices start at €90 per m² for an average location.

Rental Accommodation: There's an abundance of holiday rentals in the area, although long-term rentals can be virtually impossible to obtain unless you make arrangements well in advance. Monthly rentals range from €300 to €480 for an apartment, from €360 to €540 for a townhouse, from €450 to €720 for a small villa and from €720 to €1,200 for a villa with a private pool.

Communications

Air: Denia is 100km (60mi) from both Alicante and Valencia airports; **Gandía** is 130km (80mi) from Alicante airport and 80km (50mi) from Valencia airport; **Jávea** is 90km (55mi) from Alicante airport and 105km (65mi) from Valencia airport. (For airport details, see page 143.)

Sea: There's a regular ferry service from Denia to Palma de Majorca and Ibiza throughout the year, with increased services during the summer months.

Public Transport: The Marina Alta area is well served by the local railway running from Denia to Alicante, with stops at Teulada, Benissa and Calpe. Unfortunately, Jávea and Moraira aren't on the line. Gandía can be reached by mainline train from Valencia. Local buses connect the main areas, although services are somewhat irregular.

Roads: With the exception of Gandía, most of the Marina Alta area lies off arterial roads, and communication within the area is mainly along secondary roads, most of which are very congested in the summer (see also below).

Planned Developments

Road construction is under way in the Jávea area to provide better communications with the rest of the region. An extension to the golf course at La Sella is also in progress, and there are plans for a course at Moraira.

Employment Prospects

These are generally good, with employment available in many fields, although the tourist and service sectors dominate. Spanish speakers are at a considerable advantage.

Further Information

Useful Websites

- 💻 www.xabia.org (the official website for Jávea)
- 💻 www.deniaweb.com (information about Denia and its surroundings)
- 💻 www.gandia.net (information about Gandía)

MARINA BAJA

The Marina Baja area comprises the southern part of the Costa Blanca, including the towns of Altea, Alfas del Pi, Benidorm and Villajoyosa.

Advantages & Disadvantages

The area has excellent amenities and services and a huge variety of things to do. Drawbacks include the effects of mass tourism in the summer months, including overflowing beaches and grid-locked roads. The impact of package tourism is felt most keenly in Benidorm, Spain's busiest resort.

Major Towns & Places of Interest

Altea is one of the most unspoilt places on the Costa Blanca, known for its church's unique Moorish dome and its narrow streets and passageways. The village enjoys a wide variety of nearby scenery, including the Bernia sierra, fruit orchards and dramatic cliffs overlooking beaches and quiet coves.

Further down the coast towards Benidorm and slightly inland lies the quiet village of **Alfas del Pi**, noted for its attractive residential areas, which stretch down to the coast, where there are excellent sports facilities and a lovely beach. Construction has been strictly controlled in Alfas: no building is over four storeys and there's plenty of 'green belt' land.

Benidorm can lay claim to being the epitome (some would say nadir) of package tourism and, along with Torremolinos on the Costa del Sol (201), was Spain's first major tourist destination; today it's the country's busiest resort. The massive influx of tourists in the 1960s resulted in large-scale construction and created a resort packed with towering apartment blocks, bequeathing the town what's undoubtedly one of the ugliest skylines of any Spanish resort. But all isn't doom and gloom: Benidorm has undergone a major facelift in recent years (which almost bankrupted the local authorities), including tree planting and the extension of green areas. The town also boasts Europe's highest hotel and fifth-tallest building, opened in spring 2002 and rising to 210m (693ft). Whatever you may think of it, Benidorm is tremendously popular all year round, with visitors attracted to its beaches, thriving night life and lively atmosphere.

The town is divided into two main areas: the old town, which a traditional fishing port, and the new town built in the 1960s, where the heart of the tourist industry beats along with a proliferation of skyscrapers, shops, cafés and discotheques. Benidorm's two long, clean beaches, Levante and Poniente, are among the best in Spain. In fact, the Levante beach is considered to be one of the eight best in the world (if you ignore the crowds).

Villajoyosa lies to the south of Benidorm and, despite its small size, is the Marina Baja's area's administrative centre. The town is famous for the brightly coloured fishermen's houses which line the harbour and for its chocolate factories. Although not popular with foreign homebuyers, Villajoyosa offers a good beach and a marina and is currently undergoing a much-needed restoration programme.

Population

Benidorm: Benidorm's population is around 56,300, of which 5,750 are officially foreign residents, a third of them British. Unofficial estimates put the foreign resident population considerably higher than this, particularly during the winter months.

Alfas del Pi: Foreign residents account for just over half of the population of 15,700. The majority are British and Norwegian.

Climate

The Marina Baja is a region of climatic contrasts. The high mountain ranges of Helada and Aitana that surround Benidorm give the town a pleasant micro-climate, with an annual average temperature of around 19°C (66°F) and seldom extremes of hot and cold. Inland and away from the shelter of the mountains, however, temperatures are more extreme, much higher in summer and much lower in winter.

Crime Rate & Security

The crime rate is generally low for Spain, although petty crime and theft from hire cars are a problem in the area.

Amenities

Sports: Altea has a sailing club, and at Mascarat, a few miles up the coast towards Calpe, there's a large marina. Altea also has a 9-hole golf course. Benidorm offers an excellent range of sporting activities, including tennis, bowling, cycling and an athletics track. The town also has a marina.

Leisure: Benidorm is world famous for its nightlife, with everything from comedy to glamorous cabaret on offer practically all year round (there's no low season for clubbing!). The numerous nightclubs and discos are mainly in the new town. Benidorm also has an amphitheatre, where open-air concerts and theatre performances are held, including the International Song Festival. Villajoyosa offers a casino, Altea has recently opened a new Arts Centre, and Alfas del Pi holds an annual film festival.

The Costa Blanca's flagship theme park, Terra Mítica, is situated just outside Benidorm and offers a wealth of rides and attractions based (loosely) on a mythological theme. A sea life attraction, Seaworld, has recently opened in Benidorm and is proving popular. Aqualandia, also near Benidorm, is one of Europe's largest water-parks, open only during the summer. Cactuslandia, near Altea, boasts more than a thousand species of cacti, as well as numerous tropical birds.

English-language Cinema & Theatre: Benidorm has ten multi-screen cinemas, at which most films are shown in Spanish, although one cinema has weekly English film presentations. The town also has an active Gilbert and Sullivan Society, while Alfas del Pi has an English Theatre group, which regularly puts on plays and holds social events.

Shopping Centres & Markets: Benidorm has a wide range of shopping facilities, including a new shopping centre, La Marina. There are numerous souvenir shops, and street markets are held twice a week. Altea has a Tuesday market.

Foreign Food & Products: There's a wide choice of foreign produce, particularly British and German, in the area's supermarkets. There's also a range of specialist foreign shops.

Restaurants & Bars: Benidorm is literally packed with restaurants and bars, offering just about every sort of cuisine, although fast food dominates. Altea and Alfas del Pi also have a wide selection of places to eat and drink.

Services

International & Private Schools: Alfas del Pi has a British school and there are two in Jávea further up the coast. Benidorm has one private and two maintained Spanish schools at which fees are high, although lower than for the international schools; places are in short supply.

Hospitals & Clinics: Benidorm has a small public hospital, although many patients are treated in Alicante or Valencia, where there are larger hospitals offering specialised services. All of Marina Baja's main towns have at least one public health centre, and there are several private clinics offering a range of services, including GP consultations, dental treatment, chiropody and cosmetic surgery. Benidorm has four public health centres, where emergency treatment is also available. There are some 30 private clinics and many have English-speaking staff.

Doctors & Dentists: Many foreign doctors and dentists serve the area and most speak English and other languages. There are also several Spanish medical practices with English-speaking staff.

Tradesmen: The region has an abundance of foreign companies and workers serving just about every possible need.

English-language Press: *Look What's On*, a free booklet with information on events and venues in Benidorm, is published monthly and available in most bars. (See also page 141.)

Churches: There are Anglican, Protestant and Evangelical churches and Jewish synagogues in Benidorm, holding regular services. There are also Catholic services in English in the town. Details can be found in the local press.

Property

Property in this part of the Costa Blanca ranges from the most expensive in the whole region (in Altea) to some of the cheapest (in Benidorm).

Cost of Housing: The following prices are intended only as a guide and were current in mid-2002.

- **Alfas & Altea**
  Two-bedroom apartment: from €105,000;
  Three-bedroom apartment: from €125,000;
  Villa on a 1,000m² plot: from €220,000.

- **Benidorm**
  Two-bedroom apartment: from €100,000;
  Three-bedroom apartment: from €110,000.

Land: Plots are generally in short supply, although more are available inland. Prices start at €85 per m², depending on the location of the land.

Rental Accommodation: There's an abundance of holiday rentals in the area, although long-term rentals can be difficult to find and you should make arrangements well in advance. Monthly rentals range from €270 to €430 for a two-bedroom apartment and from €300 to €500 for a three-bedroom apartment.

Communications

Air: Altea is 65km (40mi) from Alicante airport and 100km (60mi) from Valencia airport. **Benidorm** is 45km (30mi) from Alicante airport and 120km (75mi) from Valencia airport. (For airport details see page 143.)

Public Transport: The Marina Baja is served by the 'Trenet' train service, which runs from Alicante to Denia, with stops at Altea and Benidorm. Benidorm has a good urban bus service and there are also frequent daily buses to other towns in the area.

Roads: The N-332 road is notorious for long tail-backs where it passes through Villajoyosa and Altea, and delays are long and frequent during the summer. Construction of a much-needed bypass around Villajoyosa is due to start in late 2002 and there are also plans for a bypass around Altea. Access roads to Benidorm are congested at weekends and during the summer and, as in all Spanish towns and cities, parking can only be described as a 'challenge', despite the existence of several underground car parks.

Planned Developments

Improvements to the road network are one of the region's priorities, including the bypasses around Altea and Villajoyosa. Other planned developments include a golf course and residential and hotel complexes around the Terra Mítica theme park.

Employment Prospects

In high season, employment in the tourist sector is plentiful and easy to find. Outside the summer months, regular employment may be more difficult to obtain.

Further Information

Useful Websites

⌨ www.athenea.com/benidorm (tourist information)
⌨ www.planetbenidorm.com (information about what's on in the town, with a particular emphasis on the nightlife)

ALICANTE

Alicante is a city with 3,000 years of history and has for centuries been one of Spain's most important ports. It's the 'capital' of the Costa Blanca and its main service centre. The city boasts several important monuments, including Santa Bárbara castle and the nationally famous, palm tree-lined marble promenade known as the *Explanada*. Alicante is an important congress centre and offers a wide range of hotel accommodation, although few foreign residents live in the city itself. There are several attractive beaches within the city boundaries and of particular note is San Juan beach to the east, which is over 7km (5mi) long.

Advantages & Disadvantages

Alicante's facilities and amenities are probably the best on the Costa Blanca and it also enjoys a comprehensive public transport system. There's a wide choice of leisure and cultural activities, as well as extensive sports facilities. Disadvantages include traffic congestion, noise, pollution and sometimes excessive summer heat.

Major Areas & Places of Interest

The old quarter of Alicante, known as Santa Cruz, is one of the city's most attractive, with its narrow, pedestrianised streets. Alicante's centre, with its wide range of shops, including the El Corte Inglés department store, is a popular residential area because of its proximity to the city's amenities. To the north-east is the residential area of Carolinas and to the east of the city those of Albufereta, Dos Bahías and Nuevo Alicante, the site of many high-rise apartment blocks and villas. Further east lies San Juan de Alicante, which boasts the city's best, longest beach. As a result of its proximity to the capital and range of amenities, it's a rapidly-growing commuter residential area.

Population

Alicante has a population of around 276,500, most of whom are Spanish. Among the foreign residents is a large group from France, while the British number under 300.

Climate

Along with the rest of the Costa Blanca, Alicante has a mild, pleasant climate for much of the year, although it can be very hot in the summer.

Crime Rate & Security

Alicante has a rapidly growing crime rate (Spain's fastest in 2001), a cause for concern to the authorities. Petty crime, burglary and car crime are particular problems.

Amenities

Sports: Alicante offers a wide range of sports facilities, with several municipal sports centres and many private clubs and gyms. The Royal Nautical and Regatta Club and the Alicante-Costa Blanca Nautical Club are both active in the city's marina, which has over 800 moorings. The private airfield at nearby Muchamiel offers flying in light and ultra-light aircraft. There are also three golf courses nearby, including the recently opened Playa San Juan.

Leisure: Music and theatre are important leisure activities in Alicante and there are concerts on the *Explanada* every Sunday and during the August Festival. There's also an annual Festival of Spanish Contemporary Theatre, as well as frequent plays, operas and dance programmes at the Teatro Principal. The city boasts vibrant nightlife, with a wealth of venues offering live music (jazz and salsa are popular) and a range of other entertainment. Venues are concentrated both in the old quarter, known as El Barrio, and in the more 'modern' area near the sea-front. During the summer months, many events take place on the beach, particularly San Juan beach. Alicante has a casino.

Shopping Centres & Markets: Alicante has excellent shopping facilities, with a range of department stores, shopping centres and international boutiques. The city boasts a new shopping area on Maisonnave Avenue, where many of the chain stores are now located, and several hypermarkets have opened on the city's outskirts. There are daily indoor markets selling fresh produce, and art and craft markets throughout the year.

Foreign Food & Products: Unlike the rest of the coast, foreign products aren't easy to find in Alicante, although the El Corte Inglés delicatessen section and the larger hypermarkets and supermarkets on the outskirts stock some items.

Restaurants & Bars: The city has a wide variety of places to eat and drink, particularly in the old quarter and near the promenade. Many restaurants serve typical Valencian food, based on rice and fish, including *paella*. There's also a wide selection of restaurants offering foreign cuisine, particularly Italian and Chinese.

Services

International & Private Schools: There are no international schools in Alicante, although there are schools in nearby Elche and Alfas del Pi (see page 162). There are several private and maintained Spanish schools in Alicante.

Hospitals & Clinics: Alicante has one public hospital. There are several public health centres in the city, where primary treatment is available, and there are usually facilities for emergency treatment, x-rays, physiotherapy and family planning advice. The city also has numerous private clinics, generally Spanish-run, although staff are often English-speaking.

Doctors & Dentists: Alicante's doctors and dentists are generally Spanish, although most speak English.

Tradesmen: It can be difficult to find English-speaking tradesmen in Alicante, and those working in other parts of the Costa Blanca may be reluctant to travel to the city or may charge extra for doing so. The city, however, is home to high quality Spanish professionals and, if you have a basic knowledge of Spanish, you should have no difficulty finding someone to carry out repairs, alterations and installations.

Churches: There are no English church services in Alicante, but in nearby Torrevieja and Benidorm several foreign churches are represented and hold regular services (see pages 162 and 153 for details).

Clubs: In view of Alicante's modest foreign resident population, there's little English-language club activity. Nearby resorts offer a wealth of activities (see local papers for details) and if you speak Spanish, Alicante is well served.

Property

The property market is buoyant in Alicante city centre and surrounding neighbourhoods, with property in central locations being expensive. Other prime spots include sea-front properties, and villas in Playa San Juan. Note that apartments tend to be small, although they may have three or four bedrooms.

Cost of Housing: The following prices are intended only as a guide and were current in mid-2002.

Three-bedroom apartment (around 100m²): from €90,000 (and from €120,000 in a central location);
Four-bedroom apartment (around 120m²): from €120,000 (and from €170,000 in a central location);
Bungalows: from €200,000;
Villas: from €300,000.

Land: Most available land is situated to the east and north of the city, although the choice is now very limited. Prices start at €100 per m², favourably located plots attracting much higher prices.

Rental Accommodation: There's a shortage of rental accommodation in Alicante, although out of season holiday apartments are available in nearby Albufareta and Nuevo Alicante. Monthly rents for a two-bedroom apartment start at €500 and €600 for a three-bedroom.

Communications

Air & Sea: There are excellent communications into Alicante, via air and sea (see page 143). There's also a regular boat service from Alicante Port to the Balearic Islands and Oran (Algeria), with increased services during the summer.

Public Transport: Alicante can be reached easily by train or bus from Madrid, Murcia and Valencia; there are also bus services to other areas of the Costa Blanca. Public transport within the city is efficient and inexpensive The local train ('Trenet') has frequent services as far as Denia and there are also several stops within the city. Alicante is one of the few places in Spain where trams still operate, although the routes are limited. Urban buses run along more than 25 routes and are a cheap way of getting around.

Roads: Alicante is easily accessible by road (see page 144). Within the city, however, traffic congestion and lack of parking are perennial problems.

Planned Developments

The Alicante tourist board has developed an ambitious redevelopment and refurbishment plan for the city, known as 'Alicante 2020'. Objectives include major improvements to all access areas to the city, extending its green areas, creating disabled access to the city and its transport systems, the extension of the high-speed train line (*AVE*) from Valencia and the construction of a train line to the airport.

Employment Prospects

These are generally good, although if you want to work in the city the ability to speak good Spanish is essential.

Further Information

Useful Websites

⌨ www.alicanteturismo.com (tourist website in several languages with information about the city)

⌨ www.alicante.com (general information and business listings)

SOUTHERN COSTA BLANCA

The area to the south of Alicante is completely different scenically from the northern part of the Costa Blanca. Its terrain is flat and low-lying, with several salt lagoons and extensive market gardens. The region includes the town of Guardamar del Segura, the busy and growing resort town of Torrevieja and the town of Orihuela, which lies inland but has its own coastline with several extensive holiday developments. This part of the coast is famous for its palm tree plantations.

Advantages & Disadvantages

The southern part of the Costa Blanca enjoys many advantages, including excellent beaches, which stretch for miles and some of which are practically untouched by development. The area also has good amenities and communications, and some of the least expensive property on the Costa Blanca. Disadvantages include the intense summer heat, overcrowding during the summer months and congested roads.

Major Towns & Places of Interest

Torrevieja is one of the Costa Blanca's main tourist destinations. The town is named after its large Moorish tower and is surrounded by two large, natural seawater lagoons, which form the well-known 'Salterns of Torrevieja', the largest in Europe and an important conservation area. Torrevieja is a lively town with excellent amenities and beaches and is the main service centre for the many tourist developments on this part of the Costa Blanca. It's one of Spain's most rapidly growing towns and in recent years has seen massive expansion and construction work, particularly in the north of the town. Many people find Torrevieja noisy and crowded, although even within the town itself there are quiet, green residential areas, one of the most attractive being Altos de la Bahía.

The small town of **Guardamar del Segura** lies to the north of Torrevieja. It's situated beside the river Segura and is famous for magnificent beaches backed by vast areas of pine covered dunes, which were planted in the late 19th century to protect the town from advancing sand.

Orihuela is an interesting and historic town with many well preserved monuments. It lies inland from the coast and is surrounded by market gardens, citrus plantations and contrasting scenery, with lush plantations along the Segura river and dry olive and almond groves. The town's 16km (10mi) of coastline, known as **Orihuela Costa**, has some excellent beaches, attractive coves and palm plantations. Orihuela Costa includes several large residential developments, including Dehesa de Campoamor, Cabo Roig, La Zenia, Playa Flamenca and Punta Prima, popular with both foreign residents and Spanish property owners.

Population

Guardamar del Segura: The town's total population is around 10,500, with few foreign residents.

    Torrevieja: One of Spain's fastest growing towns, with a population in 2001 of around 71,000 (an increase of 30,000 since 1998). Over 30,500 are foreign residents, the British constituting the largest group.

Climate

Although the region has the same pleasant climate as the rest of the Costa Blanca for most of the year, during the summer it's the hottest part of the coast and the heat can sometimes be overwhelming. A unique factor influencing Torrevieja's climate is the fact that two salt lakes and the sea surround the town: the air therefore contains high concentrations of salt and other minerals, which have health benefits, particularly for those suffering from respiratory and allergic problems.

Crime Rate & Security

Torrevieja's crime rate has seen a sharp increase recently. In parts of the town, the problem is so serious that some residential areas have appointed private security guards. Burglary is a particular problem, as is theft from cars.

Amenities

Sports: Torrevieja has excellent sports facilities, including a 1,500-berth marina with one of the best yacht clubs in Spain, at which the facilities were used for pre-Olympic trials in 1992. The town also has a municipal sports centre with an athletics track, and there are numerous private sports centres and tennis clubs and a flying club. The coast's other two main marinas are at Dehesa de Campoamor and Cabo Roig. Water-sports are popular everywhere. There are four golf courses in the region, including two in the coastal Villamartin development, a typically Mediterranean-style village, with extensive amenities and sports facilities.

    Leisure: Leisure activities are concentrated in Torrevieja, which has a wide choice of things to do, including a theatre, a casino and numerous clubs and bars offering live entertainment. The Habaneras International Festival in August is nationally famous. Orihuela also offers a programme of cultural events, with particular emphasis on classical music and theatre. There's a water-park to the north of Torrevieja, open only during the summer months.

English-language Cinema & Theatre: There are no English-language cinemas in the region. Torrevieja has an active Show Group, which regularly puts on plays and musicals.

Shopping Centres & Markets: Torrevieja has a wide range of shops, including many boutiques, although there are no department stores. There's also an excellent indoor market selling fresh produce and one of the largest street markets in Spain, held on Fridays. The main tourist developments on Orihuela Costa have supermarkets and a selection of small shops.

Foreign Food & Products: There's an extensive choice of foreign products in the region's supermarkets, particularly from Britain and Germany. There are also specialist foreign shops.

Restaurants & Bars: The region has numerous good value bars and eating places. Torrevieja has a wide selection of restaurants, mainly offering Spanish seafood. The coastal tourist developments also have many international restaurants and bars.

Services

International & Private Schools There's an American school in Torrevieja and a British school in Elche. Torrevieja has two private schools, both offering a Spanish curriculum.

Hospitals & Clinics: Orihuela has a small public hospital, although most cases are referred to Alicante or Valencia, which have larger hospitals offering specialised services. All of the region's main towns have at least one public health centre and there are several private clinics offering a range of services, including GP consultations, dental treatment, chiropody and cosmetic surgery.

Doctors & Dentists: A range of foreign doctors and dentists serve the region, most able to speak English and other languages. There are also several Spanish medical practices where the staff speak English.

Tradesmen: The region has an abundance of foreign companies and workers, serving most needs. The majority are concentrated around Torrevieja, although most offer their services along Orihuela Costa.

Churches: The Anglican, Christian Fellowship and Evangelical churches regularly hold services in Torrevieja, where there are also Catholic services in English. Details can be found in the local press.

Property

Torrevieja and the surrounding coast have the cheapest property on the Costa Blanca. The area has seen a boom in new construction, particularly apartment blocks, over the last decade and the town is one of the few places on the Costa Blanca where new building is still being approved. Orihuela Costa has an abundance of resale property, particularly apartments in developments such as Playa Flamenca.

Cost of Housing: The following prices are intended only as a guide and were current in mid-2002.

- **Torrevieja**
  New two-bedroom apartment: from € 75,000 to €110,000;
  Resale two-bedroom apartment: from €95,000 to €115,000;
  Three-bedroom apartment: from €100,000 to €150,000;
  Three-bedroom villa with a shared pool: from €150,000;
  Three-bedroom villa with a private pool: from €200,000.

- **Orihuela Costa**
  Two-bedroom apartment: from €80,000 to €130,000;
  Three-bedroom apartment: from €90,000;
  Two-bedroom townhouse: from €130,000;
  Three-bedroom villa: from €240,000;
  Large country house: from €200,000.

Land: Building plots are available from €65 per m^2 inland and from €200 per m^2 in desirable coastal positions. Away from the coast, large rustic plots of around 10,000m^2, with small dwellings (often little more than huts), are available from €50,000.

Rental Accommodation: Holiday lets and short-term rentals are relatively easy to find outside high season, although long-term rents (longer than a few months) are difficult to obtain. Monthly rentals start at €300 for a two-bedroom apartment and €350 for a three-bedroom apartment. Villa rentals start at €600, although all rentals in high season are around four times as high as these rates.

Communications

Air: Torrevieja is equidistant (35km/22mi) from Alicante airport and Murcia's San Javier airport. Orihuela Costa lies slightly nearer to San Javier airport.

Public Transport: Torrevieja's public transport system is limited to buses, which serve most parts of the town. Buses are also available to other parts of the coast and to Alicante.

Roads: Tail-backs are common on the N-332 along Orihuela Costa and around Torrevieja and Guardamar del Segura, although work is due to start in Guardamar del Segura in 2002 to improve circulation. During the summer months, traffic along the whole of the coast is slow and congestion frequent. The centre of Torrevieja often experiences grid-lock and parking is difficult despite several new underground car parks.

Planned Developments

Torrevieja is one of the few places on the Costa Blanca where new construction is still being approved and this looks set to continue for at least the near future. Development will also continue on Orihuela Costa and there are plans to improve services and amenities in the area. Improvements are due to be made to the N-332 (see above).

Employment Prospects

Job prospects are generally good, although mostly limited to the tourist and service sectors. Bar and restaurant work is easy to find.

THE MAR MENOR AREA

The Mar Menor is the largest salt water lake in Europe, covering an area of 170km² (105mi²). It lies at the southern end of the Costa Blanca, in the province of Murcia. The lake is surrounded on practically all sides by residential developments, the main one being at **La Manga**, a narrow wedge of land between the Mar Menor and the Mediterranean. The Mar Menor area is well known for its excellent beaches, the variety of year-round water-sports and the therapeutic benefits of its high salinity. The Mar Menor has several islands, including the large Isla Mayor (which is privately owned) and Isla Perdiguera, although these are of interest only to visitors.

Advantages & Disadvantages

The Mar Menor area has many advantages, including the pleasant climate (particularly during the winter), the area's natural beauty and its extensive water-sports facilities. There are over 40km (25mi) of beaches and at La Manga, including those surrounding the lake. Amenities are extensive and the area is easily accessible by road and by air – ever more so as San Javier airport increases its number of flights. Disadvantages include the excessive summer heat and the vast number of tourists who flock there in July and August.

Major Towns & Places of Interest

Los Alcázares is a small town on the north side of the Mar Menor. It was once a fishing port, although it's now essentially a service centre for the tourist industry and has many popular residential areas which are fully occupied during the summer, when the town's usual population of 8,500 swells to many times this figure.

Pilar de la Horadada is a small town, often considered to be the southern gateway to the Costa Blanca and well known for its excellent beaches. The town is mainly residential and it has a small marina. Tourism is the main activity, although there's also a thriving market garden export business.

La Manga is the name given to the narrow strip of land along the southern edge of the Mar Menor, which also borders the Mediterranean. The strip is 21km (13mi) long, 1.5km (less than a mile) at its widest and a mere 100m wide at its narrowest point. Most of it is taken up with high-rise hotels and apartment blocks, although the far eastern end remains undeveloped. Plaza Bohemia and Puertobello are La Manga's liveliest areas and it's one of Spain's top tourist destinations: more than half of Murcia's hotels and over 87 per cent of its apartment blocks are at La Manga!

Population

The foreign population is concentrated in La Manga, where there are large colonies of Britons and Germans. In the summer season, the area is popular with Spanish holiday-makers and property owners.

Climate

The Mar Menor area has a broadly Mediterranean climate, with less rain than the northern Costa Blanca. July and August can be very hot and the winter months are the warmest on mainland Spain. Rain, which is often torrential, falls mainly in the autumn.

Crime Rate & Security

The area has a low crime rate, although theft from hire cars is common.

Amenities

Sports: The Mar Menor is one of the world's best areas for water-sports, not least because water temperatures never drop below 11°C in winter and in summer reach 30°C. La Manga is home to four marinas and 11 sailing schools. There are classes in a variety of water-sports, including scuba diving, with many archaeological remains and sunken ships off the region's Mediterranean coast. There's also a good choice of 'dry' sports, including racket sports, horse riding and cycling, which is particularly popular because of the region's flat terrain. The nearby Cartagena Sierra and natural parks are popular with hikers and mountaineers. There are three golf courses at the western end of the Mar Menor, at Club La Manga Resort, one of Europe's largest sports and leisure resorts. There are plans for more courses in the same area.

Leisure: La Manga is one of the Mediterranean's top tourist destinations, offering a wide variety of leisure activities, particularly during the summer. Numerous restaurants, bars and nightclubs line the strip and La Manga's summer nightlife is internationally famous; there's also a casino. The area holds several important fairs and fiestas during the year and of particular importance are the Festival of the Sea in August and the International Theatre Festival. Saline mud from the Mar Menor is widely claimed to have health and beauty benefits, and several hotels in the area offer spa and mud treatments. There are no theme parks or water-parks in the area.

English-language Cinema & Theatre: Three open-air cinemas operate during the summer season, although films are shown only in Spanish.

Shopping Centres & Markets: La Manga has a wide choice of shopping facilities and there are several shopping centres along the strip. The Sunday market in Cabo de Palos, which sells fresh produce and other wares, is one of the best in the area.

Foreign Food & Products: Shops and supermarkets on La Manga stock a wide selection of foreign produce.

Restaurants & Bars: There's an extensive choice of restaurants and bars throughout the area, many of the restaurants specialising in local cuisine, although there's also a wide range of international fare.

Services

International & Private Schools: The area's only international school is the American school at La Manga. There are no private schools (the nearest are in Murcia and Cartagena).

Hospitals & Clinics: For hospital treatment you must travel either to Cartagena or Murcia, both of which have public hospitals. Several public health centres serve the area and in La Manga there are also a few private clinics with English-speaking staff.

Doctors & Dentists English-speaking medical professionals are available, including several on La Manga strip.

Property

One of the distinguishing features of property in this area is a sea view: practically all property along La Manga is beach-front. Property is in high demand and relatively short supply in La Manga, as practically all of the available land has been built on and the strip is such a popular destination. The western end of the strip is the most populated and characterised by high-rise apartment and hotel blocks, whereas the eastern end is quieter and has more townhouses and villas. Some of the Costa Blanca's cheapest property can be found in Pilar de la Horadada and on the northern side of the Mar Menor, where construction has been intense in recent years.

Cost of Housing: The following prices are intended only as a guide and were current in mid-2002.

Two-bedroom apartment: from €80,000;
Three-bedroom apartment: from €90,000;
Note that for properties with particularly good views, prices are at least double the above.
Three-bedroom villa on a small plot in La Manga: from €200,000;
Three-bedroom villa on a 1,000m^2 plot in Pilar de la Horadada: €200,000.

Land: Practically no building land is now available on La Manga, but on the other side of the Mar Menor you will pay from €60 per m^2 for inland plots and from €200 per m^2 for plots in desirable coastal locations. Away from the coast, large rustic plots of around 10,000m^2 with small dwellings (often little more than huts) are available from €50,000.

Rental Accommodation: Holiday rentals are plentiful in the Mar Menor and there are competitive offers in the winter months, when many of the resort's apartments are empty. Long-term rentals including the summer months can be difficult to obtain, although outside La Manga availability is greater. Monthly rentals start at €400 for a small apartment.

Communications

Air: San Javier Murcia is the main airport serving the area. Although it's one of Spain's smallest, air traffic has increased greatly in recent years and a growing number of daily charter flights is available to selected British and German airports as well as to Dublin. Further information is available on ☎ 968-172-000 or 🖥 www. aena.es/ae/mjv. Alicante airport is also within reasonable travelling distance (see page 143).

Public Transport: The Mar Menor has little public transport, and private transport is essential.

Roads: There's a motorway from La Manga to Cartagena, but otherwise communication by road is mainly via the N-332 and secondary roads, which tend to become congested during the high season.

Planned Developments

Given that there's little available land in La Manga, future development will be mainly in other areas around Mar Menor. There are projects for further golf courses and residential developments at the western end of the lake.

Employment Prospects

There's lots of seasonal work in the area, particularly in the tourist sector in July and August. Outside high season, however, jobs can be difficult to find.

Further Information

Useful Websites

🖥 www.marmenor.net (the main website for the area)
🖥 www.lamanga.com (Club La Manga Resort's website)

FERNANDO SCORNIK GERSTEIN

Spanish Lawyers
(abogados, lawyers, rechtsanwalt, counsellors at law)

Specialists in:

- Litigation
- company and commercial law
- immigration
- conveyance
- tax law
- investments
- probate
- personal injury
- matrimonial and family law
- criminal law
- intellectual property
- maritime law
- fiscal representation in Spain

Branches in:

- Madrid
- Gran Canaria (2)
- Lanzarote
- Tenerife

3rd Floor
32 St. James's Street
London SW1A 1HD, UK
tel. 020–7930 3593/0769 • fax: 020–7930 3385
e-mail: acedillo@fscornik.co.uk

Nerja

6.

COSTA DEL SOL
& LAS ALPUJARRAS

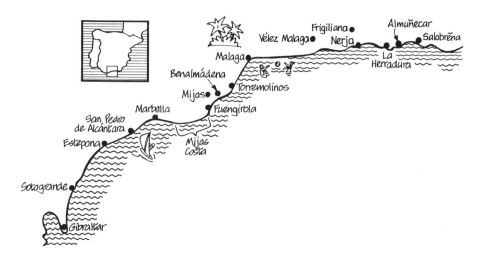

The Costa del Sol is situated on the south coast of Spain in the province of Andalusia, which is the country's most varied region. It stretches some 190km (120mi) along the Mediterranean, from its most westerly point at Sotogrande (close to Gibraltar, in the province of Cadiz) to Motril in the east in the province of Granada, although the section from Nerja to Motril is officially known as the Costa Tropical. This chapter also covers the area known as Las Alpujarras (see page 216), which is near the Costa del Sol on the southern side of the Sierra Nevada.

The heart of the Costa del Sol is in the province of Malaga, between Estepona and Nerja, where tourism is highly developed and the area's principal industry (some 8.5 million tourists visited the Costa del Sol in 2001). The scenery is dramatic, the coastline ringed by high mountain ranges along most of its length, including the Sierra Bermeja behind Estepona, the Sierra de las Nieves – with peaks rising to 3,000m (9,900ft) – which forms the backdrop to Marbella, and the high mountains of the Axarquía range, which flank much of the eastern Costa del Sol.

Most of the coast is green and lush (mainly thanks to intensive watering), and there are large wooded areas, mostly of pine and cork oaks. The eastern region is a centre for tropical fruit farming, with vast areas planted with avocados, custard apples and mango trees. The far west of the coast is the least developed part, where there are still large stretches of virgin countryside dotted with cork oaks and cattle. From Estepona eastwards, however, the area becomes ever more built-up, although gardens and green areas provide some relief from the urban sprawl.

For the purposes of this book, the Costa del Sol has been divided into eight areas: **Estepona and Sotogrande**; **Marbella**; **Fuengirola and Mijas**; **Benalmadena**; **Torremolinos**; **Malaga city**; the **Eastern Costa del Sol and Costa Tropical**; and the **inland areas**. Below is a general overview of the

Costa del Sol, followed by a detailed directory for each area. The final section of this chapter deals with **Las Alpujarras**.

Advantages & Disadvantages

The overwhelming advantage of the Costa del Sol and the main reason for its popularity with foreigners is its climate, which is warm and sunny for much of the year. Communications are another attraction, the region being easy and inexpensive to reach by air from most parts of the world. Leisure facilities are excellent all along the coast, particularly for golf and water-sports. The people of this part of Spain are known for their hospitality and are well used to foreigners, which eases their integration into the community.

The Costa del Sol's popularity has its downside, however: the region can become very crowded, particularly in July and August, when the roads become jammed and beaches swarm with bodies. Some parts of the coast have been over-developed and vast building projects threaten more of the coast. There has also been a failure to improve the region's infrastructure, which therefore hasn't kept pace with new construction and increases in population.

On balance, however, most foreigners (both residents and those with holiday homes) would agree that the Costa del Sol is generally a fine place to live. Indeed, it was ranked as the world's number one retirement destination in *International Living*'s 2001 survey.

Major Towns & Places of Interest

At the westernmost point of the Costa del Sol lies the luxury development of Sotogrande, whose nearest significant population centre to the east is the town of Estepona. Between the two and inland are the attractive white villages of Manilva and Casares. Further east along the coast is San Pedro de Alcantara (known locally as San Pedro) and to the east of that the world-famous marina at Puerto Banus and 'Golf Valley' in Nueva Andalucía, before you reach Marbella, the jewel in the Costa del Sol's crown.

Inland from San Pedro and Marbella is the village of Benahavis and the road to Ronda, along which there are many popular developments. Back on the coast, after Marbella and the leisure harbour of Cabopino, lies Mijas Costa, a long, extensively-developed (some would say over-developed) stretch of coast, extending to the town of Fuengirola. North of Fuengirola, is the hillside village of Mijas and behind the Mijas mountain range lie several rural towns, the most popular of which include Coín and Alhaurin, surrounded by citrus fruit plantations.

Back on the coast, which is almost completely built-up until past the eastern edge of Malaga, is the resort of Benalmadena, which merges to the east into one of Spain's oldest package holiday destinations, Torremolinos. The city of Malaga is next and to its east lie several smaller resorts, such as Rincón de la Victoria and Torre del Mar, which are popular with families from Malaga.

The eastern end of the Costa del Sol is much less developed than the west and building has generally been more in keeping with the surroundings. The most popular expatriate destination on the eastern side is Nerja, with beaches set in small coves and world-famous caves. Beyond Nerja lie a series of smaller resorts, each located in its own bay, such as La Herradura and Almuñécar, before the Costa del Sol ends at the town of Motril. The Axarquía mountain range to the north of Nerja is known for its attractive, well kept villages, some practically untouched by 20th century 'progress'.

Population

The Costa del Sol is one of Spain's fastest growing areas and the population has increased dramatically over recent years – to around 1.3 million – and is expected to reach 2 million by 2010. For details of foreign population numbers, see area directories below.

Climate

The Costa del Sol is renowned for its fine climate, which is usually warm and sunny, and the region enjoys over 325 days of sunshine per year. Rain falls mainly in the autumn and winter and can be torrential. Droughts also affect the region, however, and are sometimes severe, for example during the mid-1990s. The summer months are hot, with little or no rain, although there may be the occasional thunderstorm. Some parts of the coast, particularly the western side beyond Fuengirola, are cooler than the rest of the region in the summer as they're fanned by Atlantic breezes, which don't reach the rest of the coast.

Prevailing winds can be strong and come from both the Atlantic and the Mediterranean. Towns in valleys, such as Malaga and Fuengirola, sometimes also experience a hot wind blowing from inland, known as the *terral*. Winter months are cool or mild on the Costa del Sol, although heating is necessary in the evenings. It never snows on the Costa del Sol itself, although it's relatively common to see snow on the Axarquía mountains in the winter and occasionally on the mountains to the west. The Mediterranean's waters are quite warm during the summer months, but cooled throughout the rest of the year by cold currents from the Atlantic. Average temperatures on the coast are 17°C (63°F) in January and 31°C (88°F) in July.

Cost of Living

The cost of living on the Costa del Sol is around average for Spain, lower than in Madrid and Barcelona but on a par with most large cities and towns. Property is, however, very expensive – in the Marbella area, among the most expensive in the country.

Crime Rate & Security

In general, the crime rate on the Costa del Sol is low for Spain, although petty theft from property and cars is rife in the summer. You're advised never to leave valuables in your car and always to lock your property securely when you're away, even if you just pop to the swimming pool. Car theft is on the increase, particularly of expensive luxury models, which are often stolen to order. 'Mafia' crime, highly publicised and dramatised by the media, does feature on the coast (also nicknamed the 'Costa del Crime'), but rarely intrudes on everyday life. The Costa del Sol has recently become a target of the Basque separatist movement, ETA, which has planted a number of car bombs in resorts along the coast.

Amenities

Sports: There are numerous sports centres along the coast, catering for many types of sport. Most towns have at least one municipal sports centre, where membership and costs are subsidised, usually with extensive facilities and an indoor swimming pool. There are numerous private sports centres, although membership fees and hourly rates vary greatly. There are also numerous tennis clubs, including the prestigious Manolo Santana Club in Marbella and the Lew Hoad Tennis Village near Mijas.

Golf is perhaps the Costa del Sol's most popular sport and not for nothing is the coast known as the 'Costa del Golf'. The number and variety of golf courses continue to grow; in mid-2002 there were around 30, most situated at the western end of the Costa del Sol. The Valderrama Golf Club at Sotogrande is one of the most prestigious (it hosted the Ryder Cup in 1997 and the World Golf Championships in 2000). Investment in golf tourism continues and there are plans for several major new courses – including some public courses – financed and built by the regional authorities. Membership is compulsory for some courses, although the majority offer a 'pay-and-play' facility. However, golf on the Costa del Sol doesn't come cheap: the cost of a round ranges from around €70 to over €200!

Not surprisingly, water-sports are popular on the Costa del Sol, where there are several leisure harbours and marinas, most of which have a sailing club and host regattas. The coast is also within easy reach (two hours by car) of Europe's most southerly ski resort, the Sierra Nevada, which is open from December to March/April. The resort has numerous hotels and over 60km (37.5mi) of runs (it hosted the World Ski Championships in 1993).

Leisure: Leisure facilities have been vastly improved in recent years, and the Costa del Sol now has something for just about every taste and age group. One of the largest new leisure developments is the racecourse at Mijas Costa, which offers horse racing with top international names every Sunday throughout the year, except in the summer when meetings are held on Saturday evenings. There are several leisure centres in the area, including the vast Plaza Mayor complex (with numerous restaurants and a 20-screen cinema) near Malaga airport, and a new complex is currently under construction on the seafront at Marbella.

The variety of landscape and scenery on or near the Costa del Sol encourages numerous leisure pursuits, including hiking, touring, sightseeing and bird-watching. Rural tourism is popular at weekends, as is visiting the cities of Cordoba, Granada and Seville, all of which offer a wealth of monuments and cultural heritage within easy reach of the coast.

Tivoli World in Benalmadena is the Costa del Sol's oldest theme park and is a popular place for both young and old. Selwo is a huge safari park near Estepona with a large variety of animals and activities. There are also several water-parks (open only during the summer) as well as recreational parks such as El Retiro in Malaga.

English-language Cinema & Theatre: Although there are numerous cinemas along the coast, most show films only in Spanish, although Puerto Banus has regular screenings in English. Malaga and Marbella both host annual film festivals. English-language theatre groups (usually amateur) play at venues along the coast and there's a permanent theatre in Fuengirola, where most of the plays are in English.

Shopping Centres & Markets: Shopping centres have sprung up along the coast in recent years and there are plans for several more in the near future. There's an excellent range of shops in most areas and weekly open-air markets (both general and flea markets) are an essential part of life on the coast; there are also daily indoor markets where you can buy fresh produce.

Foreign Food & Products: Most supermarkets on the Costa del Sol stock a selection of foreign foods from a variety of countries, primarily Britain, the Scandinavian countries, Germany and Ireland. There are also a few foreign chain stores, including the British company Iceland (trading as Icelandia in Spain) and the Irish retailer Dunnes Stores. Most areas also have speciality shops such as British butchers and Swedish bakeries. Note, however, that despite the wide availability of imported goods, prices are sometimes high. Shopping in Gibraltar, home to many popular British stores including BHS, Marks & Spencer and Safeway, is also an option for those in search of British goods. The British bookstore, Bookworld España, has two shops on the coast, in San Pedro and Fuengirola.

Restaurants & Bars: Everywhere on the coast has plenty to offer in terms of bars, nightclubs and restaurants, serving cuisine ranging from Swedish to Thai and including the Costa del Sol's own 'culinary delicacy', fried fish. For further details, see the individual area directories below.

Services

International & Private Schools: The Costa del Sol is well served by international and British schools, and several new schools have opened in recent years in response to growing demand. The majority of schools teach a British curriculum (GCSE and A-levels or the International Baccalaureate) and some include a parallel Spanish curriculum. All schools are co-educational and most provide education from 3 to 16 or 18. Fees are generally high and for a ten-year-old may be from €1,500 per term upwards. There's also a French school (Malaga), a German school (Marbella) and Finnish, Norwegian and Swedish schools (Fuengirola). For further information, consult the European Council of International Schools (🖥 www.ecis.org) or the National Association of British Schools in Spain (🖥 www.nabss.org).

Apart from international schools, where instruction is mainly in English, there are also numerous Spanish private schools along the Costa del Sol. Some are maintained (*concertado*), which means that the fees are subsidised by the government, but the majority are non-maintained and fees are high, although generally lower than at international schools. Most private schools are co-educational; those with a religious affiliation tend to be single-sex.

Language Schools: There are numerous language schools for Spanish and most other major languages on the coast, and many town councils also offer Spanish for foreigners courses. The University of Malaga has a foreign language school and runs an extensive programme at all levels of Spanish. Private lessons are also widely available. English is spoken throughout the Costa del Sol, although to a limited extent inland and in Malaga city.

Hospitals & Clinics: The Costa del Sol is well served by several major public general hospitals in Malaga and there's also one in Marbella, where the quality of treatment and care is generally high. These hospitals include the nationally renowned children's hospital, El Materno, and the Carlos Haya, famous for its excellent cancer treatment and care. There are also many private hospitals along the coast offering a variety of treatments. A private health scheme offering emergency transfer by helicopter is also available. Most areas have at least one public health centre where you can see a GP, and many also offer emergency treatment, x-rays, family planning advice and physiotherapy. There are also numerous private clinics, ranging from those practising general medicine to more specialised operations, for example homeopathy and cosmetic surgery. Clinics sometimes cater for specific nationalities and staff usually speak English.

Doctors & Dentists: The Costa del Sol has a wealth of doctors covering most medical specialities, many with excellent reputations. Most speak English and some cater for specific nationalities. There are also many English-speaking foreign medical practitioners in the major towns, including a number practising complementary medicine such as acupuncture and chiropractic. There are also British and English-speaking foreign dentists.

Retirement Homes: Until recently, nursing and residential care homes were virtually unknown on the Costa del Sol, but in recent years several have opened, most of which are private. There are few state nursing homes in Spain and places are limited, although there are private homes in most areas as well as some residential care homes. Three new residential care establishments are under construction in Estepona (with 115 places) as well as large complexes near Alhaurin and San Pedro de Alcántara.

Tradesmen: The foreign population on the Costa del Sol is well served by expatriate tradesmen, offering a vast range of services, from plumbing to decorating and electrical work to satellite installation. Many advertise in the local English-language press, particularly *Sur in English*. While most are hard-working professionals, the Costa del Sol isn't without its 'cowboys', and you should be wary of employing anyone without a personal recommendation or references.

English-language Radio: In recent years, English-language radio has expanded and there are now several stations on the coast. Two stations linked to the BBC broadcast from Gibraltar and can be received at most places along the coast, BFBS1 (broadcasting mainly pop music) and BFBS2 (a mixture of programmes from Radio 4 and Radio 5). The longest running and most popular radio station is Onda Cero International, which broadcasts music and local news. Newer stations include Coastline Radio, Global Radio, Central FM and Spectrum, all of which mainly broadcast music.

English-language Press: English-language newspapers such as *The Express*, *The Guardian*, *The Mail*, *The Mirror*, *The Sun*, *The Telegraph* and *The Times* are printed in Madrid and are available at newsagents along the coast on the morning of publication (but aren't so easy to find inland or in the cities). Other British newspapers arrive later in the day or, in the case of some US newspapers, the following day. There's also a thriving local English-language press on the coast, most of which is distributed via supermarkets, newsagents, cafés and restaurants. The main publications include: *Absolute Marbella*, glossy free monthly magazine mainly concerned with high society in Marbella; *Andalucía Golf Magazine*, free monthly golf magazine; *Costa del Sol News*, newspaper with emphasis on cultural and social events around the coast, available every Thursday, price €0.75; *Essential Marbella*, glossy free monthly magazine mainly concerned with high society in Marbella; *The Euro Weekly News*, published on Thursdays at €1 and incorporating *The Entertainer*; *Hi!*, monthly society magazine about society on the Costa del Sol, modelled on *Hello!*; *Lookout*, free quarterly magazine about Spain; *The Reporter*, free monthly magazine about Spain and the Costa del Sol, often with an ironic twist; *Sur in English*, the flagship free English-language newspaper, published on Fridays and noted for its classified ads and *Town Crier*, free weekly newspaper published on Mondays. There are also several property publications, such as *Property News*, *Property World* and *Llave en Mano* (in Spanish).

Consulates: There are numerous consulates on the Costa del Sol, mainly in Malaga, including those representing Austria, Belgium, Brazil, Canada, Chile, Columbia, Finland, France, Germany, Italy, Monaco, the Netherlands, Norway, Switzerland and the UK. Fuengirola has consulates for Ireland, Iceland and Sweden, while the Luxembourg consulate is located in Marbella. Addresses and telephone numbers are printed in the yellow and white pages under 'Consulados'.

Churches: The Costa del Sol is well served by churches of various denominations, most of which meet at least weekly. The Church of England has churches in Malaga and Fuengirola, and regular CofE services are held in other churches in most other parts of the Costa del Sol. There are three mosques, in Fuengirola, Malaga and Marbella, and synagogues in Estepona (where there's an active Jewish Centre), Marbella and Torremolinos. Other denominations – including the Church of Scotland, Methodists, Evangelicals and Jehovah's Witnesses – are also well represented, while the Danish and Swedish Churches also meet regularly for worship. Further information can be found in the local press and on notice boards.

Clubs: The cosmopolitan nature of the Costa del Sol has spawned a wide variety of clubs, representing everything from bridge to square dancing, cycling and football, from the Conservatives Abroad to Labour clubs, and from American to South African social clubs. There are also chapters of global social clubs such as the Lions Club and the Inner Wheel. Charitable and self-help organisations such as Alcoholics Anonymous, Cudeca (cancer care) and Lux Mundi also operate on the coast. For further details, see the local press (e.g. the *Costa del Sol News*) and notice boards, or contact town halls, some of which (such as Torremolinos') have a database of clubs and associations in their area. Spanish speakers also have the option of joining a local club, of which there are many. Local town halls can provide further information.

Property

In the last few years, the property market on the Costa del Sol has been booming, with buyers spoilt for choice regarding type and location of property. Nevertheless, prices have been rising steadily and between September 2000 and September 2001 some areas saw increases of up to 25 per cent. This trend is expected to continue, at least for the next few years. Marbella, closely followed by Estepona, saw the largest rise in overseas sales in 2001: some 80 per cent of properties were purchased by foreigners, the British accounting for some 35 per cent and Germans for 30 per cent. In 2001, it was estimated that a third of all spending by foreigners on property in Spain was in the province of Malaga.

The residential market on the Costa del Sol is still in its infancy compared with other parts of Spain (until comparatively recently, many parts of the Costa del Sol which are now residential areas were farmland or open countryside), so the necessary infrastructure, i.e. transport, schools, hospitals and other essential services, is often conspicuous by its absence, although this situation should improve in the coming years.

A huge variety of property is available on the Costa del Sol, from small studios in apartment blocks to palatial mansions in large estates. There are over 400 residential developments (*urbanizaciones*) on the Costa del Sol and more than 2.6 million foreigners own homes there. Generally, prices are lower to the east of Marbella and at their cheapest in older apartment blocks in the centre of Fuengirola and Torremolinos, where the quality of construction and finish is, at best, average. The most expensive property on the coast is found in the luxury developments to the west of Marbella and in Sotogrande. There's a general shortage of quality one-bedroom and four-bedroom apartments on the Costa del Sol, where sea-front and golf course properties are also in short supply. Those that come up for sale usually attract a premium.

Recent years have seen a boom in new developments and in mid-2002 there were some 90 under construction on the western part of the coast alone. Buyers of off-plan properties on the Costa del Sol should be aware that not all new construction is carried out by reputable companies and that the resale market for newly built property is slow, despite what the promoter may tell you! New development is expected to slow in future as a result of a lack of available building land. Construction prices for villas range from €700 to €1,200 per m², depending on the quality of materials.

The property boom has resulted in a surfeit of estate agents and so-called 'middle men' on the Costa del Sol, many of whom aren't professionals. Before committing yourself to an agent, you should check that he's registered with the GIPE and if possible choose a well established one. A reliable agent won't pressure you into a sale, will offer objective advice and should insist that you're advised by an independent lawyer. Note that property prices can vary widely from one agent to another – the higher the price, the greater the agen'ts commission. You can often save yourself at least 5 per cent by buying privately (check the classified advertisements in the local press), although this is more time-consuming and potentially risky than using a registered agent.

Typical Homes: The Costa del Sol has two main types of home: apartment blocks (sometimes tower blocks) mainly located in the centres of popular residential areas, often with communal gardens and a swimming pool; and individual villas, usually set in tree-lined streets in quiet developments. The quality of construction and finish varies considerably, from below average to the best that money can buy; most new developments are of above average quality. In recent years, several companies specialising in timber homes have established themselves on the coast, although this type of property has yet to prove popular.

Rental Accommodation: The attractions of the Costa del Sol mean that there's a thriving rental market, particularly for holiday and short-term lets (under six months). An exception is Malaga city centre, which has a shortage of rental accommodation. Long-term lets are available on the coast, but more difficult to find, as returns for owners are lower than with short-term rentals and Spanish law favours tenants rather than owners. Rents have risen sharply in recent years in line with the general rise in property prices, although it's still possible to find a reasonably cheap rental in the winter. For rental rates in individual areas, see the directories on the following pages.

Communications

Air: The major airport for the Costa del Sol is Malaga's Pablo Picasso airport (8km/5mi to the west of Malaga centre), which is the third-busiest in Spain with an annual average of nearly 10 million passengers. It's well served by domestic and international flights, especially from Britain, Germany and Ireland, with between 50 and 100 flights daily. Scheduled flights operate from most major European destinations throughout the year and charter flights are also widely available, although charters from destinations such as Bristol and Edinburgh are suspended during the winter. The airport was modernised in the early 1990s and is spacious and generally efficient. A new control tower was completed in 2001 and there are plans for a second runway and terminal.

The airport is linked by bus services to central Malaga and Marbella, and there's a railway station at the terminal with regular services to Malaga and Fuengirola, stopping at most major towns on the way. Taxis are plentiful and prices are reasonable, e.g. around €40 to Marbella. Car hire companies are much in evidence at the airport; even if a company doesn't have an office at the terminal building, it will usually arrange to meet you at the airport with a car. Flight information is available on ☎ 952-048-804 and 🖥 www.aena.ed/ae/agp.

Gibraltar airport also serves the Costa del Sol, but there are few flights and they're almost exclusively to and from Britain. Queues to leave Gibraltar are often long and customs checks are lengthy. There's no public transport to Gibraltar from the Costa del Sol except taxis, which may drop you at the border (if they're willing to take you that far at all) rather than queue to get into and out of Gibraltar. Note also that you may require a visa to enter Spain from Gibraltar. For flight information ☎ 350-73026 from abroad or 956-773-026 from Spain.

Sea: Malaga port was modernised and extended in 2001, when a new 5km quay was built. The city is a popular cruise ship destination and there are also ferry services to Melilla.

Public Transport: The Costa del Sol isn't particularly well served by public transport, with the notable exception of the Malaga-Fuengirola train (see below) and Malaga city buses, and it's virtually impossible to travel quickly from one end to the other on public transport. There are, however, regular bus services from Malaga to major towns and cities in Andalusia, including Algeciras, Granada, Ronda and Seville. Local services operate along the coast from Malaga to Nerja, Malaga to Fuengirola and Fuengirola to Marbella, stopping at towns on the way. This service, currently a monopoly run by the Portillo bus company, tends to be somewhat erratic and buses are rarely punctual. Malaga has an extensive network of local buses serving most areas of the city, and most towns have their own bus services, generally providing a reasonable service, although they may be limited at weekends.

Malaga is on the main rail route from Madrid and the 600km (375mi) journey takes around four hours on comfortable Talgo trains, which operate a frequent service. The two cities will be connected by high-speed train (known as *AVE* – a French *TGV* in disguise) by around 2004, when the journey time will be cut to less than two and a half hours.

There's a local train service (*cercanías*) from Malaga to Fuengirola, stopping at most major towns and developments along the route, including Arroyo de la Miel (Benalmadena), Torremolinos and the airport. The service is known for its punctuality (trains leave every 30 minutes) and it's extremely popular. The Andalusian government has plans to extend the service to Marbella in the west and to Nerja in the east, although these are still on the drawing board and services aren't expected to be operational until 2012. There's also a local train service from Malaga to Cártama, north of the city.

Taxis are plentiful and a relatively cheap mode of transport, particularly if there are several passengers. Typical prices are around €30 from Malaga airport to Fuengirola and €45 from Malaga to Marbella. Most taxi drivers speak some English.

Roads: In recent years, there have been vast improvements to the road network along the Costa del Sol, although there's still much to be done to reduce traffic congestion. The main road (the N-340 or the *Carretera de Cádiz*) runs along the coast (it actually runs from Cadiz to Barcelona) and is a dual-carriageway from Nerja to Estepona. Work has begun on a dual-carriageway from Estepona to Sotogrande, which is expected to be completed by the end of 2002. Hold-ups are particularly common around Malaga during peak times and everywhere in the summer. The N-340 is also notoriously dangerous (it's known as the 'Road of Death' by some expatriates). Accidents are common, although fatal accidents are thankfully rare, and caution needs to be exercised at all times when using the road, an ill-conceived blend of coastal highway and town high street.

A new toll motorway, the A-7, also known as the *Autopista del Sol*, runs more or less parallel to the N-340 from Fuengirola to Estepona. It's expected to be completed by the end of 2002 with an extension to Algeciras planned for early 2003. It's fast and relatively safe, a relief after the N-340, although tolls are high (Fuengirola-Marbella and Marbella-Estepona cost around €2 to €3 and Malaga-Marbella between €2 and €4 depending on the time of year) and the motorway has just three exits, at San Pedro de Alcantara, Marbella and Calahonda. Season and frequent travel tickets are available.

Malaga is connected to Seville and Granada by a good dual-carriageway and the city has a fast ring road to the north. Both the eastern and western access roads, however, are congested at peak times and there are plans to build a further ring road as well as a second access road to the airport.

Planned Developments

The entire Costa del Sol has undergone intensive development in recent years, which will continue until at least 2010. It's estimated that the population will increase sharply in the next few years, to around 2 million. New road and rail connections are planned or under construction (see above).

Employment Prospects

Unemployment is generally low on the Costa del Sol, with the exception of central Malaga, and there are many employment opportunities for expatriates, particularly those who speak more than one language. Jobs, however, tend to be limited to the service sector, notably the catering and property industries. A working knowledge of Spanish isn't always necessary but is definitely an advantage, and a good knowledge of German is sometimes required. There are plenty of opportunities for part-time work in shops and bars, as well as voluntary work, usually helping other expatriates.

Further Information

Useful Publications

- *AA Essential Costa del Sol*, M. King (AA Publishing)

- *Costa del Sol*, S. Bryant (New Holland Publishers)
- *Costa del Sol Insight Pocket Guide* (Insight Guides)
- *The British on the Costa del Sol*, K O'Reilly (UCL Press)

Useful Websites

⌨ www.andalucia.com (Andalusia's official tourist website, with information about the whole region, including the Costa del Sol)

⌨ www.costadelsol.com (a general guide to the area)

⌨ www.costadelsolnews.es (the website of *Costa del Sol News*)

⌨ www.costaguide.com (general information)

⌨ www.surinenglish.com (the website of *Sur in English*)

⌨ www.visitacostadelsol.com (the official tourist website for the area)

ESTEPONA & SOTOGRANDE

This area lies at the western end of the Costa del Sol, part of it in the province of Cadiz. **Estepona** is a medium-sized town, which once depended on fishing for its livelihood, although nowadays tourism and a thriving industrial estate form an important part of its economy. Less developed than other coastal towns, it has retained much of its original character and is probably the most 'Spanish' of the coast's major tourist resorts.

Sotogrande is an exclusive, purpose-built development covering around 2,000ha (5,000 acres), with its own marina. Much of the property is owned by Spaniards and used as holiday accommodation, although the area is also popular with wealthy Gibraltarians, who commute daily. Stretching along the coast from San Pedro to Sotogrande is a series of developments, including Benavista, Puerto Duquesa and La Alcaidesa. The attractive white villages of Benahavís, Casares and Manilva are a short distance of the coast.

Advantages & Disadvantages

The main advantage of this area is its relative tranquillity, with fewer visitors than the rest of the Costa del Sol. Its landscape is considerably less developed and there are still large sections of unspoilt countryside. On the other hand, communications to this part of the coast are poor and public transport is virtually non-existent, making private transport essential. The main road isn't dual-carriageway and long delays are common, especially in summer. However, the A-7 motorway link is expected to be completed by 2003 and the conversion of the N-340 to dual-carriageway by 2004. Sotogrande also has few local amenities and is quiet out of season, when many holiday properties are empty.

Population

Estepona has a population of around 47,000, of which some 7,500 are foreign residents, mostly British. Sotogrande has a small resident population and is almost dead in winter.

Climate

This part of the Costa del Sol enjoys much the same warm, pleasant climate as the rest, although Sotogrande is susceptible to strong Atlantic winds.

Crime Rate & Security

Estepona has a relatively low crime rate, as does Sotogrande, which has private 24-hour security guards and gates.

Amenities

Sports: Sotogrande has the best golf courses on the Costa del Sol, including the prestigious Valderrama, where the 1997 Ryder Cup was staged. The area also has a polo club and numerous riding schools. Estepona has a reasonable selection of sports facilities, while the marinas at Sotogrande and Estepona offer sailing and water-sports.

Leisure: Leisure options in Sotogrande are mostly limited to sporting activities. Estepona, on the other hand, is an interesting town with a wide range of cultural activities, particularly art exhibitions and live music. The countryside and mountain villages around Estepona offer walking, touring and sightseeing.

English-language Cinema & Theatre: There's a small cinema in Estepona, although films are shown only in Spanish.

Shopping Centres & Markets: Estepona has a good choice of shops, including a shopping centre with a hypermarket on the outskirts. There's also a selection of nautical shops around the harbour, and a large open-air craft and gift market is held in the port on Sunday mornings.

Sotogrande has a small number of shops, mainly targeted at golf and nautical enthusiasts. For most other things you need to travel elsewhere, for example to La Linea (which has several large stores, including hypermarkets) or nearby Gibraltar. An art and furniture market is held at the marina on Sunday mornings.

Foreign Food & Products: Supermarkets have a fair selection of foreign food, mainly British and German, and there are some small specialist shops.

Restaurants & Bars: Sotogrande has a few bars and restaurants, mainly situated around the marina, although they may be closed out of season or open only at weekends. Estepona, however, has a variety of places to eat and drink, notably in the town centre and around the port, generally with lower prices than in nearby Marbella and Sotogrande. The pretty village of Benahavís is well worth a visit for its numerous excellent restaurants (it's known as the gastronomic capital of the coast). In the developments, the main choice for diners is British cuisine (some would say that this is a contradiction in terms) and there are several popular karaoke bars.

Services

International & Private Schools: Sotogrande is home to the Costa del Sol's only international boarding and day school, Sotogrande School; otherwise you must travel to Marbella. The same applies to private schools, which are situated in and around Marbella.

Hospitals & Clinics: One of the disadvantages of Estepona is that it has no local hospital (the nearest is in Marbella), although the town does have a number of health centres. The choice of private clinics in Estepona is limited and you may need to travel to Marbella.

Doctors & Dentists: A few English-speaking doctors practise in Estepona and there are several dental clinics where English is spoken.

English-language Radio & Press: See page 178.

Property

Sotogrande has some of the most expensive property on the Costa del Sol, as well as some of the most exclusive. Most property consists of villas set in large grounds or luxury apartments in the marina. Although construction in the area is restricted, there are several new developments under way, including a man-made island in the marina – Isla Tortuga – with over 50 apartments and moorings. Property is cheaper in Estepona, particularly in the centre, where you can still pick up a bargain, although the area of the coast mid-way between Estepona and Marbella, known as the 'New Golden Mile', contains mostly premium properties.

Cost of Housing: The following prices are intended only as a guide and were current in mid-2002.

- **Sotogrande**
  Apartments: from €320,000 to €570,000;
  Villas: from €425,000 (note that most villas are large, with plots of at least 2,000m²).

- **Estepona**
  Two-bedroom apartment: average €140,000;
  Three-bedroom apartment: average €160,000, although new duplex apartments on the 'New Golden Mile' cost from €850,000;
  Three-bedroom townhouse: average €210,000;
  Villa on a 1,000m² plot: average €300,000.

Land: Estepona has an abundance of land, although most of it is in the surrounding countryside and classified as 'rustic', which means that plots are generally large (at least 2,500m²). Prices start at €15 per m², although plots in popular locations are €80 per m².

Rental Accommodation: There's a chronic shortage of rental properties in the Estepona area, particularly long-term rentals and townhouses and villas. Rents for a two-bedroom apartment range from €600 to €900 per month. There's little rental accommodation in Sotogrande except holiday lets.

Communications

Air: Estepona is approximately 80km (50mi) and Sotogrande 100km (60mi) from Malaga airport (see page 181). The journey time to Sotogrande outside the high season is around 90 minutes, although this will be reduced to under an hour when the A-7 motorway link is completed in 2003.

Public Transport: Public transport is poor and private transport essential if you choose to live in Sotogrande. Estepona has a limited local bus service.

Roads: This part of the Costa del Sol has poor road communications, although these will be greatly improved by the end of 2002 when the motorway from Estepona to Algeciras and the conversion of the N-340 to a dual-carriageway have been completed. At present, the N-340 from Estepona to Sotogrande has some of the worst tail-backs on the coast, which extend for miles at weekends and during the high season.

Planned Developments

Once the A-7 motorway link and the widening of the N-340 are completed, it's predicted that the area will be one of the fastest-growing on the coast, the area around the villages of Casares and Manilva being expected to develop significantly, with several important construction projects planned.

Employment Prospects

Job prospects are generally good, particularly if you have a good knowledge of Spanish, although jobs tend to be limited to the tourist and service sectors.

Further Information

Useful Websites

⌨ http://marbella2000.com/estepona (useful information about the town, including cultural listings)

MARBELLA

In common with most places on the Costa del Sol, until the 1960s Marbella was a quiet fishing village. Then it was 'discovered', deemed ripe for up-market tourism and quickly became an exclusive resort for the jet set. The town lies beneath the spectacular Sierra Blanca mountain range, whose main peak – known as the *Concha* (shell) – rises to over 1,000m (3,300ft). Marbella is divided into two main parts: the old town, confined by the Moorish fortress walls, with its quiet, narrow streets and the Orange Square in the centre; and the new town, with its high-rise blocks and wide avenues lined with trees and shrubs.

Marbella is surrounded by exclusive developments, including Hacienda Las Chapas, El Rosario and Los Monteros on the eastern side, and Nagüeles, the so-called 'Golden Mile' and Nueva Andalucía with its 'Golf Valley' to the west. These developments are packed with luxury mansions, often owned by the rich and famous, although there are occasional apartment blocks. The world-famous leisure marina of Puerto Banus with its floating gin palaces lies to the west of the city and receives around 5 million visitors a year. The area around the marina has seen massive development in recent years and now boasts many luxury apartment blocks and good shopping facilities.

The town of San Pedro de Alcantara (known locally as San Pedro) to the west of Marbella is generally quieter and has retained much of its original Spanish character. The exclusive residential area of Guadalmina lies to the west of the town.

Advantages & Disadvantages

The main advantage of Marbella and its surroundings is the high quality of the area and its amenities; it's considerably more up-market than popular resorts such as Fuengirola or Torremolinos. The down side, however, is the high cost of living, including higher municipal taxes, in addition to which (and in common with the rest of the Costa del Sol) it's extremely crowded in high season, particularly in August.

Population

The population of Marbella is around 106,000, of which some 21,000 are foreigners, mainly British and German.

Climate

Like the rest of the Costa del Sol, Marbella enjoys pleasant weather all year round. The area's micro-climate means that it's generally milder than the rest of the Costa del Sol, rarely too hot or too cold.

Crime Rate & Security

Marbella's emblematic and controversial former mayor, Jesus Gil, made security one of his priorities when he came to power in the early 1990s. Consequently, Marbella has one of the largest local police forces in Spain, particularly around the main tourist areas, and crime is generally low. Many developments have their own security guards and services.

Amenities

Sports: Marbella has several municipal sports centres, including an indoor swimming pool, tennis centre and rugby pitch. There are also many private sports centres, particularly tennis clubs, and the port has a sailing club. Several golf courses are located around the city, and the nearby area of Nueva Andalucía (known as 'Golf Valley') is noted for its fine golf clubs.

Leisure: Marbella has a nationally famous museum of engraving and a bonsai museum. There are also many private art galleries. The town's nightlife is spread over three main areas: the old town, which is crammed with small bars and restaurants; the new town, with its stylish pubs and clubs; and the port, where there are numerous clubs and discos, most of them open-air. There are also several exclusive clubs, including Oh! Marbella and the sophisticated (and expensive) Olivia Valère. Puerto Banus also has a lively social scene, with something to suit all tastes, ranging from fast-food outlets to luxury restaurants, piano bars and discos. Puerto Banus is still *the* place to see and be seen in Marbella. Bear in mind that prices in Marbella and Puerto Banus are among the highest on the coast and that many bars and clubs either close out of high season or open only at weekends. There are no theme parks within the city, but those in other parts of the Costa del Sol are within easy reach.

English-language Cinema & Theatre: The cinema complex at Puerto Banus shows a recently released film in English with Spanish subtitles, usually twice a day. It also hosts the annual Marbella Film Festival in the autumn. There's another cinema complex at La Cañada shopping centre, although all films are shown in Spanish. A large theatre opened in Marbella in 2001, featuring frequent plays and shows, although they're in Spanish. There are also several small amateur theatrical groups which perform in English at various venues around the area.

Shopping Centres & Markets: Marbella has extensive shopping facilities and is probably the best place on the coast to buy clothes, with numerous boutiques, many stocking designer names. There are also many furniture stores and art galleries in the city. The La Cañada shopping centre to the north of Marbella is popular and houses a number of chain stores, and around Marbella there are several hypermarkets and DIY stores. Puerto Banus is home to a large El Corte Inglés department store (which for some reason is known as the 'Costa Marbella'), and recent development has seen the opening of many other stores, selling everything from household goods to designer shoes. Puerto Banus is also a good place to shop for designer clothes. An open-air market is held in Marbella on Mondays and Nueva Andalucía has an antiques and crafts market on Saturday mornings.

Foreign Food & Products: Virtually all supermarkets and grocery shops in Marbella sell a wide choice of foreign food, with particular emphasis on Arabic, British and German foods. There are also several specialist shops.

Restaurants & Bars: Marbella offers a wide choice of restaurants and bars, although prices tend to be higher than elsewhere on the coast; some of the town's restaurants are top quality. Puerto Banus also has a good range of restaurants, plus many fast-food outlets, particularly in the area around the cinema. Marbella is also known for its beach bars (called *chiringuitos*), serving mainly fish dishes and *paella*. Bars, often with an international theme and live music, are plentiful throughout the city.

Services

International & Private Schools: Marbella has several international schools within its boundaries and is home to the only German school on the coast. Marbella offers a wide choice of private Spanish schools, including several maintained schools.

Hospitals & Clinics: Marbella is home to the main general hospital on the coast, the Hospital Costa del Sol, which is one of the few independent Spanish hospitals. It's generally well run and has a volunteer translation service for foreign patients. Marbella also has a small private hospital. There are numerous private clinics in Marbella, including several clinics offering cosmetic surgery and spa treatments.

Doctors & Dentists: Doctors and dentists from many countries practise in Marbella.

English-language Radio & Press: See page 178.

Property

In 2001, Marbella led the property boom on the Costa del Sol, with the largest increases in residential tourism seen on the coast. Construction has been continuing apace, particularly on the northern periphery of the city at the foot of the Sierra Blanca. Marbella has the most expensive property on the Costa del Sol and the greatest number of luxury developments, notably the so-called 'Golden Mile' (where the King of Saudi Arabia has a palace), Nagüeles (lined with luxurious mansions) and Hacienda Las Chapas in the east. Of the developments around Marbella, Nueva Andalucía is the 'cheapest' and Nagüeles the most expensive. The city centre has many apartment blocks, where property is sometimes cheaper, but it's difficult to find a bargain in Marbella.

Cost of Housing: The following prices are intended only as a guide and were current in mid-2002.

● **West side** (including San Pedro, Nueva Andalucía, Nagüeles)
Two-bedroom apartment: average €325,000;
Three-bedroom apartment: average €415,000;
Three-bedroom townhouse: average €385,000;
Villa on a 1,000m² plot: average €550,000.

● **East side** (including Los Monteros, El Rosario)
Two-bedroom apartment: average €265,000;
Three-bedroom apartment: average €400,000;
Three-bedroom townhouse: average €320,000;
Villa on a 1,000m² plot: average €425,000.

Land: The little available land costs from €120 to €240 per m².

Rental Accommodation: In recent years, rental accommodation has been in increasingly short supply in Marbella and it's difficult to find long-term rentals, particularly apartments. The monthly rent for a two-bedroom apartment starts at around €450.

Communications

Air: It's around 50km (30mi) to Marbella and around 55km (35mi) to Puerto Banus from Malaga airport (see page 181).

Public Transport: Marbella's public transport system is limited to a reasonably efficient network of buses, which serve most areas of the city, San

Pedro and Puerto Banus. There's a new bus station on the northern outskirts from where a service operates to the city centre.

Roads: Marbella's road system is generally good and not too congested, except during the summer. The city has a main bypass to the north (A-7) and a secondary one (N-340) around the centre. In common with most of the coast's towns, on-street parking is virtually impossible and underground car parks are expensive.

Planned Developments

Marbella has been one of the coast's major growth areas, and development – particularly to the north and west of the city – has been spectacular in recent years. This growth, however, is now slowing and further development is likely to be restricted.

Employment Prospects

Job prospects are generally good, although as in other areas of the Costa del Sol they're mainly limited to the tourist and service sectors, particularly the property market.

Further Information

Useful Websites

▣ http://marbella2000.com (the city's official website containing general information)
▣ www.marbella.com (a general guide)

FUENGIROLA & MIJAS

Fuengirola has traditionally been popular with British and Spanish tourists, although recent years have also seen an influx of other nationalities, making it one of the most cosmopolitan towns on the Costa del Sol. It's extensively built-up and its long beaches and wide promenade, which stretch for over 8km (5mi), are flanked by high-rise apartment blocks and hotels. There's also a small town centre, where traditional squares with white houses survive. Fuengirola is always busy, being an active town in its own right as well as a tourist resort. The area to the east of the town and the dry river, known as Los Boliches, is particularly popular with foreigners.

Mijas is a typical Andalusian white village with attractive narrow streets, situated in the mountains above Fuengirola. Mijas village is the administrative centre for Mijas Costa, which stretches from Fuengirola to the port of Cabopino in the west and includes many developments, such as Calahonda, Riviera del Sol, Miraflores, Torrevieja, El Chaparral, El Faro and La Cala, which lies in a long sandy bay and remains a quiet fishing village in spite of the developments surrounding it. The prestigious Cala Golf Resort is a few miles north of the village.

Advantages & Disadvantages

The area is generally cosmopolitan, although some parts, such as Calahonda and Riviera del Sol, are inhabited mainly by British residents, making communication and daily life easy for English-speakers. This can, however, be a disadvantage if you wish to practise your Spanish and integrate into the local community. Fuengirola's surrounding developments also offer a quieter residential existence, away from the hustle and bustle of the town itself. In the winter, however, some of these residential areas can be very quiet. Fuengirola offers many amenities and is one of the less expensive parts of the Costa del Sol, although traffic and human congestion are problems all year round and younger people sometimes feel outnumbered in the winter, when it attracts hordes of retirees fleeing the northern European winter. Mijas is an attractive village but has very steep streets and is crowded with tourists in high season.

Population

Fuengirola has a total population of around 53,000, of which some 11,000 are foreign residents, the majority British. Mijas and Mijas Costa have a total population of around 45,000; there's a similar number of foreigners, mostly British, as in Fuengirola.

Climate

The area generally enjoys the same climate as the rest of the Costa del Sol, although in the summer Fuengirola can be several degrees warmer than Mijas Costa because of the hot winds that blow across the town from inland.

Crime Rate & Security

Both Fuengirola and Mijas have relatively low crime rates and are generally safe. Many developments employ private security companies.

Amenities

Sports: Both Fuengirola and Mijas have public indoor sports centres, with well patronised swimming and football clubs. There are also numerous private clubs, including tennis clubs and gyms, and Fuengirola has an active sailing club. Several golf courses are within easy reach of the area and there are plans for more in the near future.

Leisure: Fuengirola and Mijas offer a variety of leisure options, many organised by the area's expatriate groups. The culture departments of the town councils also have a full programme of exhibitions, concerts and other events all year round, and the Foreigners' Department of Mijas council organises many events and outings for local residents. Fuengirola has many bars, offering a variety of live music, while the Fuengirola fair in October and the Mijas fair in September are popular events. Fuengirola has a small, innovative zoo (recently revamped) and a water-park, which opens only in the summer.

English-language Cinema & Theatre: The local cinemas don't screen English-language films, although the Mijas Costa cinema plans to do so in the near future. Fuengirola is home to the Salon Varietés, an expatriate theatrical group offering a full programme of plays and musicals in English year-round. There are also several amateur theatre groups in the area and Mijas has an annual theatre festival in summer.

Shopping Centres & Markets: Fuengirola has a wide variety of shops, a large number aimed at tourists, and many supermarkets, and offers some of the best value shopping on the coast. It's well served by Spanish chain stores selling quality clothes, and there are also many furniture and household shops. One disadvantage is that parking can be a problem, although more spaces are being created, including an underground car park in the centre (the construction of which will, however, cause temporary chaos!). El Corte Inglés has plans to open a large department store in Fuengirola and there are also advanced plans for a major shopping centre near the castle.

Mijas village has limited shopping, mainly restricted to souvenir shops and small grocery shops. La Cala has an ever-growing selection of shops (a new shopping centre has recently opened). Mijas Costa has a variety of supermarkets, mostly in Calahonda.

Fuengirola hosts the largest open-air market on the coast, which takes place at the fairground on Tuesdays, where a large flea market is also held on Saturdays, and there's a small market in the port on Sunday mornings. Mijas Costa has markets on Wednesdays and Fridays at Calypso (behind Calahonda and Riviera) and there's a large Saturday market in La Cala.

Foreign Food & Products: There's an excellent choice of foreign products, particularly British, Scandinavian and German. The Irish store Dunnes has two branches in Fuengirola and the British frozen food company Iceland (called Icelandia in Spain) also operates two stores in the area.

Restaurants & Bars: Fuengirola is literally packed with places to eat and drink, serving fare from around the world at reasonable prices. The streets around the old town behind the sea front are the main restaurant area. Mijas has several quality restaurants and Mijas Costa is home to a variety of restaurants and bars.

Services

International & Private Schools: Fuengirola has a number of international schools, both British and Scandinavian (Finnish and Swedish). There are several private Spanish schools in Fuengirola, although places are limited.

Hospitals & Clinics: There are no hospitals in Fuengirola or Mijas and patients are referred to Marbella or Malaga for treatment. There are, however, several health centres in the locality. Fuengirola has numerous private clinics, covering a wide range of specialities.

Doctors & Dentists: Many private doctors and dentists from various countries practise in Fuengirola and the surrounding area, and many Spanish doctors and dentists in the area also speak English.

Tradesmen: The area has an abundance of foreign companies and tradesmen providing for just about every need.

English-language Radio & Press: See page 178.

Property

The housing market in this area is booming and new construction, particularly of apartments and townhouses, is under way in most parts of Mijas Costa and on the little remaining building land in Fuengirola and Mijas. Fuengirola has some of the least expensive property on the Costa del Sol, although this consists mostly of small apartments in older blocks; townhouses and villas in the popular Pueblo Lopez and Pueblo Lucia developments cost as much as those in the more exclusive parts of the coast. New construction in areas immediately surrounding the town, such as Las Lagunas, Los Pacos and Torreblanca, is considerably cheaper than in other towns on the coast, and the popular developments of Calahonda and Riviera del Sol also offer good value. However, the white village of Mijas has become quite expensive and congested in recent years, and there's little room for expansion.

Cost of Housing: The following prices are intended only as a guide and were current in mid-2002.

- **Fuengirola**
  Two-bedroom apartment: from €90,000;
  Three-bedroom apartment: from €110,000;
  Three-bedroom townhouse: from €150,000;

Villa on a 1,000m² plot: from €210,000.
Fuengirola has some of the cheapest property on the Costa del Sol, although properties in attractive central locations and beach-front apartments attract a premium of at least 50 per cent over the above prices.

● **Mijas Village**
Two-bedroom apartment: average €160,000;
Three-bedroom apartment: average €175,000;
Three-bedroom townhouse: average €240,000;
Villa on a 1,000 m² plot: average €350,000.

● **Mijas Costa**
Two-bedroom apartment: average €140,000;
Three-bedroom apartment: average €190,000;
Three-bedroom townhouse: average €200,000;
Villa on a 1,000 m² plot: average €400,000.

Land: Virtually no land is available in Fuengirola, which has an acute shortage of building space. There are a variety of plots for sale in Mijas Costa, where prices start at around €120 per m² rising to €200 per m² for prime positions.

Rental Accommodation: Rental accommodation is generally quite easy to find in the area, particularly in Fuengirola, which has a plethora of apartments for rent, although long-term rentals including the summer months can be difficult to find. Detached villas are also in short supply. Rents average around €500 per month for a one or two-bedroom apartment and start at €600 for three bedrooms.

Communications

Air: Malaga airport (see page 181) is around 25km (15mi) from Fuengirola and Mijas.

Public Transport: Fuengirola enjoys some of the coast's best public transport. The efficient local train service from Malaga to Fuengirola stops at four places within the area: the Fuengirola centre, Los Boliches, Torreblanca and Carvajal. There's also a municipal bus service, with several routes serving most of the town, including El Faro to the west and Cerros del Aguila to the north-west. In the summer, buses run from the town centre to the water-park. Buses also run from Fuengirola to Malaga, Mijas and Marbella, services generally running every half an hour on weekdays.

Roads: Traffic congestion is a chronic problem in Fuengirola, which is far too small for the volume of traffic it handles. Traffic jams are common throughout the day in the town centre, where parking spaces are in short supply. It's best either to use public transport or to park on the outskirts and walk to the centre.

Puerto Colom, Majorca (© Marc Castejon)

▲ *Sagovia, Castilla y León*
  (© Dennis Kelsall)

▼ *Montgo, Costa Blanca* (© Molino Villas)

▼ *Marbella, Costa del Sol*
  (© Patrick Hickey)

▲ *Surfing, Tenerife*
  (© Horizon)

◄ *Villa, Costa Blanca*
  (© Molino Villas)

▲ *Moraira, Costa Brava*
  (© Molino Villas)

▼ *Peñaranda de Duero, Castilla y León*
  (© Dennis Kelsall)

▲ *Near Corcubión, Galicia*
  (© Dennis Kelsall)

▲ *Retamor, Costa del Sol*
  (© Patrick Hickey)

Parque de Río Duratón,
Castilla y León
(© Dennis Kelsall) ▶

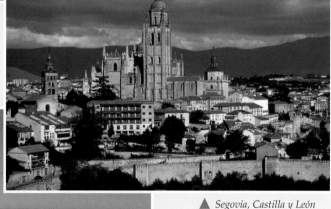

▲ *Cristianos Beach, Tenerife*
(© Horizon)

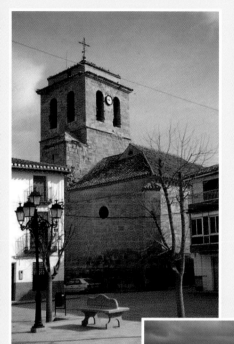

▲ *Galera, Costa del Sol*
(© Patrick Hickey)

▲ *Segovia, Castilla y León*
(© Dennis Kelsall)

◀ *Playa de Amadores,*
Gran Canaria
(© Katy Stjernström)

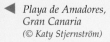

Playa de la Lanzada, Galicia
(© Dennis Kelsall)

Monasterio Lluc, Majorca
(© Marc Castejon)

Gormaz, Castilla y León
(© Dennis Kelsall)

Arro, Aragón
(© Dennis Kelsall)

Alcala de las Cazules, Costa del Sol
(© Patrick Hickey)

Planned Developments

Fuengirola is expanding along the river to the north of the castle. In addition to a residential area, there will be several hotels and a large shopping complex with a cinema. A new road from the town centre will be constructed to improve access to the shopping centre. There are also advanced plans for a major re-development of Fuengirola port and for an underground car park beneath the central Church square.

Employment Prospects

Job prospects are generally good, although they're mainly limited to the tourist and service sectors, particularly the property market.

Further Information

Useful Websites

🖥 www.fuengirola.org (the official tourist website, in several languages)
🖥 www.ayto-mijas.com (the Mijas Town Council website)

BENALMADENA

Benalmadena is one of the Costa del Sol's newest and fastest-growing resorts, already the area's second most popular tourist destination after Torremolinos. It's split into three parts: the village, which sits on a mountain, Arroyo de la Miel, between the village and the coast; and Benalmadena Costa, which is on the coast. The village is the administrative centre for the area and has preserved a traditional, quiet character, although there are many new developments (mostly townhouses and villas) surrounding it. Arroyo has many shops and businesses, as well as the town's railway station and a range of accommodation. Benalmadena Costa has a plethora of hotels and apartment blocks, as well as a prestigious, spectacular marina – Puerto Marina – which has twice won the Best International Port in the World award (in 1995 and 1997). The marina includes a series of man-made islands, each with exclusive apartments and moorings, plus shops, bars and restaurants.

Advantages & Disadvantages

One of Benalmadena's main advantages is that it's a dynamic town with plenty going on all year round. The growth of the area also means that there's a wide choice of accommodation, although it becomes very crowded in the summer and can be noisy.

Population

The total population is 37,000, of which 6,000 are foreigners, mainly British.

Crime Rate & Security

The crime rate is very low for the Costa del Sol.

Amenities

Sports: The public sports centre in the village offers a wide range of activities. There are also numerous private tennis and sports clubs in the vicinity, and Benalmadena has several golf courses, including the renowned Torrequebrada, with more under construction.

Leisure: Benalmadena has plenty to offer in terms of leisure opportunities, including a casino and cabaret at Torrequebrada. Nightlife is centred around the marina and the so-called '24-Hour Square', where there are several lively nightclubs and a variety of bars. Benalmadena has more theme parks than elsewhere on the coast, including the Costa del Sol's oldest, Tivoli World, which is situated just north of Arroyo. As well as fairground attractions, the park offers cabaret shows and concerts at weekends, often starring top Spanish singers. On Sunday mornings, it hosts a popular market, while Benalmadena's cable car, just outside the park, offers rides to the top of the mountains behind the town, providing spectacular, panoramic views of the coast. In the marina is Sealife, with an extensive collection of marine life and a marine research centre, and June 2002 saw the opening of the Selwo Marina Park, whose attractions include dolphins.

English-language Cinema & Theatre: None.

Shopping Centres & Markets: Benalmadena has a wide variety of shops, especially in Arroyo, and several large supermarkets. The area around the marina has shops specialising in nautical equipment.

Foreign Food & Products: Foreign products are easily obtainable, most supermarkets stocking a selection.

Restaurants & Bars: There are several good restaurants in the village and a wide choice in Arroyo and on the coast. The marina also offers a range of restaurants, bars and pubs.

Services

International & Private Schools: There are two new British schools in the area. Benalmadena has a limited number of private Spanish schools.

Hospitals & Clinics: Residents of Benalmadena receive hospital treatment in nearby Malaga (see page 206). There are no private hospitals. As well as public health centres, there are several private clinics in Benalmadena, some of which are foreign-run and staffed.

Doctors & Dentists: There's a reasonable choice of doctors and dentists, most of them English-speaking, although some people prefer to travel to Malaga or Fuengirola for a wider choice.

English-language Radio & Press: See page 178.

Property

The area north of Benalmadena is currently undergoing major development, most projects consisting largely of townhouses, although there will also be some apartments and villas. Property is generally reasonably priced, although homes in the marina and around Torrequebrada fetch premium prices.

Cost of Housing: The following prices are intended only as a guide and were current in mid-2002.

Two-bedroom apartment: from €110,000;
Three-bedroom apartment: from €150,000;

Three-bedroom apartment in Puerto Marina or a beach-front apartment in Torrequebrada: from €300,000;
Three-bedroom townhouse: from €180,000;
Villa on 1,000m² plot: from €240,000.

Land: Some building plots are still available close to the amenities, although the majority of land for sale is in the countryside to the west of Benalmadena. Prices range from around €100 to €150 per m² according to the plot's proximity to the village or town.

Rental Accommodation: There's generally little problem finding rented accommodation in Benalmadena, except in the village. Rents range from around €600 per month for a two-bedroom apartment in Arroyo de la Miel to €900 for a sea-front location.

Communications

Air: Malaga airport (see page 181) is just 12km (7.5mi) away.

Public Transport: Public transport is generally good in Benalmadena, which is one of the main stops on the Fuengirola to Malaga train line (the station is in Arroyo). There are also municipal bus services to and from the marina and Arroyo de la Miel, and the council has plans for a light railway along the same route, although there's strong local opposition to the project.

Roads: Benalmadena is sandwiched between the new section of the N-340 (labelled the N-340/A-7), which bypasses the town to the north, and the old N-340, which runs along the coast. The old section has been converted into a pleasant, tree-lined boulevard dotted with roundabouts, which is generally quiet except at main junctions, particularly with the access roads to the marina. Most roads in the area are wide and traffic runs smoothly, with the exception of the village, where congestion is common along the narrow streets and parking can be difficult.

Planned Developments

Benalmadena is one of the fastest-growing areas on the coast and there are major development plans for the northern part of the town, much of the which is already under construction.

Further Information

Useful Websites

⌨ www.benalmadena.com (the town's official website)

TORREMOLINOS

Spain's third-busiest resort, Torremolinos was one of the first places in Spain to open itself to tourism, in the early 1960s, and consists of rows of high-rise apartment and hotel blocks, the typical image of a package-holiday destination, although the area to the west of the town centre has residential streets of townhouses and villas. Torremolinos is also a major conference centre and has the most extensive range of hotels on the coast. It boasts clean beaches, an almost infinite range of bars, restaurants and shops, as well as the best variety of nightlife and entertainment on the coast. The old fishermen's quarter, La Carihuela, is the best place on the coast to eat fried fish.

Advantages & Disadvantages

Torremolinos is a friendly, vibrant town all year round, with plenty of things to do. It has a wealth of amenities and is well maintained, with particular emphasis on cleanliness and parks. A key advantage is its relatively low property prices. On the other hand, Torremolinos becomes exceptionally crowded in the summer, when package holidaymakers descend in their thousands, and parts of the town can be very noisy.

Population

The total population is around 41,000, of which some 15 per cent are foreigners, mainly British.

Crime Rate & Security

The crime rate is generally low for Spain.

Amenities

Sports: Torremolinos has a large, well-equipped public sports centre, which includes an athletics track. There are also number of private sports centres and gyms, and several golf courses within easy reach of the town.

Leisure: Torremolinos has a vibrant nightlife, centred mainly around San Miguel street, which has several large discos and clubs. There's also a vibrant gay scene, and many bars include drag shows. Torremolinos has a water-park, which is open only during the summer months.

English-language Cinema & Theatre: None.

Shopping Centres & Markets: Torremolinos has plenty to offer the shopper and is particularly good for souvenirs and leather goods. There are numerous supermarkets and chain stores, most of which are located in the main street, San Miguel. There's a market on Thursdays and a car boot sale on Sundays.

Foreign Food & Products: The town offers a wide range of foreign products and there are several specialist shops.

Restaurants & Bars: Torremolinos boasts the densest concentration of bars and restaurants on the Costa del Sol – over 500 of them! The variety is endless and caters for all pockets and tastes, although of particular note are the fish restaurants along the seafront in the area known as La Carihuela.

Services

International & Private Schools: Torremolinos has one international school, Sunnyview, which is one of the longest-established on the coast. There are also a few private schools.

Hospitals & Clinics: There are no public health service hospitals and the area is served by those in Malaga (see page 206). There are many private clinics in the town, most of them with English-speaking staff.

Doctors & Dentists: Torremolinos has a large number of English-speaking doctors and dentists.

English-language Radio & Press: See page 178.

Property

Torremolinos has some of the cheapest property on the Costa de Sol, although beach-front apartments command premium prices and townhouses and villas in the Montemar area are also quite expensive. Bargains can still be found in the older apartment blocks in the centre built in the 1960s and 1970s, although they may require extensive modernisation and the quality of construction may be poor. New construction is under way to the east of the town between the centre and the airport, particularly in the Los Alamos residential area.

Cost of Housing: The following prices are intended only as a guide and were current in mid-2002.

Two-bedroom apartment: from €100,000;
Three-bedroom apartment: from €120,000;
Three-bedroom townhouse: from €150,000;
Villa on a small plot: from €190,000.

Land: There are few available building plots in Torremolinos.

Rental Accommodation: Rental accommodation is generally easy to find, particularly during the winter. Monthly rents for a two or three-bedroom apartment range from around €600 in the residential area of Montemar to around €800 for a sea-front location.

Communications

Air: Malaga airport (see page 181) is just 6km (3.5mi) from Torremolinos.

Public Transport: The town is well served by public transport and is one of the stops on the Fuengirola to Malaga train line. There are also frequent bus services to and from nearby towns.

Roads: The roads of Torremolinos can become very congested, particularly the beach access roads at weekends and during the summer. There's a shortage of car parks, and parking can be a problem in both the town centre and along the sea front.

Planned Developments

Torremolinos has grown about as much as is possible and there's little room for further development.

Employment Prospects

There are plenty of job opportunities, although they're limited to the tourist and service sectors.

MALAGA

Spain's fifth largest city, Malaga is the capital of the Costa del Sol and a major Mediterranean port. It's one of the most cosmopolitan cities in Spain and for centuries has been a popular destination for foreigners, as the names of many of the city's districts and streets testify. During the 19th century, Malaga was a thriving winter resort for wealthy Europeans.

Malaga has, however, been largely untouched by mass tourism and remains a genuine Andalusian city. The city's Moorish history, as with many other Andalusian capitals, can clearly be seen in the Alcazaba fortress and the Gibralfaro castle, now home to a luxury Parador hotel. Pablo Picasso was born in Malaga (the airport is named after him), and a major museum housing a selection of his works will open in 2003.

Advantages & Disadvantages

One of Malaga's main advantages is that it has the best amenities and facilities on the Costa del Sol. Public transport is generally excellent and reasonably priced, and the city has a vibrant cultural scene, with concerts and other events all year round. It also has excellent shopping facilities. Although Malaga is busy, it doesn't become as crowded as other parts of the coast and in summer it's a relative oasis of calm. Malaga is typically Spanish and not an expatriate 'bubble' like many areas of the Costa del Sol. This can, however, be a disadvantage if you aren't prepared or able to learn Spanish. Other disadvantages are traffic congestion, rising crime and the summer heat, especially when the hot inland wind blows.

Population

The total population of Malaga is around 530,000; there are few foreign residents.

Major Areas & Places of Interest

In recent years, large-scale development has taken place in the north and west of the city. To the west of the centre lies the Teatinos district, home to the university and the scientific and technological park. It's currently undergoing major expansion and is expected to become a major centre in its own right. Behind Teatinos and almost in the mountains are the exclusive areas of Colonia de Santa Inés and Puerto de la Torre, where there are many villas and townhouses.

The modern 'centre' of Malaga is situated on the west side of the Guadalmedina river around the El Corte Inglés department store and the Larios shopping centre, which encompasses many of the city's amenities, including the bus and railway stations. The old town centre, which is full of narrow streets around the cathedral, is currently being extensively restored. To the east of the centre are the exclusive residential areas of Malagueta, Limonar, Pedregalejo and Cerrado de Calderón. These are the most expensive districts of Malaga with many old colonial-style mansions.

Climate

Because of its location and aspect, facing east and at the end of a long mountain valley, Malaga can be several degrees hotter than the rest of the Costa del Sol in summer, particularly when an offshore wind blows.

Crime Rate & Security

Malaga has the highest crime rate on the Costa del Sol and petty crime has risen alarmingly in recent years. Bag snatching is common, particularly around the old town and at night. You should be wary of walking alone or in poorly-lit areas.

Amenities

Sports: Malaga has some of the best sports facilities in the area, including a new sports pavilion on the west side of the city, where the leading Malaga basketball team (Unicaja) plays. The city also has a first division football team, based at the Rosaleda stadium to the north of the city. In and around Malaga are numerous sports centres, gyms and swimming and tennis clubs, as well as two sailing clubs. There are two golf courses on the outskirts of the city, at the Parador near the airport and the Añoreta Club to the east, and most of the coast's other courses are within easy reach.

Leisure: Malaga has a wide variety of leisure options, including good beaches, interesting walks around the old town and the harbour, excellent shopping and a lively cultural scene. The nationally famous summer fair lasts for several days at the beginning of August. Malaga also has annual cinema and jazz festivals. The Cervantes Theatre in the old town is the Costa del Sol's main cultural base and home to the prestigious Malaga Philharmonic Orchestra. The Cervantes has annual opera, jazz and classical concert seasons, as well as plays and other music all year round. There are also several smaller theatres in Malaga. The Alameda Park is one of the world's most renowned botanical gardens and there are two other botanical parks on the outskirts of the city.

English-language Cinema & Theatre: Malaga has many multi-screen cinemas, where you can see the latest American blockbusters, as well as several smaller cinemas showing Spanish and European films. Films are usually shown in Spanish and only occasionally in the original version.

Shopping Centres & Markets: Shopping in Malaga has improved markedly in recent years and it's now the best place on the coast for shopaholics. The city has several shopping centres with large hypermarkets on its periphery and two in the centre. The main shopping areas are concentrated around the old town, where there's a wealth of boutiques, and around the new centre where the large El Corte Inglés department store is situated. The two areas are within easy walking distance of each other. All the main Spanish chain stores have branches in Malaga and the Irish store Dunnes also has a large department store in the Larios centre.

Foreign Food & Products: Foreign goods aren't as easy to find in Malaga as they are on the rest of the Costa del Sol, although some hypermarkets have a small selection and El Corte Inglés' delicatessen stocks a limited supply of foreign produce.

Restaurants & Bars: Malaga has an excellent choice of restaurants and bars, particularly those offering Spanish cuisine. Around the Pedregalejo area in the east there are many restaurants serving fried fish, the Malaga delicacy, while the old town is a popular place for *tapas* bars and Irish-style pubs. Most bars and pubs are open until the small hours and there's also a vibrant club scene. Prices in bars, restaurants and clubs in Malaga are lower than in most other places on the Costa del Sol.

Services

International & Private Schools: A French lycée and two international schools (both using a British curriculum) are the only options in or near Malaga. However, Malaga has the best and most varied selection of private Spanish schools on the Costa del Sol.

Hospitals & Clinics: The coast's best hospitals and clinics are found in Malaga, which has several large public hospitals, including the university teaching hospital and numerous smaller private hospitals and clinics.

Doctors & Dentists: Malaga has many excellent doctors and dentists, in both the public and private health sectors, most of them Spanish. Many speak at least some English.

Tradesmen: It can be difficult to find English-speaking workers in Malaga, and those based in other parts of the coast may be reluctant to travel to Malaga or will charge extra to do so. However, the city has excellent Spanish artisans and if you have a basic knowledge of Spanish you should have no difficulty in finding someone to carry out repairs and installations.

English-language Radio & Press: See page 178.

Property

The housing market is healthy in Malaga and much more stable than on the rest of the Costa del Sol, as most property in the capital consists of primary residences rather than holiday homes. Prices, therefore, tend to be less susceptible to the sharp rises seen in other parts of the coast, although they have risen steadily in recent years.

Most property is considerably cheaper in Malaga than on the rest of the coast, except for the districts on the east side of the city and along the seafront, where resale property is in short supply. New developments are plentiful to the west of Malaga, particularly in Teatinos, although the choice tends to be limited to apartment blocks. Note that most property in Malaga consists of apartments and the choice of townhouses and houses is limited to developments on the outskirts or the Limonar area.

Cost of Housing: The following prices are intended only as a guide and were current in mid-2002.

Two-bedroom apartment: €50,000 to €150,000 in the centre and from €120,000 on the east side;

Three-bedroom apartment: from €80,000 in the centre and from €150,000 on the east side;

House: from €350,000.

Rental Accommodation: Malaga has a large university population and as a consequence there's a shortage of rental accommodation. Rents range from around €500 per month for a two-bedroom apartment to €600 for a three-bedroom apartment.

Communications

Communications are generally excellent in Malaga, although traffic congestion is a problem at peak times.

Air: Malaga airport (see page 181) is around 8km (5mi) from the city centre.

Public Transport: Buses serve all parts of the city and a light railway system with four lines is planned. The bus and railway stations, both recently renovated, are in the city centre (near the Larios centre) and there are frequent services to other parts of the coast and region and to Madrid.

Roads: The road network around Malaga is generally good and all access roads are dual-carriageways. Construction is under way on a second ring road around the north and west sides of the city, as well as a second airport access. Travelling times by road from Malaga to other major cities are: Granada: 1hr 30m, Seville: 2hrs 30m and Madrid 5hrs.

Planned Developments

Malaga is a growth area and major development work is in progress or planned for the near future, including a large congress centre, currently under construction. The area around the port will be extensively remodelled and house an auditorium, museum, shopping centre and leisure complex. Construction is under way on a second ring road around the north and west sides of the city, as well as a second airport access.

Employment Prospects

Malaga has the most varied employment opportunities on the Costa del Sol. There are job opportunities in just about every sector, particularly in the fast-developing technology park, where many major international companies are based. Note, however, that a good knowledge of Spanish is essential if you wish to find work in Malaga.

Further Information

Useful Websites

🖥 www.malagaturismo.com (the official tourist website for the city)
🖥 www.malaga.com (general information, with business listings)

EASTERN COSTA DEL SOL & COSTA TROPICAL

The eastern Costa del Sol and the Costa Tropical are markedly different from the western Costa del Sol, which has dominated the region's tourist industry and – to a certain extent – overshadowed the eastern side. Despite this, the eastern Costa del Sol and Costa Tropical are popular with tourists, many of whom prefer their relative tranquillity and more authentically Spanish character. This part of the coast is dominated by the high mountain ranges of the Axarquía, and much of the land is devoted to tropical orchards (avocado, custard apple and mango) and vines. The resorts to the east of Malaga are more like suburbs of the city than tourist resorts, and indeed many people commute to the city from this area. Further east is the popular resort of Nerja, which marks the limit of Malaga province. East of Nerja, the Costa Tropical begins and includes the resort of La Herradura and the towns of Almuñécar, Salobreña and Motril.

Advantages & Disadvantages

The main advantages of this part of the coast are tranquillity (for most of the year) and that it has preserved its traditional character. Property (with the exception of Nerja) is considerably cheaper than on the western coast. Disadvantages include the relative isolation of the area from the rest of the Costa del Sol and few amenities, although these are improving. This means that you must travel to Malaga for hospitals, major shops, etc, although the journey time is relatively short. Communications, particularly along the Costa Tropical, are slow and most resorts are very crowded in the summer.

Main Towns & Places of Interest

Rincón de la Victoria and **Torre del Mar** are two towns/resorts that cater mainly for Malaga commuters and Spanish tourists, although Torre del Mar has grown in popularity over recent years with foreign buyers. Both have good beaches and amenities, particularly Torre del Mar, which is close to nearby **Vélez-Málaga**, one of the largest towns in the area. Both resorts have many high-rise apartment and hotel blocks.

Nerja is the jewel of the eastern Costa del Sol and the town, once a quiet fishing village, retains its original charm with relatively few high-rise apartment blocks. Nerja has attracted a different sort of tourism from that of other Costa del Sol resorts and is popular with those in search of a quieter, more authentically Spanish holiday or home. The town's backdrop is the high mountains of the Sierra Almijara, site of the attractive white villages of the Axarquía, and has 16km (10mi) of beaches, mostly set in pretty coves. The spectacular Nerja caves, which are used as a concert hall in summer, are the Costa del Sol's most visited attraction and house prehistoric paintings (although they aren't currently on public view). **Frigiliana**, one of the Costa del Sol's most beautiful villages, in the foothills behind Nerja, is increasingly popular with foreign buyers seeking a typically Spanish environment.

Beyond Nerja lies the **Costa Tropical**, which offers several resorts. **La Herradura** is an attractive small town with an exclusive marina (Marina del Este) and quiet residential developments in the foothills. Further east, **Almuñécar** has a good beach lined with high-rise apartment blocks and popular with people from Granada, many of whom own a second home there. **Salobreña** is a spectacular white village perched on a rocky outcrop topped with a Moorish castle and has attractive beaches; it has seen a surge in holiday home developments in recent years.

Population

The population of Nerja is around 16,000, of which some 2,500 are foreigners, mainly British.

Crime Rate & Security

The crime rate is generally very low for Spain.

Amenities

Sports: Water-sports are popular in the area, particularly sailing and scuba diving. Salobreña has an artificial reef off the coast, which is increasingly popular with divers, and Marina del Este has a sailing club. There are also numerous tennis and riding clubs in the area. Unlike the western Costa del Sol, the eastern side has few golf courses, although there are plans to build more. At present there are only two, at Rincón de la Victoria and at Salobreña.

Leisure: Nerja has a reasonably good choice of cultural activities, including its internationally famous Music and Ballet Festival, held in the auditorium of the Nerja caves in the summer. There are annual international classical music and jazz festivals in Almuñécar, which has a water-park, open only during the summer months. There's also a Parrot and Cactus Park in the area.

English-language Cinema & Theatre: None of the area's cinemas, in Torre del Mar, Almuñécar and Motril, show films in English. English-language plays are often performed in Nerja.

Shopping Centres & Markets: Nerja has a reasonably good choice of small supermarkets and shops, although for more variety you must travel to the nearby shopping centres at Vélez-Málaga, Torre del Mar and La Cala del Moral or to Malaga itself. The El Ingenio shopping centre – which recently opened at Vélez-Málaga – is one of the largest in the province. Almuñécar has limited shopping facilities and the smaller resorts have only a few modest shops. Note that some shops in resort areas may be closed outside high season.

Weekly markets are held on Tuesdays in Nerja, Thursdays in Frigiliana and Vélez-Málaga, and on Fridays in Almuñécar and Salobreña. Nerja also has a Sunday flea market.

Foreign Food & Products: The shops and supermarkets in the area, particularly Nerja, stock a wide choice of foreign foods. There are also a few specialist foreign shops in Nerja. At the El Ingenio shopping centre in Vélez-Málaga, there's a branch of the Irish department store, Dunnes.

Restaurants & Bars: The area boasts numerous restaurants and bars, particularly Nerja, which has a wide selection of international restaurants. Beach restaurants are popular in this area, although in the smaller resorts bars and restaurants may be closed outside the main tourist season.

Services

International & Private Schools: A new international school has recently opened in Rincón de la Victoria and there's also one in Almuñécar. There are no international schools in the vicinity of Nerja, the nearest being in Malaga and Almuñécar. There are no private schools in the area and state schools are the only choice, unless you travel to Malaga.

Hospitals & Clinics: There's a small provincial hospital at Vélez-Málaga, serving the eastern Costa del Sol. The main towns each have a public health centre, although in the smaller resorts opening hours may be restricted. Vélez-Málaga has several private clinics.

Doctors & Dentists: The area has a limited choice of doctors and dentists, and for specialist treatment you need to travel to Malaga.

Tradesmen: While the eastern end of the Costa del Sol isn't as well served as the western end, there's a range of foreign companies and tradesmen in the area offering most services.

English-language Radio & Press: See page 178.

Property

The property market at this end of the coast is as buoyant as it is at the western end and, although property is generally cheaper, prices have been rising fast recently and look set to catch up with those in the west. New construction is booming, particularly in Rincón de la Victoria and Nerja.

Cost of Housing: The following prices are intended only as a guide and were current in mid-2002.

- **Almuñécar**
  Two-bedroom apartment: from €80,000;
  Three-bedroom apartment: from €85,000;
  Villa on a small plot: from €225,000.

- **Nerja**
  Two-bedroom apartment: from €120,000 to €160,000;
  Three-bedroom apartment: from €130,000 to €220,000;
  Three-bedroom townhouse: from €160,000;
  Villa on a small plot: from €250,000.

- **Torre del Mar**
  Two-bedroom apartment: from €80,000;
  Three-bedroom apartment: from €90,000;
  Villa on a small plot: from €250,000.

Land: There are few building plots on this part of the coast, although inland there's a wide choice. Plots near the coastal resorts cost from €250 per m², while inland they cost from around €80 per m².

Rental Accommodation: Rental accommodation is generally quite easy to find in the area, particularly in Torre del Mar and Almuñécar, where there's an abundance of apartments for rent. However, finding a long-term rental which includes the summer months can be difficult, and villas are in short supply. Rents average around €500 per month for a two-bedroom apartment and start at €600 for three bedrooms. Prices in Nerja are around 10 to 15 per cent higher.

Communications

Air: Malaga airport (see page 181) is 55km (35mi) from Nerja and 80km (50mi) from Almuñécar.

Public Transport: Public transport in the area is generally poor and restricted to local buses. Nerja has a limited bus service operating in the town (e.g. to and from the caves). Private transport is essential for most journeys

Roads: In the summer of 2001, the N-340 dual-carriageway from Malaga was completed as far as Nerja, meaning that previous through traffic now bypasses the coastal towns and resorts. As a result, the area is considerably quieter and traffic congestion has been reduced. In Nerja, a series of roundabouts is currently being built, both in the town and around the main access areas, which will further alleviate congestion.

Beyond Nerja, the N-340 is mostly single lane and characterised by a progression of winding bends following the coastal contours. As a consequence, progress is slow and long delays are common during the summer months. Plans are progressing for extending the dual-carriageway as far as Almuñécar, although they're still on the drawing board. The Costa Tropical is connected to Granada in the north by the N-323, which is dual-carriageway except for the first stretch, where tail-backs are common at weekends and during the summer.

Planned Developments

The area's major project is road improvements, particularly the completion of the dual-carriageway from Nerja to Almuñécar. There are also long-term plans for a railway service from Malaga to Nerja.

Employment Prospects

Given the modest size of the area's resorts and their relatively small population, especially in the winter, long-term employment prospects are limited. Short-term employment is relatively easy to find in the summer.

Further Information

Useful Websites

🖳 www.nerjanow.com (general information and business listings)
🖳 www.nerja.org (the official tourist site for the town, with good general information)

INLAND COSTA DEL SOL

Away from the coastal resorts, there are many small towns, villages and country areas that are popular with foreign property buyers. The main centres are: Manilva and Casares, which are near Estepona in the west of the region; Ojén, behind Marbella; Alhaurín El Grande and Coín, behind the Mijas mountain range; and villages in the Axarquía, inland from the eastern end of the Costa del Sol. Most of these villages and towns are untouched by large-scale tourism, although many of their foreign residents work on the Costa del Sol in tourist-related businesses.

Advantages & Disadvantages

The main advantages of living inland are the tranquillity, the spectacular natural surroundings and the fact that you can escape the hordes of tourists. Property prices and the cost of living are also generally lower than on the coast. On the negative side are the lack of amenities, the remoteness of some places and the poor infrastructure, including roads which can be impassable after heavy rain. A good knowledge of Spanish is also essential if you wish to make a success of life inland.

Major Towns & Places of Interest: Manilva is a small town noted for its sweet grapes, Casares a spectacular white village perched on a rocky crag, while Ojén is an attractive white village used as the gateway to the Sierra de las Nieves natural park. Coín is a small, busy town set in an agricultural landscape and Alhaurín El Grande is a large, bustling town serving as a satellite residential area for Malaga. Cómpeta and Frigiliana are small, typical white villages set in vineyards, from whose grapes sweet Malaga wine is made.

Population

Manilva has a population of around 5,000 people, Coín, 17,500 and Cómpeta some 2,700. Relatively few foreign residents live inland.

Climate

The inland Costa del Sol generally enjoys the same pleasant climate as the coast, with two important differences: winter is considerably cooler, especially in the mountains, and summer can be noticeably hotter. Rainfall can also be much heavier and more frequent in mountain areas, particularly at the western end of the Costa del Sol, where the Alcornocales National Park has Spain's highest annual rainfall.

Crime Rate & Security

The crime rate inland is generally very low, particularly in villages where an unofficial 'neighbourhood watch' system operates.

Amenities

Amenities are generally lacking inland, and most residents find that they must travel to the coastal resorts for anything other than basic shopping.

Sports: Most villages offer limited sporting facilities, although some have a public swimming pool and larger towns may have a tennis club or gym. Several of the Costa del Sol's golf courses are inland.

Leisure: Again, leisure options are limited and mostly consist of outdoor activities such as walking. If you speak Spanish, however, you can participate in the activities and classes organised by the village or town council. Some towns have annual events, such as the Flamenco festival in Ojén, and all have an annual fair, often lasting several days.

English-language Cinema & Theatre: None of the towns inland has a cinema or theatre.

Shopping Centres & Markets: Shopping facilities are usually limited in villages, where the only option may be a small store or a weekly visit from a van. Larger towns have more to offer, but again the choice is limited. There are weekly markets on Wednesdays in Alhaurin de la Torre and Istán, Thursdays in Frigiliana and Saturdays in Coín.

Foreign Food & Products: The choice is extremely limited or non-existent in many villages.

Restaurants & Bars: Although the choice is mainly limited to Spanish cuisine, there's no shortage of bars and roadside eateries (known as *ventas*), where the food is usually good and prices considerably lower than on the coast.

Services

International & Private Schools: None.

Hospitals & Clinics: Hospital treatment isn't available inland and you must travel to the coast. Most localities have a health centre, although surgery hours may be restricted (the same applies to clinics).

Doctors & Dentists: Few private doctors and dentists practise inland, and it may be difficult to find an English-speaking practitioner.

Tradesmen: Few foreign service companies or workers are based inland and those on the coast may be reluctant to travel too far or will charge significantly more to do so. For more unusual jobs, this may also apply to Spanish service companies.

English-language Radio: Given the mountainous nature of the region, reception can sometimes be poor, but you may be able to receive the coastal English-language stations.

English-language Press: Larger localities may receive English-language publications, although often sporadically. Subscriptions to English-language publications are possible, but whether you receive them will depend on the postal service, which is often little better than non-existent in some rural areas!

Property

There's a variety of housing available for sale inland, although most foreigners are attracted to rustic property, often on large plots. Houses range from basic shepherds' huts to large villas. Buying land to build on is also popular (you can even buy a whole valley), although you should bear in mind that the regulations regarding what and how large a house you can build are different inland from on the coast. This is mainly because most land in the countryside is classed as 'rustic' and the minimum plot requirement is at least 2,000m^2 for a medium-sized house. **You should take extra care with title deeds and boundaries, which need careful checking by an experienced professional.**

Cost of Housing: In recent years there has been increased interest in inland property and prices have risen, although it's still considerably cheaper than on the coast. Two-bedroom village or town centre apartments start at around €50,000 and townhouses are available from €60,000. Country houses (known as *fincas*) with a large (e.g. 3,000m^2) plot range from €120,000 to over €250,000.

Land: The price of land varies considerably, from as little as €2 per m^2 for very large plots in remote areas to €60 per m^2 for small plots nearer the coast.

Rental Accommodation: Rentals are available in most inland areas, although you won't find a large choice of properties. The monthly rent for a small apartment in a popular town starts at around €350 and for a small country property at around €600.

Communications

Air: Malaga airport (see page 181) is 93km (58mi) from Manilva, 28km (17.5mi) from Coín and 55km (34mi) from Cómpeta.

Public Transport: Public transport away from the Costa del Sol generally leaves much to be desired, with infrequent, slow services. **Private transport is an absolute must if you decide to live inland.**

Roads: Away from the coast, road conditions vary from reasonable to little more than vague marks on the ground ('tracks' would be too grand a description). Roads between most of the main towns and villages, however, are acceptable. The mountainous nature of the terrain means that roads can be tortuous and progress slow, while landslides and road subsidence are often a problem in bad weather.

Planned Developments

Road access to the towns and villages in the vicinity of Malaga is currently being improved.

Employment Prospects

Poor, although considerably improved if you have a good command of Spanish or are prepared to commute to the coast.

LAS ALPUJARRAS

The region of Las Alpujarras, just to the north of the Costa del Sol, is divided between the provinces of Granada to the west and Almería to the east. The perpetually snow-capped mountains of the Sierra Nevada lie to the north, the dramatic Gador mountains to the east and the Mediterranean to the south. The area is traversed by the Guadalfeo river. Average altitude is over 1,000m (3,300ft), in one of the most beautiful, unspoilt parts of Spain, with snowy peaks, deep valley gorges and tree-lined slopes. Las Alpujarras is famous for its mini-ecosystem, irrigated by melting snows and boasting the purest air in Europe and some of the most spectacular views in Spain (on clear days you can see the Rif mountains in Morocco). The traditional way of life in some places has continued virtually unchanged for hundreds of years.

The region, particularly the western (Granadan) area, is increasingly popular with both Spanish tourists and foreigners in search of the 'real' Spain, and weekends and holidays are particularly busy. Most tourists, however, rarely venture beyond the route connecting the villages of Pampaneira, Bubión and Capileira, and many also visit Trevélez.

Advantages & Disadvantages

The area's main advantages are the unique natural surroundings, tranquillity (in Las Alpujarras you *really* can get away from it all) and the friendliness and hospitality of the local population. Disadvantages include the area's isolation, lack of amenities and services, poor communications and harsh climate. Conditions in the Alpujarras can be extreme and before deciding to move there you should carefully consider the implications of life in one of the most undeveloped parts of western Europe.

Major Towns & Places of Interest

Lanjarón, famous for its spring water and spa, lies at the western entrance to the Alpujarras. The busy market town of **Orgiva** is the 'capital' of the Alpujarras and has an interesting church and good amenities. Other towns in the area include **Albuñol** in the south-east, which is small but has a range of amenities, and **Berja** in the far east of the area (in Almería province), which is the largest town in the Alpujarras.

Pampaneira, **Bubión** and **Capileira** are widely considered to be among the most attractive of the villages in the region. As a result, they're also among the most popular with visitors and at weekends are packed with cars and coaches. All three have a wide choice of bars and restaurants, as well as a wealth of craft shops. **Trevélez**, at an altitude of 1,500m (almost 5,000ft), is Europe's highest village and famous for its cured hams (*jamón serrano*). Other villages of note include **Bérchules**, **Pitres** and **Yegen**, where the writer Gerard Brenan made his home during the 1920s and 1930s (see **Useful Publications** on page 183).

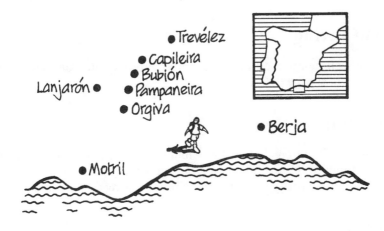

Population

Outside the three principal towns, Berja (pop. 13,000), Albuñol (pop. 5,500) and Orgiva (pop. 5,000), the population is sparse (many villages scarcely number 500 inhabitants) and decreases annually as many locals, particularly younger people, emigrate to the coast or the cities. There are few foreign residents, although the area does have a large colony of hippies, based mainly around Orgiva.

Climate

The Alpujarras have an extreme climate with harsh winters, during which much of the northern part is snow-covered, and hot summers, although the region's high altitude makes the heat less oppressive than in the rest of inland Andalusia. The southern villages enjoy a more temperate climate, although night temperatures everywhere are low all year round. Spring and autumn are the best seasons, with warm, sunny weather.

Language

The Alpujarras are typically Spanish and, although some of the more accessible villages are popular tourist spots, little English is spoken by the locals, many of whom are elderly. The ability to speak reasonable Spanish is essential if you want to make a success of life in the area. You may find the local accent difficult to understand, which is the case in much of Andalusia, although the naturally hospitable nature of the people means that they will do their utmost to help you with the language.

Cost of Living

Generally well below the Spanish average. Property and land are relatively inexpensive (see page 220).

Crime Rate & Security

The crime rate is extremely low, Las Alpujarras being one of the last places in Spain (and indeed the world) where you can leave your door unlocked when you go out and be pretty sure nothing will be missing when you come back.

Amenities

The remoteness of the region means that amenities are limited and in the case of smaller villages, virtually non-existent.

Sports: The towns and some of the larger villages have football pitches and public swimming pools, but no other sports facilities. Climbing in the mountains is popular, as are riding and adventure sports such as hang-gliding and abseiling. Note, however, that although the Prado Llano ski resort in the Sierra Nevada is quite near, there's no direct access to it from Las Alpujarras.

Leisure: Practically all of the leisure activities available in the Alpujarras take advantage of the magnificent natural surroundings. These, together with the unique flora and fauna, form a paradise for hikers and ornithologists. Rural tourism is increasingly popular and an important source of local income, and many foreign residents offer residential classes in drawing, painting and ceramics. All villages have annual fairs and festivities, one of the best known and unusual being the New Year's Eve celebration in the village of Bérchules – which takes place in August!

English-language Cinema & Theatre: None. Orgiva has a small cinema showing films in Spanish.

Shopping Centres & Markets: Towns such as Orgiva and Lanjarón have a reasonable selection of shops, including small supermarkets, bakeries and butchers'. Other villages may have just a small general store or rely on visits from a mobile shop. There's an abundance of local produce, and many people grow their own vegetables and fruit. Most villages have a visiting market twice a month. Orgiva has a market on Thursdays and a hippy market.

Foreign Food & Products: Foreign produce isn't generally available in Las Alpujarras and you must travel to the Costa Tropical (see page 208) or Costa de Almería (see page 226) to find it.

Restaurants & Bars: Despite the small size of the towns and villages, there's a good choice of restaurants and bars offering local specialities, including a free *tapa* with every alcoholic drink. Vegetarian cuisine is popular among the local foreign population and there are several vegetarian restaurants of note in the area.

Services

The area's isolation and small population mean that services are limited.

International & Private Schools: There are none in the area and the only education option is Spanish state schools, which are situated in the larger towns.

Hospitals & Cinics: There's a small public hospital in Pitres and larger hospitals in Almería and Granada, to which most cases are transferred. Granada also has several small private hospitals. There are public health centres in Albuñol, Berja, Lanjarón, Orgiva and Pitres, and a doctor usually visits the larger villages once a week.

Doctors & Dntists: If you wish to be treated by an English-speaking doctor or dentist, your only option is to travel to either Granada or Almería, or even to Nerja or Malaga for some ailments.

Tradesmen: Some foreign workers offer services in the area, although they tend to be specialist craftsmen and limited to a small range of skills. Local expertise, however, is generally good, particularly for construction and agricultural work.

English-language Radio: None.

English-language Press: Many English newspapers are printed in Madrid and available daily at newsagents along the neighbouring Costa del Sol, although they may not be available in the Alpujarras until the afternoon or the following day (if at all). There's also a thriving local English-language press on the coast (see page 178) and many publications provide subscriptions, although delivery to the Alpujarras may take several days.

Churches: Apart from those at a Buddhist monastery, the only religious services in the area are Catholic masses in Spanish.

Property

The property market has grown in recent years as a result of increased interest in the area from foreign property buyers and prices have risen. Nevertheless, the cost of property and land is generally low and Las Alpujarras is one of the last areas of near-coastal Spain where it's still possible to find a bargain (although many a bargain turns out to be the opposite once expensive restoration work has been done).

When deciding where to live in the Alpujarras, you should bear in mind that properties in higher locations are cooler in the summer but more isolated. Also note that tracks can become impassable in wet weather, as well as ruining your car, and that valleys can be dark and cold in winter. Therefore, although an isolated farmhouse in the mountains may appear attractive in the spring sunshine, you should fully consider the implications of living there in winter, when you can be cut off from local amenities for weeks at a time.

Typical Homes: The Alpujarras have a unique architecture, reminiscent of that found in Berber villages in the Rif and Atlas mountains in North Africa. Houses in the towns and villages are adapted perfectly to the steeply terraced terrain, being cube-shaped with flat roofs and prominent chimneys. They're almost always painted white and usually have two storeys, with animals and stores housed below and living quarters above. Older houses may have elaborate iron grilles in front of the windows and huge double doors opening onto a courtyard, where there may be lots of plants and a fountain. Also typical of the region, and indeed of the whole of Andalusia, are large, usually white farmhouses (known as *cortijos*), which tend to be made of local stone, with thick walls and small windows. Many have a central courtyard and are set in large areas of land, which may incorporate olive groves or vineyards.

Cost of Housing: The cost of property varies with the condition and location (town and village properties are more expensive). Properties with mains water and electricity attract a premium, as does land with irrigation. Townhouses in good condition with two or three bedrooms and a roof terrace start at around €30,000. *Cortijos* in need of restoration and without mains services start at around €70,000; *cortijos* in good condition and with mains electricity and water start at around €100,000.

Land: There's plenty of land for sale in the Alpujarras, although plots in towns and villages are in short supply. Bear in mind that there are strict local regulations in villages regarding the height and size (area) of buildings, and in some localities roof terraces aren't permitted. In the countryside there are also regulations governing the type of building allowed. **Before committing yourself to the purchase of a plot, ensure that a building licence will be issued and that the conditions of the licence are adequate.** Land within a town or village costs around €60 per m^2 and outside, where plots are usually at least 2,000m^2, from around €12 per m^2.

Rental Accommodation: Rental accommodation is generally widely available, although long-term rentals are harder to find, as many locals prefer the higher rental returns from weekend and holiday lets. Long-term rents are generally reasonable, e.g. €500 per month for a *cortijo*.

Communications

One of the major disadvantages of the Alpujarras is the area's poor communications, although many locals would argue that this is actually an advantage because it keeps the crowds away! Journeys are, however, slow and long, and private transport is essential, particularly if you choose to live outside the towns of Lanjarón and Orgiva.

Air: There are three airports within striking distance of Las Alpujarras. Granada is the closest but handles few international flights, so it's often necessary to take an expensive connecting flight from either Barcelona or Madrid (information ☎ 958-245-200). Almería airport (see page 247) has a reasonable selection of flights, many from Britain and Germany, although journey times from the airport to the western part of Las Alpujarras are long (information ☎ 950-213-836). Malaga (see page 181) is served by frequent, inexpensive flights from many international destinations (information ☎ 952-048-804) but is around two and a half hours drive from Orgiva.

Public Transport: Public transport is limited to buses, which run to Orgiva, Lanjarón and Trevelez from Granada, and there are only a few a day. Some local buses connect the region's villages and towns, although for most journeys private transport is essential.

Roads: There are main roads (dual-carriageway) from Granada and the coast to the gateway of Las Alpujarras, although once you leave them progress slows considerably. Local roads are narrow and winding, making driving hazardous for the unwary and inexperienced. Road conditions between the main towns and villages are generally good, although bad weather or snow in winter can make some of them impassable. Roads to more remote villages and areas are often little more than tracks and suitable only for 4WD vehicles. Petrol stations are few and far between.

Planned Developments

Given the area's inaccessibility and isolation, plus the fact that much of it lies within the National Park of the Sierra Nevada, major future development is unlikely and will be limited to improving tourist facilities such as hotels and car parks.

Employment Prospects

Job opportunities are generally limited to self-employment in areas such as arts and crafts, and rural tourism providing self-catering or bed and breakfast accommodation. Seasonal work in agriculture may also be available. A good knowledge of Spanish is essential if you plan to work in Las Alpujarras.

Further Information

Useful Publications

- *South of Granada*, Gerard Brenan (Penguin) – a classic account of life in the village of Yegen during the 1920s and 1930s
- *Driving over Lemons*, Chris Stewart (Sort of Books) – a modern account of life in Las Alpujarras

Useful Websites

🖳 www.lasalpujarras.com (general information, plus business listings)

Galician fishing village

7.

OTHER COSTAS & THE
CANTABRIAN COAST

This chapter looks at other coastal areas of Spain that are popular with foreign buyers: the Costa Brava and Costa Dorada (north-east), the Costa de Almería (south-east), the Costa de la Luz (south-west) and the Cantabrian coast (north-west).

COSTA BRAVA

The Costa Brava (Wild Coast) runs for 220km (137mi) along the north-east coast of Spain, from the town of Portbou on the border with France to the resort town of Blanes, 60km (37mi) north of Barcelona. It's almost entirely within the province of Girona (which is within the region of Catalonia) and lays claim to be the home of package tourism in Spain: this started in the 1950s, when the first British and Scandinavian sun-seekers arrived. But the Costa Brava has a far longer history, having attracted settlers from many ancient cultures, including the Iberians from North Africa, the Greeks and the Romans, and the coastline was often plundered by pirates, forcing the natives to establish towns and villages inland.

The spectacular Greco-Roman city ruins at Ampurias are some of the best in Europe and there are also numerous other archaeological sites on the coast. Towns such as Tossa de Mar and Pals have preserved their medieval architecture and the area has many baroque monuments. More recent art and architecture is also represented; the artist Salvador Dalí was born at Figueres, where there's now a Dalí Museum, housed in a building as surreal as the exhibits themselves and the second most visited museum in Spain.

The Costa Brava is a curious mix of long stretches of wild, rugged coastline, sprawling holiday resorts such as Blanes, Lloret De Mar and Platja d'Aro, and picturesque fishing villages such as Cadaqués, Calella de Palafrugell and Tamariu. The coastline is characterised by tall, pine-clad cliffs, virtually inaccessible coves and river deltas incorporating important nature reserves and sandy beaches. The seven small, uninhabited Medas Islands near L'Estarit form part of a highly protected marine and nature reserve, with spectacular flora and fauna.

Although the Costa Brava officially ends at Blanes, many people include in it the coastline south of the resort, as far as Barcelona. This area is mainly flat with long, sandy beaches and is home to textile firms and an important agricultural industry, including vineyards (much of Spain's Cava is made here), horticulture and cut flowers. Extensive areas along the coast are under greenhouses or plastic.

The Costa Brava is one of Spain's top tourist destinations and is growing in popularity, with both foreign and Spanish visitors (numbers rose by almost 12 per cent in 2001).

Advantages & Disadvantages

Advantages include the area's spectacular scenery and beautiful coastline, its good communications and amenities, and the relatively low property prices. The Costa Brava doesn't become as crowded as the Costa Blanca and the Costa del Sol in the summer and it's relatively easy to escape from the tourist hordes. Barcelona (see page 106), one of the liveliest cities in Europe, with a vast range of leisure and cultural opportunities, is also within easy reach. Among the disadvantages are the sometimes harsh winter climate, the effects of mass tourism in some of the resorts in the summer and the relatively poor accessibility of some parts of the coast.

Major Towns & Places of Interest

Blanes, the southern starting point of the Costa Brava, is a built-up resort, popular with Spanish holidaymakers, with good amenities and many villa developments set in pine forests. **Lloret de Mar** is one of Spain's urban eye-sores, as synonymous with package tourism as are Benidorm and Torremolinos. It's crammed with high-rise apartments, making it one of the ugliest parts of the coast, although it's popular with foreign holiday makers (the British in particular), has a wide choice of services and amenities, and has recently undergone a facelift, including the addition of an attractive palm-tree lined promenade.

Tossa de Mar is also popular with foreign holidaymakers and, although built-up, it has preserved its attractive medieval town centre with narrow, winding streets. Further north are the busy resorts of **Sant Feliu de Guixols** and **Platja d'Aro**, the latter being one of the most developed on the coast, and the town of **Palamòs**, which is a major service centre and the third most important port in Catalonia. **Calella de Palafrugell**, **Llafranc** and **Tamariu** are attractive fishing villages set against a backdrop of dramatic cliffs, which have all managed to preserve their original character.

Further north still are several large resorts such as **L'Estartit** and **L'Escala**, and there are many villa developments under construction in the area. Ampuriabrava, near the famous ruins of Ampurias, boasts the unusual 'water town' of **Urb. Marina Residencia**, where two main canals and more than 20 arterial canals have been built and lined with apartments and villas, each with a private mooring. The nearby resorts of **Urb. Santa Margarida** and **Rosas** are popular with north Europeans and have a wide choice of leisure activities, particularly nightlife.

At the northern end of the coast are **Cadaqués** and **Port de la Selva**, two attractive fishing villages which, because of their poor accessibility, have remained largely unspoilt and undeveloped. Cadaqués is one of Spain's trendiest resorts and is crowded and expensive in high season. **Llança**, the last town before Portbou at the border, is an important commercial centre with several developments and an excellent variety of restaurants.

At the other end of the coast, to the south of Blanes, are numerous resorts, many serving as commuter bases for Barcelona, including **Calella**, which is popular with foreigners, and **Arenas de Mar**, an important commercial centre for this part of the coast.

Population

Compared to other coastal areas of Spain, the Costa Brava has a relatively small foreign population, although resorts such as Lloret de Mar and Tossa de Mar are home to a number of foreigners. The area is particularly popular with the British, Dutch, French and Germans.

Climate

The Costa Brava has a broadly Mediterranean climate, although autumn and winter are considerably cooler than on the more southern Costa Dorada and Costa Blanca, and central heating is necessary in winter. Summers are generally hot and dry. The area is susceptible to high winds from all directions, and the particularly unpleasant north wind, known as the *Tramontana*, can blow for days at a time. Winter storms can be fierce, especially on exposed areas of the coast. Average temperatures are 8°C (47°F) in January and 27°C (80°F) in July.

Language

Catalan is one of Spain's four official languages and Europe's seventh most spoken language, used by around 7 million people in Spain and parts of

France and Italy. Spanish and Catalan are the official languages of Catalonia and the vast majority of inhabitants are bi-lingual. Instruction in Catalan is compulsory in all schools. The Catalans have a strong feeling of 'national' identity and in many areas the Catalan language dominates. Although everyone speaks Spanish, integration into Catalan society and culture is easier and quicker if you also speak Catalan. There are several Catalan-only newspapers and television channels.

Cost of Living

The Costa Brava generally has a low cost of living and some of the cheapest property on the Spanish coast. In summer, however, prices tend to rise sharply. The city of Girona, inland from the Costa Brava, annually tops statistics for the highest standard of living in Spain.

Crime Rate & Security

The crime rate is generally low, that in the province of Girona being one of the lowest in Spain. Theft from hire cars and holiday apartments is, however, quite common in the resorts and you should take the necessary precautions.

Amenities

Sports: Most large towns have at least one public sports centre, usually with an indoor swimming pool, and there are numerous private clubs. Tennis clubs and riding stables are particularly popular. Water-sports are a major activity on the Costa Brava, which has numerous marinas, including the large Marina Residencia and the marina at Port d'Aro, situated inland. Most marinas have sailing clubs and hold competitions and regattas. Sailing is a major activity and many of the coast's coves can be reached only by boat. Scuba diving is also popular; the area around the Medas Islands offers unique marine life, and shipwrecks, many of them unexplored, line the coast.

Several ski resorts in the Pyrenees are within a hour's drive of the Costa Brava. As well as downhill and cross-country skiing, the resorts offer other 'white' sports, such as ice-skating. The area has seven golf courses, all of them at least 18-hole, and more are being built. Most courses offer 'pay-and-play' facilities and a round costs from €55. The Rally of Catalonia is held in the area every spring.

Leisure: There's an excellent choice of leisure activities in the area and most towns offer a year-round programme of cultural events, including International Music Festivals held at Cadaqués, Castell de Peralada and Tossa de Mar. Many events are based on Catalan culture, although others have a distinctly international theme, such as the Cuban Habaneras Festival held at Blanes. The town of Calella to the south of Blanes organises an extensive programme of sporting and cultural activities in the summer, known as Calella Activa. All towns celebrate annual festivals, often in honour of the Virgin of the Carmen, the patron saint of fishermen, and Saint George, patron saint of Catalonia. The festivals are colourful and lively, and usually last for several days. Calella also holds a beer festival in October, based on the Munich *Oktoberfest*, while Blanes holds a prestigious annual Firework Contest in July.

Most resorts have a lively nightlife during the summer, with a variety of discos and nightclubs. Lloret de Mar has the liveliest, although some people may find it too noisy and brash. Out of season, bars and nightclubs in smaller resorts such as Cadaqués and Marina Residencia may close. Lloret de Mar also has a casino.

Santa Margarida and Lloret de Mar have theme parks with funfair-like attractions. Lloret also has a water-park, open only in the summer, and Marineland near Blanes offers dolphin shows. Port Aventura near Salou on the Costa Dorada (see page 234) is one of Spain's flagship theme parks and there are regular trips there from the Costa Brava resorts, although the journey can take two hours or more.

English-language Cinema & Theatre: Generally none, except the occasional visiting theatre group. Barcelona has several cinemas which show films in English with Spanish or Catalan sub-titles (see page 109).

Shopping Centres & Markets: Shopping facilities in the area are generally good. Both Barcelona (see page 109) and Girona have an excellent range of shops and are within easy reach of most parts of the Costa Brava. Blanes is the commercial centre of the southern Costa Brava and has many shops, including large supermarkets. Lloret de Mar and Tossa de Mar also have a good variety of shopping facilities. Smaller resorts are less well provided for, although all have at least one supermarket, and shops may close out of season.

Large towns in the area have daily indoor markets selling fresh food and some, such as Blanes, also have a daily outdoor food market. Some towns have weekly general produce markets (Blanes has one on Mondays), and craft fairs are held regularly.

Foreign Food & Products: Most supermarkets in the resorts stock a wide selection of foreign produce, with particular emphasis on British, Dutch and German food.

Restaurants & Bars: There are hundreds of bars and restaurants in the area (Blanes alone has some 95 restaurants!), many of which serve Catalan cuisine, widely considered to be one of the best in Spain, with dishes based on local produce, particularly vegetables, seafood and fish. Some of Spain's most prestigious restaurants, such as El Bulli near Montjoi, are found in the area. In resorts popular with foreigners, such as Lloret de Mar and Tossa de Mar, international cuisine reigns supreme, with the emphasis on fast food, and there are numerous British pubs and Dutch bars.

Services

International & Private Schools: There are no international schools on the Costa Brava, although those in Barcelona are within easy travelling distance (see page 109). The main towns all have private schools, most of which offer a Spanish curriculum, with instruction in Catalan and Spanish. Many have a religious affiliation.

Language Schools: There are a number of language schools offering Spanish and Catalan classes to foreigners, as well as private lessons.

Hospitals & Clinics: There are public hospitals at Blanes, Calella and Palamòs, as well as three in Girona and several in Barcelona. Emergency treatment is available at all hospitals. There are no private hospitals on the coast, although Barcelona has a number (see page 109). Most towns have a public health centre where emergency treatment may be available. Larger health centres offer facilities such as family planning advice, physiotherapy and x-rays. There are also several health spas of note on the Costa Brava and private clinics in most of the larger towns.

Doctors & Dentists: English-speaking medical professionals are available throughout the area.

Retirement Homes: There are few nursing or residential care homes on the Costa Brava.

Tradesmen: A number of foreign professionals and artisans offer services on the coast, although far fewer than on the Costa Blanca or the Costa del Sol. You will find a better choice in Barcelona, although foreigners based there may not be willing to travel to the Costa Brava or will charge extra to do so.

English-language Radio: None.

English-language Press: Most English newspapers are printed in Madrid and are available at international newsagents in the area. Other English and foreign newspapers may arrive later in the day or, in the case of some US newspapers, the following day. There are no local English-language publications.

Consulates: Many countries have consular representation in Barcelona (see page 110).

Churches: The only church services available on the Costa Brava itself are in Spanish and most are Catholic. Barcelona has a number of foreign churches with weekly services in English (see page 110).

Clubs: Unlike other Spanish resort areas, the Costa Brava doesn't have an active expatriate club scene, although international clubs such as the Rotary Club and the Lions Club are present in the area. Barcelona has a wide range of club activities (see page 106).

Property

The Costa Brava is one of the few places on the Spanish coast where you can still buy a bargain property (another is the Costa Dorada – see page 234), although over the last few years prices have risen considerably (nearly 1.5 per cent per month in some places), reflecting increased interest in the area from foreign buyers, particularly Dutch and German and, to a lesser extent, British. This trend is expected to continue, and property on the Costa Brava is therefore considered to be an excellent investment. Many new constructions are under way, particularly on the more accessible parts of the coast and in the countryside around towns such as Sant Feliu de Guixols.

Typical Homes: A typical Catalonian building is known as a *masía*, a large stone mansion set in extensive grounds. *Masías* many several centuries old are available for purchase around the Costa Brava, although prices for a restored one can reach several million euros. Bear in mind that the price of an unrestored *masía* will increase significantly once you start work on it. Many villages and towns on the Costa Brava also have large, almost palatial residences known as *Casas de Indianos*, which were built in the 19th century by rich Catalan emigrants returning from the Americas.

Cost of Housing: Note that the prices given below aren't for sea-front or golf course property, for which you should expect to pay at least double.

Two-bedroom apartment: from €60,000;
Three-bedroom apartment: from €75,000;
Three-bedroom townhouse: from €80,000;
Three-bedroom villa with an 800m² plot: from €200,000;
Masía with extensive grounds: from €350,000.

Land: A good choice of plots is available on the Costa Brava, where prices range from €30 per m² for inland plots to €200 per m² and upwards for plots on the coast with good views. Plots vary in size, although they tend to be over 800m².

Rental Accommodation: Like all popular holiday regions, the Costa Brava has a wealth of rental property for short-term and holiday lets, although long-term accommodation (longer than six months) is difficult to find because many property owners prefer the higher returns from holiday lets. Monthly rents start at around €450 for a small apartment and at €600 for a small townhouse. Rents during high season are considerably higher.

Communications

Air: The Costa Brava can be reached from four main airports, two of them in France (Montpelier and Perpignan), all of which are served by charter and scheduled flights from Britain. In Spain, the Costa Brava's main airport is Girona (28km/17.5mi from Blanes), which is small but served by a variety of charter flights, mainly from Britain and Germany. Note that the number of flights is greatly reduced during low season. Airport information is available from ☎ 972-186-600.

Barcelona airport (75km/47mi from Blanes) also serves the area, with many charter and scheduled flights from various international destinations. Airport information can be obtained from ☎ 932-983-838 or 🖥 www.aena. es/ae/bcn.

Sea: Barcelona is a major port, with daily ferry sailings to the Balearic Islands and weekly sailings to Genoa in Italy. Many resorts on the Costa Brava have marinas and fishing ports, and from May to October, small ferries act as 'water buses' along the coast, stopping at the resorts. Boat trips are also available to the Medas Islands.

Public Transport: Public transport is generally good in the region. The train line from Barcelona to Portbou (which includes Spain's oldest railway, originally built in 1848) stops at many resorts south of Blanes and Blanes itself before it runs inland to Girona and back to the coast at Llança. Trains travel to Barcelona from Blanes every 30 minutes. Barcelona can be reached by train from France (journey times will be considerably reduced when the extension to the high-speed track is finished), as well as from Madrid and Valencia. Work on the high-speed line from Madrid to Barcelona (known as the *AVE*) is under way and expected to be finished by 2004.

Buses, both local and regional, serve the area and generally offer a good service. Large towns and resorts have their own local bus routes: Lloret, for example, has three bus lines, and services have recently been improved. In more remote parts of the coast, public transport services are few and far between or non-existent, so private transport is essential.

Roads: Two toll motorways serve the area, the A-7 from Barcelona to the French border and the A-19 from Barcelona to Blanes. The N-II lies inland from Blanes and has many branch roads serving the resorts; they're mainly secondary and single-carriageway and become crowded in high season and at weekends. Road access to some resorts such as Cadaqués is poor and journey times are long. Because of the rugged nature of the terrain, large sections of the Costa Brava cannot be reached by car and, apart from the road running along the coast from Blanes to Palamòs, you usually cannot drive along the coast. Road access to the Costa Brava from France is quick and easy, and journey times from Britain are around 12 hours.

Planned Developments

No significant developments were planned in mid-2002.

Employment Prospects

Catalonia has one of Spain's lowest unemployment rates and the coast is no exception. Employment prospects are generally good, although the ability to speak Spanish and other languages (particularly Dutch and German) is a major advantage.

Further Information

Useful Publications

- *AA Essential Costa Brava*, T. Kelly (AA Publishing)
- *Costa Brava Insight Pocket Guide* (Insight Guides)
- *Lonely Planet: Catalunya and the Costa Brava*, D. Simonis (Lonely Planet Publications)
- *The Rough Guide to the Costa Brava*, C. Lloyd (Rough Guides)

Useful Websites

- www.costabrava.org (the area's official tourist website, in several languages)
- www.costabrava.com (a general guide and business directory)
- www.blanes.net (the official guide, with useful information about the town and surrounding area)
- www.lloretguide.com (information about the resort)
- www.tossademar.com (information about the resort)

COSTA DORADA

The Costa Dorada (Golden Coast) runs for over 300km (187mi) along the southern Catalonian coast in north-east Spain. It's a mainly flat region, characterised by long golden beaches (hence the name) that run for miles, including some of the best in the country. The Costa Dorada isn't as popular as some of Spain's other coasts, although July and August are busy, with both foreign and Spanish visitors.

The coast has a rich history and is home to some of the best preserved Roman sites in Europe. Tarragona was one of the most important cities in the

Roman Empire, with remains to prove it, and the region also has some notable medieval monuments, such as the castle at Calafell. This part of Spain is a land of contrast: between its ancient architectural legacy and its busy, modern tourist resorts such as Salou and Sitges. Industry is also found along the coast, and there are two nuclear power stations just south of Tarragona (one of which is in the process of being dismantled).

At the southern end of the coast lies the Ebro River Delta, one of the Mediterranean's most important marine reserves and a highly protected area. The delta is home to numerous species of bird and has extensive areas planted with rice. At the northern end of the coast is the Garraf National Park, a large area of typical Mediterranean vegetation.

Advantages & Disadvantages

The Costa Dorada has excellent beaches, a pleasant climate, efficient communications and a wide range of leisure options. Apart from the larger resorts, most of the coast is quiet, and Barcelona, one of the liveliest cities in Europe and with a vast range of leisure and cultural opportunities, is within easy reach (see page 108). Drawbacks include a lack of amenities and services outside high season, when many resorts practically close down, and the fact that both the railway line and the N-340 run parallel to the beach for much of the southern section of the coast, making beach access both difficult and dangerous.

Major Towns & Places of Interest

Much of the southern part of the coast remains relatively undeveloped and construction has been limited to villa developments such as Riumar, Cabo Roig and Lastres Calas, which have few services and amenities. **L'Ampolla**, **L'Ametlla de Mar** and **L'Hospitalet de l'Infant** are small towns which were once fishing communities, although they're now mainly reliant on tourism. L'Hospitalet has good beaches, a marina and lively nightlife during the high season. **Miami Playa** resort is one of the largest on this part of the coast and is heavily built-up, mainly with apartment blocks, and well known for its excellent summer nightlife. The area is currently undergoing a construction boom, with many new projects under way.

Cambrils is an attractive town surrounded by developments such as Vilafortuny, which has many apartment blocks. **Salou**, further north, is one of the Costa Dorada's most famous resorts and is a busy, lively town, popular with Spanish and foreign tourists alike. It has a beautiful, palm-lined promenade and good services and amenities. The large city of **Tarragona** is one of Catalonia's industrial centres and has an important port and oil refinery. It also has numerous Roman ruins, including a forum and theatre, as well as several important medieval monuments, such as the imposing cathedral. Tarragona's northern beaches are particularly attractive and the coastline has large areas of pine forest.

North of Tarragona are several towns, such as **Altafulla,** with its old walled town centre, and **Torredembarra,** which has excellent beaches and an interesting old fishing quarter. Popular developments here include Urb. Bara and Urb. Costa Daurada. **Calafell** is popular with foreign residents, with many apartment blocks, an interesting medieval town and castle, and a large marina at Segur de Calafell. **Cunit** is a small resort with eight cove-like beaches, and **Cubelles,** further north, is an upmarket residential villa development.

Vilanova I La Geltrú is one of the Costa Dorada's most important commercial and industrial centres, although the town also has an important tourist industry. The old quarter boasts many attractive monuments, and the town's marina is considered to be one of the best on the Catalan coast. **Sitges** is the jewel in the Costa Dorada's crown and one of Spain's best known resorts, offering a wide range of leisure activities. The town has many interesting monuments and the view of the old quarter from the sea is particularly attractive. Sitges is popular with both foreign and Spanish tourists, and has a large gay community. North of Sitges lie developments such as Les Botigues de Sitges and La Rosa, before you reach **Castelldefels,** a large commuter town of Barcelona, with excellent beaches and good amenities and services.

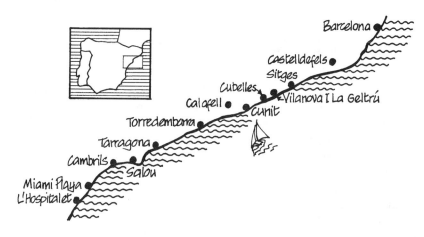

Population

The Costa Dorada has a small foreign population, mainly concentrated around the resorts on the northern part of the coast. The area is popular with the British, French and Germans.

Climate

The Costa Dorada's climate is broadly Mediterranean, with average temperatures of around 9°C (4°F) in the winter and 24°C (75°F) in the summer, when the weather usually sunny. Temperatures inland are somewhat lower in winter and higher in summer. Humidity tends to be low and there's often a sea breeze. Rain falls mainly in the spring and autumn and is occasionally torrential.

Language

Catalan is one of Spain's four official languages and Europe's seventh most spoken, used by around 7 million people in Spain and parts of France and Italy. Spanish and Catalan are the official languages of Catalonia and the vast majority of inhabitants are bi-lingual. Instruction in Catalan is compulsory in all schools. The Catalans have a strong sense of 'national' identity and in many areas the Catalan language dominates. Although everyone speaks Spanish, integration into Catalan society and culture can be easier and quicker if you also speak Catalan. There are several Catalan-only newspapers and television channels.

Cost of Living

The Costa Dorada generally has a low cost of living and some of the cheapest property on the Spanish coast.

Crime Rate & Security

The crime rate is generally low, although theft from hire cars and holiday apartments is quite common in the resorts.

Amenities

Sports: Most large towns have at least one public sports centre, usually with an indoor swimming pool, and there are numerous private clubs. Tennis and riding are particularly popular. The Costa Dorada also has several marinas, the one at Vilanova of particular note. Port Ginesta at Castelldefels was built to host the water-sports at the 1992 Olympics and its world-class installations offer the chance to practise a wide range of water-sports, including rowing and canoeing. Windsurfing is popular in the area, the sea breezes at Cunit being particularly favourable, and conditions are suitable for scuba diving.

Adventure sports are also popular, with a wide range of activities on offer, from rock climbing to mountain biking. The Costa Dorada has four golf courses, including the prestigious Bonmont Terres Noves course. All are 18-hole and offer 'pay-and-play' facilities.

Leisure: The Costa Dorada has a varied range of cultural events throughout the year, although most take place during the summer. Sitges celebrates an International Theatre Festival and a prestigious International Film Festival annually, while Calafell holds an International Music Festival against the spectacular backdrop of its medieval castle. All towns hold annual fairs and festivities, often lasting for several days, and of particular note are the Carnival celebrations at Sitges in February, Saint John festivities in June throughout the area and the fair in honour of Saint Tecla at Tarragona in September.

Port Aventura, near Salou, claims to be Europe's largest theme park, visited by several million visitors per year. It boasts the world's 'largest' roller-coaster and has two hotel complexes. Sitges and La Pineda (north of Salou) both have water-parks open in the summer, while Aqualeon at El Vendrell combines a water-park with safari and marine attractions.

Other popular leisure pursuits are visiting the region's towns and villages and the wide range of activities offered at the Ebro Delta National Park, including guided tours and bird-watching, and. The many Roman remains throughout the region are much visited. Nightlife on the Costa Dorada is lively during the summer, when resorts such as Salou, Sitges and Port Ginesta offer some of the best clubbing in Spain.

English-language Cinema & Theatre: None, with the exception of the occasional visiting theatre group. Barcclona has several cinemas which show films in English with Spanish or Catalan sub-titles (see page 109).

Shopping Centres & Markets: Shopping facilities in the area are generally good and Reus and Tarragona, as well as Barcelona (see page 109), all have an extensive range of shops and are within easy reach of the coastal resorts. Sitges is the commercial centre of the northern Costa Dorada and has many shops, including large supermarkets. Large resorts such as Torredelbarra and La Pineda have reasonable shopping facilities, but smaller resorts are less well provided for, although all have at least one supermarket; shops may close out of season. The region's large towns have daily indoor markets selling fresh food and also usually have weekly general markets (e.g. Tarragona on Saturdays and Salou on Sundays).

Foreign Food & Products: Most supermarkets in the resorts stock a wide selection of foreign produce, particularly British and German food.

Restaurants & Bars: There are numerous bars and restaurants in the area (Salou alone has over 100!), many of which offer local Catalan cuisine, widely considered to be one of Spain's best. Dishes are based on local produce, particularly rice (grown in the nearby Ebro delta), vegetables, seafood and fish. In resorts popular with foreigners, such as Salou and Sitges, international cuisine reigns supreme, with an emphasis on fast food, and there are numerous British pubs and German bars.

Services

International & Private Schools: Castelldefels has an Anglo-American school and other schools are found in Barcelona (see page 109). The main towns all have private schools, most of which offer a Spanish curriculum with instruction in Catalan and Spanish. Many of the schools have a religious affiliation.

Language Schools: There are a number of language schools offering Spanish and Catalan classes to foreigners, and private classes are also available.

Hospitals & Clinics: Tarragona's two public hospitals serve the area and there are also public hospitals inland at Tortosa and Reus, and several in Barcelona. Emergency treatment is available at all hospitals. There are no private hospitals on the coast, although Barcelona has a number. Most of the main towns have a public health centre where emergency treatment may be available. Larger health centres offer facilities such as family planning, physiotherapy and x-rays. There are also private clinics, mainly in the larger towns.

Doctors & Dentists: English-speaking medical professionals are found throughout the region.

Retirement Homes: There are few nursing or residential care homes on the Costa Dorada.

Tradesmen: A number of foreign professionals offer services in the area, although far fewer than on the Costa Blanca and the Costa del Sol. You may find a better choice in Barcelona, although the foreigners based in the city may not be willing to travel to the Costa Dorada or may charge extra to do so.

English-language Radio: None.

English-language Press: Most English newspapers are printed in Madrid and are available on the morning of publication at international newsagents in the area, although out of season you may need to order them. Other English and foreign newspapers may arrive later in the day or, in the case of some US newspapers, the following day. The Costa Dorada has no local English-language publications.

Consulates: Several countries have consular representation in Tarragona, among them Belgium, France, Germany and Norway. Most other countries, including Britain and the USA, are represented in Barcelona (see page 110).

Churches: The only services available on the Costa Dorada are in Spanish and most are Catholic. Barcelona has a number of foreign churches with weekly services in English (see page 110).

Clubs: The Costa Dorada doesn't have as active an expatriate club scene as other Spanish coasts, although international clubs such as the Rotary Club and the Lions Club are represented in the area. Barcelona has a wide range of clubs (see page 106).

Property

The Costa Dorada, like the Costa Brava (see page 234), is one of the last places on the Spanish coast where you can still buy a bargain property. The region has fewer foreign property buyers than some other *costas* and holiday homeowners tend to be Spanish. Prices have, however, risen in recent years, although not as much as in other parts of Spain, e.g. the Costa del Sol and the Canary Islands. Beach-front properties attract a premium of at least 25 per cent. Many new constructions are under way, particularly around Salou and the resorts in the south, such as Miami Playa.

Typical Homes: A typical Catalonian building is known as a *masía*, a large stone mansion set in extensive grounds. There are fewer *masías* here than on the Costa Brava, and most property consits of modern villas and apartment blocks.

Cost of Housing: The following prices are intended only as a guide and were current in mid-2002.

Two-bedroom apartment: from €90,000;
Three-bedroom apartment: from €120,000;
Townhouse: from €130,000;
Villa with a 1,000m² plot: from €180,000;
Country house with extensive land (more than 2,500m²): from €90,000.

Land: There isn't much available building land on the Costa Dorada. Most plots are large and inland, often with a dwelling, which may be little more than a ruin.

Rental Accommodation: The Costa Dorada has a wide choice of rental property for short-term and holiday lets, although long-term accommodation (longer than six months) is difficult to find because many property owners prefer the higher returns from holiday lets. Monthly rents start at around €400 for a small apartment and €550 for a small townhouse. Rents during high season are considerably higher.

Communications

Air: Reus airport near Tarragona is one of Spain's smallest, although its passenger numbers increase annually (over 600,000 in 2001). It handles scheduled and charter flights to Spanish and European destinations (airport information is available from ☎ 977-779-847). Barcelona airport (see page

111), which is an hour's drive from Salou, also serves the area, handling a wide range of charter and scheduled flights from international flights. Airport information can be obtained from ☎ 932-983-838 and 🖳 www.aena.es/ae/bcn.

Sea: The port at Tarragona is one of Spain's busiest for cargo, although it has no passenger ferries. Barcelona is a major port, with daily ferry sailings to the Balearic Islands and weekly sailings to Genoa in Italy. Car and passenger ferries cross the Ebro river delta.

Public Transport: The Barcelona-Valencia train line runs the length of the Costa Dorada along the coast (with excellent views of the beaches) and has stops at the main towns and resorts, including L'Ametlla, Miami Playa, Salou, Tarragona, Torredembarra, Segur de Calafell and Sitges. The journey time from Barcelona to Sitges is under 30 minutes.

Barcelona can be reached by train from France and from Madrid and Valencia. Work on the high-speed line from Madrid to Barcelona (known as the *AVE*) is under way and expected to be finished by 2004, when journey times will be considerably reduced.

Regular bus services link the region with other main centres in Catalonia and the rest of Spain. The larger towns on the Costa Dorada are also served by local bus services.

Roads: The region's road network is generally good and, although all stretches of motorway are toll roads, fares are reasonable. The A-7 motorway runs the length of the southern stretch of the Costa Dorada to El Vendrell, near Calafell, and has numerous exits to the main towns and resorts. The A-16 motorway runs the remaining length of the coast up to Castelldefels and has greatly improved communications, particularly from Barcelona to Sitges.

The N-340 runs the length of the coast to Calafell but is single-carriageway and passes directly through many towns and resorts, meaning that progress is slow. The northern part of the coast is served by a local road (the C-246), which is particularly slow as it winds its way through the Garraf National Park. Roads around the resorts become crowded at weekends and during the summer. Needless to say, parking is difficult in the main towns.

Planned Developments

Major residential developments are under wat around Sitges, Tarragona and the resort area at Miami Playa.

Employment Prospects

Catalonia has one of Spain's lowest unemployment rates and the coast is no exception. Employment prospects are generally good, although the ability to speak Spanish well is essential. Most jobs are in the tourist sector and may be available only during high season.

Further Information

Useful Publications

● *Costa Dorada and Tarragona Pocket Guide* (Berlitz)

Useful Websites

▭ www.costadaurada.org (the official tourist information website for the area)
▭ www.salou.org (the resort's official website)

COSTA DE ALMERIA

The town of Almería (which means 'mirror of the sea') is in south-eastern Spain in the province of Andalusia and its holiday resorts are known as the Costa de Almería. The area is one of contrasts, between busy tourist resorts and starkly beautiful, practically untouched land. It's also one of Spain's wealthiest regions, owing to a large agricultural industry; there are more than 10,000ha (24,000 acres) of vegetables and flowers under plastic greenhouses.

The area includes the national park of Cabo de Gata, a unique marine reserve with beautiful virgin beaches and rocky coves. Inland, the landscape is practically uninhabited, comprising desert and sandstone rock formations, the setting for many Wild West movies. In the west of the province and inland lie the remote villages of the southern Alpujarras in Sierra Nevada (see page 172). Almería is also home to Europe's largest, most powerful telescope, a major astronomical observatory, and the area is a pioneer of solar power.

Advantages & Disadvantages

The Costa de Almería has several advantages, including its excellent climate and unspoilt countryside. The region is also ideal for water sports, walking and bird-watching. On the other hand, it has poor communications with the rest of Spain and out of season many resorts are quiet, with amenities closed. Some people also find that the arid, almost treeless landscape loses its appeal after a while.

Major Towns & Places of Interest

Almería is a modern city which has managed to preserve much of its old town, including a Moorish fortress. To the west lies a series of resorts: **Aquadulce**, the first to be developed, has a marina and many holiday apartment blocks; **Roquetas del Mar** and **Playa Serena** form the Costa de Almería's largest resort and the area's main package holiday destination; and **Almerimar** is a purpose-built holiday resort with a large marina and good beaches.

Further to the west, close to the province of Granada, is the town of **Adra**. Inland lies the large town of **El Ejido**, practically indistinguishable from the 'fields' of plastic greenhouses surrounding it. To the east of Almería lies the **Cabo de Gata** national park, dotted with small villages such as San José and Níjar. On the east coast is the town of Caboneras, once a small fishing village but now a commercial port and industrial centre.

Set inland, in the mountains, is the Moorish village of **Mojacar**, one of the area's most attractive places. It suffered massive emigration during the 1960s and the mayor, in an attempt to halt the exodus, gave land to anyone who promised to build on it! Within a year, a picturesque artists' colony had established itself in the village and Mojacar now has the largest number of foreign residents in the area. Its resort, Mojacar Playa, has a variety of apartment and hotel complexes along its 9km (5mi) of beaches and is growing in popularity with foreign buyers. Further to the north is the rapidly developing village of Garrucha and the resort of Vera, with its extensive naturist beaches and facilities.

The **Sierra de Gador** behind Almería has several attractive villages in the lower foothills, including Vícar, Enix and Félix, where the mountain landscapes and fruit and almond orchards make them popular with foreign buyers. La Envia golf complex has good amenities and there are plans for another course and complex in the area.

Population

The total population of the area is around 500,000 (Almería has over 150,000 inhabitants) and foreign residents make up a substantial proportion, most of them immigrant workers from Eastern Europe and Africa employed in greenhouse agriculture. Roquetas del Mar has a total population of around 47,600, of which 3,600 are foreign residents. The town's population is expected to double by 2010. Of the 5,000 inhabitants of Mojacar almost half are foreign residents, mainly German and British.

Climate

The province of Almería is the hottest in Spain and boasts the highest number of sunshine hours in Europe, with over 3,100 annually. The weather is usually warm and pleasant from early March to November. Rainfall is scarce and most parts register less than 200mm per year, meaning that there are often droughts. Average temperatures are 16°C (61°F) in January and 32°C (90°F) in July.

Cost of Living

Almería is one of the richest provinces in Spain and this can be seen by the proportion of luxury cars on the roads and the number of banks in the main towns. Some things, such as dining out, are expensive, while others such as property are relatively inexpensive compared with other Spanish coasts.

Crime Rate & Security

In most parts of the Costa de Almería the crime rate is low. Some areas, however, particularly El Ejido, experience occasional outbreaks of racial violence between the residents and African immigrants working in the greenhouses. Race relations are tense in the province generally, although they've improved recently.

Amenities

Generally, amenities are limited in comparison with the main *costas* because of the region's relative remoteness.

Sports: The Costa de Almería offers a wide variety of sporting activities, with water-sports the most common. There are several marinas and ports in the area, most of which have a sailing club. The pristine waters make it a prime spot for scuba diving, considered to be among the best in Spain. Horse riding is popular and there are many riding schools. There are 18-hole golf courses at Almerimar and Roquetas del Mar and others inland. The city of Almería will host the Mediterranean Athletic Games in 2005.

Leisure: A primary leisure attraction on the Costa de Almería is its spectacular natural surroundings and there are numerous opportunities for walking, hiking and bird-watching (with flamingos and rare water-birds on the salt lagoons). Cycling is another popular pastime. All villages and towns have annual fairs and the Almería fair held during the last two weeks of August is of particular note.

Almería's main attraction, and its major claim to fame, is the Mini Hollywood theme park at Tabernas. It has the original film sets for many of the Westerns filmed here, including *The Good, the Bad and the Ugly*. Roquetas del Mar has a water-park, open only during the summer.

Shopping Centres & Markets: Most towns and villages have a selection of small supermarkets and shops, although the choice of goods can be limited. In some resorts, shops may close out of season. Almería and Murcia are better options for shopping and both have several large stores and hypermarkets. Note that the quality of the water on the Costa de Almería is poor and you're advised to drink only bottled water.

Foreign Food & Products: Supermarkets in the resorts usually stock foreign produce, although prices tend to be high and outside the high season availability may be limited.

Restaurants & Bars: Almería city has a wealth of bars and restaurants, particularly *tapas* bars. The resorts offer a variety of restaurants, often serving international food. Local cuisine consists mostly of fish dishes. There's also a reasonable choice of pubs and clubs on the Costa de Almería, although out of season some open only at weekends, while others close. Note that eating out is expensive on the Costa de Almería.

Services

International & Private Schools: There are no international schools in Almería. There are several private schools in the capital, all offering a Spanish curriculum, many with a religious affiliation.

Hospitals & Clinics: Almería has two public hospitals and one private one. El Ejido also has a private hospital. The Roquetas del Mar authorities are currently petitioning for a hospital. All main areas have a public health centre, although in more remote areas, opening hours may be restricted. There are also several private clinics, mainly in the capital.

Doctors & Dentists: Several English-speaking doctors and dentists are available in the area, particularly in the resorts.

Retirement Homes: There are few nursing or residential care homes on the Costa de Almería.

Tradesmen: Foreign expertise isn't always easy to come by, although local expertise is good.

English-language Radio: Broadcasts can be received from the English-language radio stations on the Costa del Sol (see page 178)

English-language Press: Most major English newspapers are printed in Madrid and are available at newsagents in the main resorts on the morning of publication, although out of season you may need to place an order. Some English and foreign newspapers may arrive later in the day or, in the case of some US newspapers, the following day. The Costa del Sol's main newspaper, *Sur in English*, can be obtained at some outlets or on subscription, as can *The Euro Weekly News*.

Consulates: The only consulate is the German one at Roquetas del Mar. Other consulates are in Malaga (see page 179).

Property

The property market is generally buoyant and many new complexes have been built or are under construction. Prices are generally lower than on the Costa del Sol, although they've risen considerably over the last few years. The cheapest area is around Mojacar Playa and there's increasing demand for inland country properties.

Typical Homes: The Costa de Almería's architecture is distinctive, characterised by whitewashed 'sugar cube' square houses stacked on top of each other. Windows are usually small to keep out the heat and the architecture is reminiscent of Morocco. In some inland parts of the province, caves have been dug into hill and mountain sides and are used as dwellings. These caves are often spacious and have the advantage of being warm in winter and cool in summer.

Cost of Housing: The following prices are intended only as a guide and were current in mid-2002.

● **Roquetas del Mar**
  Two-bedroom apartment: from €90,000;
  Three-bedroom apartment: from €105,000;
  Villa: from €270,000.

● **Mojacar**
  Two-bedroom apartment: from €60,000;
  Two-bedroom townhouse: from €95,000;
  Villa: from €180,000.

● **Sierra de Gador**
  Country house: from €110,000.

Land: As is the case everywhere, the cost of land varies considerably according to its location. A plot near the coast and all its amenities will cost in the region of €150 per m², while plots inland are considerably cheaper. Bear in mind that some parts of the Costa de Almería, such as Cabo de Gata, are protected and building regulations are strict. **Check with the local authorities before committing yourself to the purchase of land.**

Rental Accommodation: Holiday and short-term rentals are generally easy to come by, although prices in summer are high. Long-term accommodation (longer than six months) is more difficult to find, particularly in the resorts, although winter lets are generally good value. Typical monthly rents are from €400 for a two-bedroom apartment, from €480 for a three-bedroom apartment and from €1,000 for a villa with private pool.

Communications

Air: The Costa de Almería is easily reached from three airports. Almería airport is located just outside the city and has a modest number of flights, mainly from Britain and Germany (the service is much reduced out of season). From winter 2002, however, there will also be a weekly scheduled flight from Gatwick, with extra flights during high season. Almería airport also has flights to several Spanish destinations, although in 2001 Iberia reduced the service and tickets are some 20 per cent more expensive than at other airports. Almerimar is 30km (19mi) from the airport, Mojacar 98km (61mi) and Roquetas 20km (12.5mi).

Murcia airport (San Javier) is around 45 minutes from Mojacar. It's a small airport, with a limited number of charter flights, mainly from Britain, although the choice is growing. Alicante airport, which is around two hours from Mojacar, is a larger airport, with a wide selection of flights to and from many European destinations.

For information: Almería airport ☎ 950-213-709; San Javier Murcia ☎ 968-172-000, 🖳 www.aena.es/ae/mjv; Alicante airport ☎ 966-919-000.

Sea: There's a summer service from Almería to the Spanish enclave of Melilla in north Africa.

Public Transport: Public transport on the Costa de Almería is poor and in many areas private transport is essential. Almería has a railway station, from which you can travel to Granada and Madrid, although in 2001 the number of trains was reduces and the night train to Madrid cancelled. Bus travel is another option to Granada, Malaga and Murcia, although services are infrequent. There are limited bus services within the region itself.

Roads: For many years, Almería was both undeveloped and out on a limb because of a lack of good roads linking the city with the rest of Andalusia. The situation has improved dramatically in recent years, although there's still much to be done, particularly regarding the connection with Granada. At present, the Costa de Almería is linked to the Costa del Sol by the N-340, which is dual-carriageway only in parts, meaning that journey times can be long.

The A-92 runs from Granada to Almería, although it's dual-carriageway only as far as Guadix, the rest of the journey consisting of a narrow winding road, most of it presently dug up. The completion of the dual-carriageway is forecast for 2003, while the main road from Almería to Mojacar is mostly dual-carriageway already. Within the rest of the region, roads are reasonable, although because of the mountainous terrain, progress can be slow.

Planned Developments

The 2005 Mediterranean Games mean that new infrastructure and sports facilities will be needed, particularly around the city of Almería, and it's expected that the Games will put the region on the map. Other developments include more golf courses and the building of tourist complexes in the foothills of the Sierra de Gador. The area between the resorts of Roquetas del Mar and Aguadulce is currently expanding and the two towns are expected to be joined by 2012. Building work includes the largest shopping centre in the province, a theatre-auditorium, an aquarium and several thousand homes.

Employment Prospects

Almería has the lowest unemployment rate in Andalusia, mainly because of the jobs provided by agriculture and tourism. The ability to speak Spanish and German is a distinct advantage.

Further Information

Useful Websites

💻 www.almeria-turismo.org (the official tourist website)
💻 www.almeriainthesun.com (a useful tourist website)

COSTA DE LA LUZ

The Costa de la Luz (Coast of Light) is in south-western Spain and comprises the Atlantic coast of Andalusia. It stretches from Tarifa, the southern tip of Spain, to the Portuguese border and is divided by the Guadalquivir River, which also forms the border between Cadiz and Huelva provinces (to get from one province to the other, you must travel via Seville, 100km/60mi to the north). Along with the Costa de Almería and the Cantabrian coasts, this is one of Spain's most 'authentic' coastlines, virtually untouched by mass tourism. It's noted for its magnificent sand dunes, windswept marshes, sleepy villages and delicious seafood.

Although the Costa de la Luz is one of Spain's quieter stretches of coast, construction has increased in recent years and August is busy, particularly in the main resorts, such as Matalascañas. The section of the Costa de la Luz in the province of Cadiz is more popular with foreign buyers and residents. Europe's largest nature reserve, the Doñana National Park (Coto de Doñana), lies near Cadiz, in the delta of the Guadalquivir river and is one of the most highly protected areas in the world.

Most coastal resorts are popular with Spanish tourists, particularly in the summer. There are few foreign residents and only limited amenities and services specifically for foreigners. If you choose to live in this part of Spain, the ability to speak Spanish is essential.

Advantages & Disadvantages

Advantages of this area include peace and quiet, some of Spain's best beaches and world-class windsurfing. Disadvantages include strong winds virtually all year round, poor communications and few amenities and services outside the large towns.

Major Towns & Places of Interest

Tarifa is mainland Europe's southernmost tip and the point at which the waters of the Mediterranean meet those of the Atlantic. Until the mid-1980s it was a quiet fishing village, when water-sports enthusiasts discovered that the strong winds blowing almost permanently along the coast could be put to good use. Tarifa is now a popular resort, ranking among the top three windsurfing destinations in the world. Further up the coast, there are magnificent sandy beaches and the tiny village of Bolonia, with its exceptionally well-preserved Roman ruins.

Barbate near Cape Trafalgar is the area's main town, although it's little more than a fishing village. Between Barbate and the city of Cadiz there are a few isolated coastal developments as well as the villages of **Caños de Meca** and **Conil de la Frontera**, both increasingly popular with foreigners. Before reaching Cadiz, one comes to the large, busy town of **Chiclana** with its up-and-coming resort of Novo Sancti Petri on the coast. **Cadiz** is one of Spain's great maritime cities and has a rich history and an attractive old quarter with many fine monuments.

North-west of Cadiz lies the pretty town of **El Puerto de Santa María** (known simply as El Puerto), famous for its magnificent sea food and *manzanilla* (a tangy dry sherry). Further up the coast there are several developments, including Urb. Vistahermosa and Urb. Fuentebravia, popular with Spanish holiday makers, although practically empty outside high season. **Rota,** with its American naval base, and **Chipiona** are two large towns to the north of Cadiz, before you reach the attractive town of **Sanlúcar de Barrameda,** which lies at the mouth of the Guadalquivir River and has some fine beaches. Development along the coast is then interrupted by the Doñana National Park, which has a long stretch of protected coastline.

North of Doñana are the popular resorts of **Matalascañas** and **Playa de Mazagón,** where holidaymakers from Seville flock during weekends and holidays. The industrial city of **Huelva** has several attractive resorts nearby, including **Punta Umbría** with its marina, **Playa de la Antilla** and **Isla Cristina,** which lies practically on the Portuguese border. Inland is the busy city of **Jerez de la Frontera** (known as Jerez), which serves as a service centre for much of the area and is one of the popular excursion destinations from the Costa del Sol and Gibraltar. The city has many interesting monuments and is famous for its sherry industry (the word 'sherry' is an Anglicised corruption of Jerez) and dancing horses.

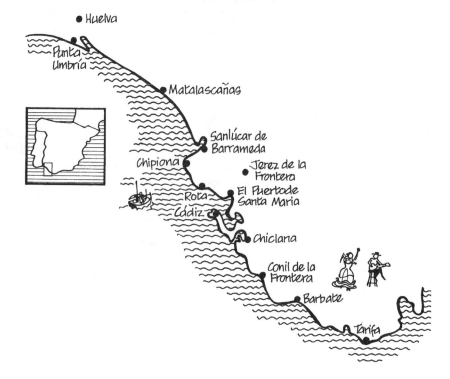

Population

The three largest towns in the region are Jerez (pop. 185,000), Huelva (pop. 140,000) and Cadiz (pop. 138,000). The foreign population is low.

Climate

The Costa de la Luz enjoys more than 3,000 hours of sunshine per year and the climate is generally warm and pleasant. Most of the rain falls in the autumn and winter. Because the coast is exposed to the Atlantic, strong winds blow almost continually and the easterly wind known as the *Levante* is particularly unpleasant.

Cost of Living

The cost of living on the Costa de la Luz is generally low for Spain, and property is also relatively cheap (see page 253).

Crime Rate & Security

The crime rate is generally low, although the coastline is infamous for tobacco and drug smuggling, much of which enters Spain via Gibraltar. Petty crime is common in towns such as Tarifa and Barbate.

Amenities

This part of Spain has considerably fewer amenities than the neighbouring Costa del Sol. During the winter, much of the area is quiet and some resorts are practically empty, with no services. Leisure activities are extremely limited out of season and it's wise to visit the area in winter as well as during the high season before committing yourself to buying a property.

Sports: The area's small towns have limited sports facilities, with some modest public sports centres, private gyms and tennis clubs. Water-sports reign supreme, the windsurfing and surfing conditions being among the world's best. Tarifa and the surrounding area is the windsurfing capital and the town has many specialist shops and clubs. Other popular water-sports include sailing (there are several marinas in the area) and scuba diving. Horse riding is also popular, there are many riding clubs and competitions are held regularly. Jerez, with its Formula 1 race course, is on the motor-racing circuit. The area has many golf courses, which generally offer a 'pay-and-play' facility, including Montecastillo, home to the Volvo Masters event, and Sancti

Petri, designed by Severiano Ballesteros. Several more are currently under construction.

Leisure: Leisure activities are outdoor-oriented, to take advantage of the spectacular coastline and countryside. Ornithologists in particular find much to attract them, especially in the autumn when millions of migrating birds gather over the Straits. Doñana National Park also provides unique animal and bird watching, although special permission is required to enter the park. Walking and hiking are also popular.

The area has many attractive towns and villages, the White Villages of Cadiz of particular note, while the magnificent city of Seville (see page 124) is within easy reach. All of the region's towns and villages have annual fairs and festivities, and the Carnival celebrations at Cadiz in February are nationally famous for their *chirigotas* – songs parodying current affairs. There are no theme parks on the Costa de la Luz, although the Isla Mágica in Seville is within easy reach.

English-language Cinema & Theatre: None.

Shopping Centres & Markets: Shopping facilities in the smaller towns are often limited to a selection of modest supermarkets and shops, with even less in the villages. Note that shops in the resorts may be closed out of season. Large towns and cities such as Algeciras, Jerez and Cadiz have good shopping facilities, with shopping centres and hypermarkets, and Seville (see page 124) has an excellent range of shops. If you're at the eastern end of the coast, you can also visit Gibraltar, which has many British shops, including a large supermarket. Towns in the region often have daily indoor markets selling fresh food and there are also weekly general markets at most of them.

Foreign Food & Products: Some supermarkets in the popular resorts stock a small selection of foreign produce, although the choice is limited and prices are high. For those at the eastern end of the coast, Gibraltar has a wide selection of British goods, and shops including Marks & Spencer, Mothercare and Safeway. Bear in mind that queues to enter and leave Gibraltar by car can be horrendous.

Restaurants & Bars: There's an abundance of bars and restaurants in the region, most serving Spanish cuisine, with the emphasis on seafood and fresh fish. Cadiz, El Puerto and Sanlúcar are particularly famous for their excellent seafood, especially prawns and lobster. Note that bars and restaurants in the resorts may be closed out of season.

Services

International & Private Schools: El Altillo international school in Jerez offers a Spanish curriculum within a bi-lingual (Spanish-English) environment. Otherwise, the nearest international school is Sotogrande on the nearby Costa del Sol, which offers a British curriculum. Large towns such as Cadiz, Jerez and San Fernando have several private schools, all offering a Spanish curriculum and many with a religious affiliation.

Language Schools: Language schools offering Spanish for foreigners are found in the larger towns and cities, and private classes are also available.

Hospitals & Clinics: There are public hospitals in Cadiz, Jerez, Puerto Real and Tarifa, and all hospitals offer emergency treatment. Algeciras and Seville (see page 126) have larger hospitals. The larger towns and smaller ones such as Barbate, Chiclana, Conil and Tarifa all have at least one public health centre, where emergency treatment may be available. Cadiz has some small private clinics.

Doctors & Dentists: Most of the region's doctors and dentists are Spanish, although many speak English.

Retirement Homes: There are few nursing or residential care homes on the Costa de la Luz.

Tradesmen: Few foreign workers serve the area, although local artisans are excellent and reliable.

English-language Radio: No English-language stations broadcast from the area, although at its eastern end you can pick up programmes broadcast from stations on the Costa del Sol and Gibraltar (see page 178).

English-language Press: Most major English newspapers are printed in Madrid and are available on the morning of publication at newsagents in the main towns, although you may need to place an order. Some English and foreign newspapers may arrive later in the day or, in the case of some US newspapers, the following day. There are no local English-language publications.

Consulates: The nearest consulates for most countries are in Malaga (see page 179) and Seville (see page 127).

Churches: English-language church services are generally unavailable in the area.

Clubs: As a result of the small foreign population, there are few clubs specifically for foreigners. There are, however, many social and sporting activities organised by the local authorities, although you need to have a reasonable grasp of Spanish to become properly involved.

Property

The Costa de la Luz has a healthy property market and, although there isn't as wide a choice of buildings as on the neighbouring Costa de Sol, prices are considerably lower. Indeed, the Costa de la Luz has some of the cheapest coastal property in Spain, although ever-increasing interest in the area, from both foreign and Spanish buyers, means that this is unlikely to continue for much longer. Many new developments are under construction along the coast.

Typical Homes: As throughout Andalusia, older houses may have elaborate iron grilles in front of the windows and huge double doors opening onto a courtyard, where there may be lots of plants and a fountain. Also typical of the region are large, usually white farmhouses (known as *cortijos*), which tend to be made of local stone, with thick walls and small windows. Many have a central courtyard and are set in large areas of land, which may incorporate olive groves or vineyards.

Cost of Housing: The following prices are intended only as a guide and were current in mid-2002.

Two-bedroom apartment: from €100,000;
Three-bedroom apartment: from €135,000;
Two-bedroom townhouse: from €140,000;
Three-bedroom villa with a 1,000m^2 plot: from €230,000.

Land: Unlike many coastal areas of Spain, the Costa de la Luz still has a lot of land available for building, although regulations regarding height and size of construction are strict. Plots are generally large (at least 1,500m^2) and prices start at around €125 per m^2.

Rental Accommodation: The Costa de la Luz has a good choice of rental property for short-term and holiday lets, although long-term accommodation (longer than six months) is difficult to find, as many owners prefer the higher rental returns from holiday lets. Monthly rents start at around €450 for a small apartment and at €600 for a small townhouse. Rents during high season are considerably higher.

Communications

Communications both to and within the Costa de la Luz, particularly by road and public transport, are generally poor.

Air: Both Jerez and Seville (see page 106) have airports, although they're small and flights are mainly domestic (there may be the occasional international charter flight to Seville). Gibraltar also has an airport, its flights mainly to and from Britain. Malaga airport offers the best option, with frequent flights to and from many European destinations, although the journey time to the airport is long, particularly from the Huelva section of the Costa de la Luz. If you need to fly to or from this part of the Costa de la Luz, it may be quicker to use Faro airport on the Algarve in Portugal.

For information: Gibraltar ☎ 350-73026 from abroad or 956-773-026 from Spain; Jerez ☎ 956-150-000; Malaga ☎ 952-048-804, 🖳 www.aena. es/ae/agp; Seville ☎ 954-449-023.

Sea: Ferry services sail from Cadiz to Gran Canaria and from Tarifa to Tangier in Morocco.

Public Transport: Public transport in the area is generally poor and the only option is bus travel, which if you wish to travel any distance is time-consuming and involves several changes. Cadiz, Jerez and Seville are well connected by frequent bus services, although otherwise private transport is essential.

Roads: Apart from the area around Cadiz and Jerez, which is served by dual-carriageways, and the motorways from Cadiz to Seville (toll) and from Seville to the Portuguese border, roads in the region are generally single-carriageway and journey times are long. The main road from Tarifa to Cadiz is the slow N-340, although there are advanced plans for its upgrade to dual carriageway. To travel the length of the Costa de la Luz is time-consuming and involves a lengthy drive via Seville, as traffic isn't allowed to cross the Doñana National Park.

Planned Developments

These include the regeneration of the port at Cadiz, the conversion of the N-340 to dual-carriageway and the completion by 2005 of a dual-carriageway connecting Vejer de la Frontera and Jerez, which will improve communications between the southern Costa de la Luz and inland Andalusia. Much of the area is highly protected and construction is strictly regulated, so it seems unlikely there will a great deal more development on the coast other than the completion of a number of golf courses.

Employment Prospects

Job prospects are poor, particularly in areas such as Barbate and Tarifa, where there's high unemployment because of cut-backs in the fishing industry. Cadiz also has high unemployment because of the depressed shipping industry. A working knowledge of Spanish is essential if you want to work in the region.

Further Information

Useful Websites

⌨ www.andalucia.com (general site about Andalusia, including information about the Costa de la Luz)

⌨ www.tarifa.net (information about Tarifa, with emphasis on windsurfing)

THE CANTABRIAN COAST

The Cantabrian coast runs the length of northern, Atlantic Spain. It's around 750km (470mi) long and includes the provinces of Galicia in the west, Asturias, Cantabria and the Basque Country. The region is one of Spain's most beautiful, certainly the greenest. Several mountain ranges back onto the coastline, including the Pyrenees and the spectacular Picos de Europa, which has some stunning bays and beaches. The famous pilgrim route to the shrine of St James the Apostle runs the length of the coast, from the French border to Santiago de Compostela.

The Cantabrian coast has a rich, ancient legacy, dating back over 20,000 years, as the numerous cave paintings (the best-known are at Altamira) testify. Well preserved Roman monuments are also found throughout the area, although unlike the rest of Spain it wasn't home to either the Romans or the Moors for long.

The region receives a lot less tourism than Spain's other coasts, although its resorts are popular with Spanish visitors during the summer months. Much of the area is economically dependent on agriculture and heavy industry, particularly central Asturias, where there are coal mines, and around Bilbao. The region is a curious mixture of the ultra-modern, e.g. the spectacular titanium Guggenheim Museum in Bilbao and the recently refurbished port at Santander, and the traditionally rural, including areas where time seems to have stood still. The latter aspect is best seen in the hundreds of tiny villages where the land is still tilled by hand and many locals speak the local dialect.

Galicia is one of Spain's poorest regions, a rural province heavily reliant on agriculture. Geographically, it's unlike anywhere else in Spain, reminiscent of the west coast of Ireland, with a rugged coastline dotted with small coves and long sandy beaches. Galicia's cliffs are particularly spectacular, although dangerous (many ships have been wrecked along the coast). Inland, Galicia is hilly and green, with a plethora of eucalyptus forests and a vast network of rivers. The region has a rich Celtic heritage and Galician, closely resembling Portuguese and one of Spain's four official languages, is widely spoken (see page 228).

Asturias also relies heavily on agriculture, although the province also has a wealth of industry, based mainly in the central valleys and the city of Avilés. The coastline is known as the Costa Verde (Green Coast), one of the most beautiful and undeveloped in Spain. Inland, the terrain is mountainous and much of the province's land is part of protected national parks, with unique flora and fauna, including western Europe's only significant brown bear population. Asturias also has many important historic sites, including the Sanctuary of Covadonga, a site of pilgrimage for many Catholics, and numerous churches. Like Galicia, the region has a rich Celtic heritage, and the *Asturianos* (as the inhabitants are known) are well known for their hospitality.

Cantabria is one of Spain's smallest regions and is well known for its vast array of prehistoric remains, particularly caves, and its spectacular sandy beaches, some of which stretch for several miles. It also has some beautiful medieval villages and attractive fishing harbours. The Cantabrian countryside is green and mountainous like neighbouring Asturias, and the area relies mainly on agriculture, particularly livestock farming. Many tourists pass through the region, although most are heading south and Cantabria is unspoilt and quiet for most of the year.

The **Basque Country** (known as *Euskadi* by its inhabitants) is a small region in northern Spain on the border with France. It has traditionally relied on agriculture and heavy industry and is the most industrialised part of Spain, although much of the area remains unspoilt. The countryside is mountainous (although less so than Cantabria and Asturias), green and thickly forested, while the rugged coastline is dotted with small coves and bays and is home to an important fishing industry. The Basque Country feels different from the rest of Spain and the language (*Euskera*), one of Europe's oldest tongues and apparently unrelated to any other language in the world, is still spoken (along with Spanish), although its complexity means that it's spoken only by a minority. Basques have traditionally been fiercely independent and the area is home to Spain's most virulent 'nationalism', expressed violently by the terrorist group ETA, whose existence is one of Spain's most pressing social and political problems. The Basques are also famous for their hospitality and gastronomy, the latter widely considered to be one of the best in Spain.

The Cantabrian coast is essentially Spanish, with few foreign residents, and there are few amenities and services specifically for foreigners. If you choose to live there, the ability to speak reasonably fluent Spanish is essential.

Advantages & Disadvantages

Advantages include the area's tranquillity, some of Spain's best beaches and most spectacular countryside, and a generally low cost of living. Disadvantages include the relatively cool, wet climate, poor communications in the west of the region and the lack of amenities and services away from the large cities.

Major Towns & Places of Interest

Galicia's major cities are its four regional capitals: **A Coruña** (formerly known as La Coruña), an attractive city on the west coast with a rich maritime history and good amenities; **Lugo**, a charming town situated inland from A Coruña and almost entirely enclosed by Roman walls; **Ourense,** in the south and mainly industrial; and **Pontevedra**, an attractive city on the coast near the Portuguese border with important fishing and seafood industries. **Santiago de Compostela** is the jewel in Galicia's crown, lying at the end of one of the most important Catholic pilgrimages. It's one of the most beautiful cities in Spain, with an imposing Romanesque cathedral, where St James the Apostle is allegedly buried.

Asturias has three main cities: **Avilés**, which is mostly industrial; **Gijón**, one of Spain's shipping centres and an attractive seaside city, extensively refurbished in recent years, with a new marina; and **Oviedo**, a beautiful city, famous for its university and spectacular Gothic cathedral. Asturias also has some popular seaside resorts, including the fishing village of **Luarca** in the west, and **Ribadesella** and **Llanes** to the east. All are attractive, mainly unspoilt resorts with good amenities, although they're quiet out of season.

Cantabria's main city and capital is the busy port of **Santander**, one of Spain's leading seaside resorts, popularised by the Spanish aristocracy a hundred years ago. It has an attractive old quarter, a fine sea-front and several impressive beaches. The port, which has recently been expanded, is one of Spain's main points of entry and nearly 150,000 visitors arrive at Santander by ferry every year. Other places of note in Cantabria are the coastal resorts of **Castro Urdiales**, **Comillas**, **Laredo** and **Santona**, traditional fishing villages all popular with Spanish visitors and holiday home owners. Inland lie the beautiful medieval villages of **Santillana de Mar** and **Barcena La Mayor**, the latter reputed to be Europe's oldest village.

The Basque Country's most beautiful city is **San Sebastian** (also considered to be one of the most beautiful in Spain), popularised by Spanish aristocrats and royalty at the turn of the century. Set in a rounded bay known as La Concha (the shell), the city has many attractive monuments and excellent shopping facilities. **Vitoria**, situated inland, is the capital and seat of the Basque government, an attractive town with one of the highest standards of living in Spain. **Bilbao** is Spain's sixth-largest city and home to the country's largest port. Much of the city is heavily industrialised, although the old quarter and town centre, as well as the port and airport, have been extensively refurbished and are attractive (Bilbao is home to the striking, emblematic Guggenheim Museum). Nearby coastal resorts include **Zarautz** and **Zumaia**.

Much of the Cantabrian coast is frequented by Spanish and foreign tourists in the summer, but for the rest of the year tourists are few and far between.

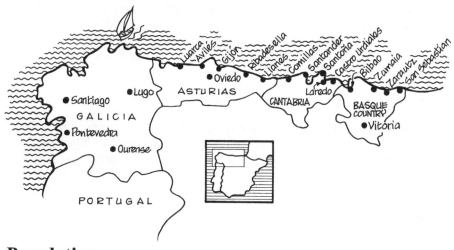

Population

The foreign population of the Cantabrian coast is very small.

Climate

The Cantabrian coast is the coolest, wettest region of Spain, hence its verdant countryside. There's rain throughout the year, although slightly less in the summer and Cantabria and the Basque Country receive less rain than Galicia and Asturias. High winds are common, especially in Galicia, whose western coastline is particularly susceptible to storms.

The summer months are generally refreshingly cooler than the rest of Spain, although inland areas of the Basque Country and Galicia can be hot and humid. Winters tend to be mild on the coast, although in mountainous inland areas the snows arrive early, often staying until spring and mountain communities are frequently cut off. Average temperatures at Pontevedra are 14°C (58°F) in January and 25°C (77°F) in July, and at Santander 12°C (54°F) in January and 22°C (72°F) in July.

Language

Spanish is spoken all along the Cantabrian coast, although in the Basque Country and Galicia *Euskera* and *Gallego* respectively are also official languages. *Gallego*, similar to Portuguese, is widely spoken by most inhabitants and is taught in schools. Most signposts and notices in the region are in both Spanish and *Gallego*. *Euskera*, on the other hand, isn't widely spoken, except in the area around San Sebastian and in some villages, and doesn't form part of compulsory education except in special Basque schools. Both regions have local television stations, which broadcast in the local languages. There are also 'nationalist' movements in Asturias, which promote *Asturiano*, a dialect of Spanish, although not many people speak it.

Cost of Living

This part of Spain is one of the cheapest, particularly Asturias and Galicia. Cantabria and the Basque Country are more expensive, although general daily expenses are still reasonable, while Santander and San Sebastian have notably high property prices.

Crime Rate & Security

The crime rate is very low in most of the region, and in village communities crime is virtually unheard of. Car related crime is common in the large cities and you should take care not to leave any valuables in your vehicle.

Terrorist violence is a feature of the Basque Country and, although most residents are usually unaffected, in many Basque towns and cities vandalism and violence in support of *ETA* are common, particularly at night, when you should avoid certain areas. You will also have to put up with the ubiquitous graffiti and flags supporting Basque terrorists and prisoners.

Amenities

Outside the main cities, this part of Spain has few amenities, and during the winter months much of the area is very quiet and resorts are practically empty, with a bare minimum of services. Leisure activities are also limited out of season. It's therefore wise to visit the area in winter as well as during the season, to give yourself a good idea of what's available and what life is like when the tourists are away.

Sports: Most cities and large towns have several public sports centres, usually with an indoor swimming pool, and there are also numerous private clubs throughout the region. Tennis clubs and riding stables are popular, while water-sports are one of the region's prime sporting activities, both along the coast and on the numerous rivers. Sailing is popular and many resorts have marinas with sailing clubs, which host competitions and regattas during the summer.

Windsurfing and scuba diving are found on the coast, while on the region's rivers, canoeing and rowing are popular; the annual Descent of the Sella River in August is one of the major international canoeing events. Salt and freshwater fishing are both excellent (the trout fishing in Asturias ranks among the best in Europe).

There's a small ski resort in the Picos de Europa mountain range, and several ski resorts in the Pyrenees are an easy car journey from the eastern end of the Cantabrian coast. Mountaineering, rock climbing and related adventure sports are some of the region's main attractions and there are many specialised clubs and groups offering mountain-related pursuits. Note that these aren't for the inexperienced, because conditions can change quickly at high altitude and even experienced shepherds have been known to lose their way. Numerous accidents and several fatalities occur every year.

Rural tourism is a major growth industry in the region, which offers a range of overnight and weekend accommodation in typical local houses. The Cantabrian coast also has a few peculiar sporting activities. Lifting and throwing impossibly heavy objects such as tree trunks and boulders is, for some reason, particularly popular and regular competitions are held. *Pelota* is widely practised in Basque communities and *boules* is popular along most of the coast.

The region has many golf courses, particularly around Santander (where Severiano Ballesteros was born) and several more are planned, although there are fewer courses in Galicia. Courses generally offer a 'pay-and-play' facility.

Leisure: Most of the major cities offer an extensive range of cultural activities, especially during the summer. San Sebastian is probably the cultural capital of the area, with concerts, recitals, operas and plays available at the city's concert hall and theatres. It hosts a nationally renowned Jazz Festival in July and an acclaimed International Film Festival in September.

Santander also has plenty to offer culturally, including the prestigious International Music Festival and its excellent Summer University Courses. It also has a casino. Other cities such as Bilbao, Oviedo and Santiago also have lively cultural scenes.

Away from the main cities, leisure activities are generally out-of-doors to take advantage of the spectacular coastline and countryside. Walking and hiking are particularly popular and the St James Pilgrims' Way to Santiago is busy all year round. Ornithologists and botanists will find much to attract them in the area and some of the bird and plant life in the Picos de Europa is unique.

All areas, however small, have annual fairs or festivities, which often last for several days. Even tiny, remote villages spend a fortune on entertainment and fireworks for their annual fair. Festivities of particular note include the annual fairs at Bilbao, San Sebastian (with its international firework competition) and Vitoria in August, the Feast of St James in Santiago in July, the breaking in of wild horses at numerous locations in Galicia and Asturias in the summer, and the infamous San Fermin bull running held at nearby Pamplona in July.

Year-round attractions include the Cabarceno wildlife safari park near Santander and the Altamira Caves visitor centre, where an exact replica of the caves have been constructed (access to the real caves is extremely limited and there's a waiting list of years). Santander also has a zoo, while San Sebastian has an interesting aquarium and a rather 'tame' amusement park.

English-language Cinema & Theatre: None, with the exception of foreign films shown at the San Sebastian Film Festival in September and the occasional performance by visiting theatre groups.

Shopping Centres & Markets: Shopping facilities in the main cities are generally good. San Sebastian is particularly strong for designer shops, although the city has no department stores. Most cities have a branch of El Corte Inglés, Spain's flagship department store, and also have shopping centres, usually containing a hypermarket. Larger towns tend to have a good selection of shops too, including the large supermarkets. Smaller towns are less well provided for, although all have at least one supermarket, and some shops may close out of season. Villages often don't have any shopping facilities at all and are dependent on visits from mobile shops.

The region's cities and large towns have daily indoor markets selling fresh produce and some also have daily outdoor food markets. Most towns have weekly general produce markets, and craft fairs are held regularly. Rural towns also hold regular farmers' markets.

Foreign Food & Products: Foreign produce isn't generally available, except in specialist shops in the large cities or in the delicatessen sections of hypermarkets and El Corte Inglés department stores.

Restaurants & Bars: One of the joys of life in this part of Spain is eating out, the local cuisine being nationally acclaimed. There's an abundance of bars and restaurants, most of which offer Spanish cuisine, with an emphasis on seafood. Basque food is of particular note, and touring the bars in the old quarter of San Sebastian sampling the numerous *tapas* is one of Spain's great culinary experiences. International menus are also available, the emphasis on Italian and Chinese fare. Eating out is generally cheap in the region, with the added advantage of generous portions (the Cantabrian Coast isn't a good place to live if you're on a diet).

Services

International & Private Schools: International schools are thin on the ground in this part of Spain and the only options are the American school at Bilbao and the English School of Asturias. All the region's cities and large towns have several private schools, offering a Spanish curriculum; many have a religious affiliation.

Language Schools: Language schools offering Spanish for foreigners are found in all the large towns and cities, and private classes are also available.

Hospitals & Clinics: There are public hospitals in all the main cities, those in the Basque Country being particularly prestigious. Private hospitals are also found in the larger cities, those in the region of Navarra being nationally acclaimed. Cities and main towns all have at least one public health centre, where emergency treatment may be available. Out of the main towns, there are generally greatly reduced health facilities and some villages have no services at all. Private clinics are available in most cities and large towns.

Doctors & Dentists: Most doctors and dentists in the region are Spanish, although some may speak English, especially in the cities.

Retirement Homes: There are few nursing or residential care homes on the Cantabrian coast.

Tradesmen: Virtually no foreign workers serve the area.

English-language Radio: None.

English-language Press: Most English newspapers are printed in Madrid and may be available at international newsagents in the major cities and large towns, although you may need to place an order. Other English and foreign newspapers may arrive at the end of the day of publication or, in the case of some US newspapers, the following day. There are no local English-language publications.

Consulates: There are foreign consulates in the following towns in the region: Asturias (Brazil, Hungary and Mexico); Bilbao (numerous consulates, including Britain, France, Germany and Ireland); A Coruña (several, including Belgium and the USA; Ourense: Portugal); Pontevedra (Britain,

Germany and Portugal); San Sebastian (several, including Germany); Santander (Italy).

For addresses and phone numbers, look in the white or yellow pages under '*Consulados*'.

Churches: English-language church services are rare.

Clubs: Because of the small foreign population, there are few clubs specifically for foreigners. There are, however, many social and sporting activities organised by the local authorities, although you need to speak reasonable Spanish to participate.

Property

The Cantabrian coast has a healthy property market, although there isn't as wide a choice as on other Spanish coasts and property specifically designed for use as a second home isn't available. Property is generally cheap, however, and this is one of the last places in coastal Spain where you can still find a bargain, although rental returns aren't as good here as on the other coasts. On the other hand, Santander (particularly the popular Sardinero area) has very expensive property, and property in the city of San Sebastian is the most expensive in Spain – almost three times as much per square metre as that of other Spanish cities. Overall, property prices in the region have been rising steadily over the last few years and this is expected to continue, so property is regarded as a good investment.

Typical Homes: In Galicia, typical houses are large stone mansions, known as *pazos*, often with wooden balconies. Asturian and Cantabrian towns and villages have many palatial houses known as *casas de Indianos*, built by rich immigrants returning from the Americas in the 19th century. They're built of stone and usually have large, covered balconies on the upper floors, enclosed in stained glass set in wrought iron. Typical village homes are also made of stone, with stables and grain stores on the ground floor and the living quarters upstairs. In the Basque Country, typical houses are built in a French style, with white facades decorated with painted gables, shutters and eaves.

Cost of Housing: The following prices are intended only as a guide and were current in mid-2002.

Small apartment: from €100,000;
Large apartment: from €150,000;
(Note that prices for a beach-front property or one or in Santander or San Sebastian are at least double.)
House: from €200,000;
Country house with land: from around €50,000 (note that, although an old country house may appear to be a bargain, restoration costs will considerably increase the initial price).

Land: Unlike many coastal areas of Spain, the Cantabrian coast still has lots of land available for building, although regulations regarding the height and size of what you can build are strict. Land is often cheap and plots are generally large (at least 1,500m²). Prices for urban plots start at €50 per m². Rural plots are cheaper, although they may lack utility connections.

Rental Accommodation: The region has a reasonably healthy rental market, with the exception of San Sebastian, where there's a shortage and prices are high. In small towns and villages you may also find it difficult to rent long term (more than six months), because many properties are let for weekends and short holidays. Monthly rentals for a two-bedroom apartment start at around €480 and for a small house at €550. Rates during high season and in San Sebastian, Santander and Vitoria are considerably higher.

Communications

A blend of the extremely good (among the best in Spain) and the very poor, particularly in the mountain areas and the west of the region.

Air: Several airports serve the area, although all are small and offer few international flights. Bear in mind also that connecting flights from other Spanish airports to the region are often expensive. Bilbao airport, 8km (5mi) north of the city, is the largest in the region, offers the best selection of international flights and is served by most main European destinations. Information is available from ☎ 944-869-301.

Santander's Parayas airport is small, with domestic flights only. Airport information is available from ☎ 942-202-100. Asturias airport, 47km (30mi) west of Gijón and Avilés, is also small and handles only domestic flights. Airport information is available from ☎ 985-127-500. Labacolla airport, 12km (7.5mi) east of Santiago, is also modest, but has flights to several European destinations, including Amsterdam, London and Paris, as well as to most domestic airports. Information is available from ☎ 981-547-500.

Sea: The Port of Santander is one of Spain's main entry points, receiving nearly 150,000 ferry passengers per year. Ferries sail several times a week from the British port of Plymouth, with a journey time of around 24 hours. In the summer months, ferries also travel from to Bilbao from Portsmouth, which takes around 35 hours. Ferry travel isn't cheap, although discounts and special offers are often available. Note that the Bay of Biscay is notoriously rough at all times of year; take your seasickness pills!

Public Transport: The standard of public transport varies greatly and, unless you choose to live in one of the cities or larger towns, private transport is essential. A train service, known as *FEVE*, runs along the coast from Bilbao to Ferrol, stopping at numerous places along the way. The journey, although picturesque, is slow and is more of a tourist attraction than an efficient means of getting around. Train services link the main towns with Madrid, and within the Basque Country there are local train services run by Euskotren, which are extremely popular and used by millions of passengers per year. Bilbao has an ultra-modern metropolitan train service (with two lines designed by Norman Foster), most of which travels underground. Both lines are currently being extended.

Buses run throughout the region, although to travel from one end of the Cantabrian coast to the other is virtually impossible without numerous changes. Within each area, buses connect the cities and main towns, and there are limited services to larger villages. Note, however, that most villages off the main roads aren't on the bus network. All the main cities also have urban bus networks.

Roads: The Cantabrian coast generally has good communications with the rest of Spain, although the mountain ranges that separate it from the middle of the country make progress slow and the passes are occasionally closed by snow. Some parts of the region, i.e. around the main cities in the Basque Country and Asturias, and along the coast from the French border as far as central Asturias, have excellent roads, although many stretches of motorway are toll.

In other parts of the region, most roads are single-carriageway and traffic is heavy and progress slow, even though road conditions are good. Roads in remote parts, particularly the mountains, are generally narrow and tortuous, often closed in winter. Many parts of the western Cantabrian coast have poor road communications and you should expect journeys to be slow. Roads connecting busy tourist spots, such as the Picos de Europa access roads and roads to popular seaside resorts, can be horribly crowded in July and August.

Planned Developments

Many of the region's cities are undergoing major restoration work. For example, Gijón's city centre is currently being restored. Improving the region's infrastructure is the main impending project, particularly the roads. The Cantabrian Highway (the A-8) is currently under construction in Asturias and will eventually run from Irún on the border to Oviedo. It's expected to be finished in 2004.

Employment Prospects

Unemployment is quite high throughout much of the region and job prospects for foreigners aren't particularly good, unless you wish to be self-employed in the tourist sector. A good knowledge of Spanish is essential if you wish to work in the region.

Further Information

Useful Publications

● *Vacances: Basque Country*, Y. Maznik (Cassell Illustrated)

Useful Websites

⌨ www.asturnor.com (the official tourist site for Asturias)
⌨ www.basquecountry-tourism.com (the official tourist site for the Basque Country)
⌨ http://turismo.cantabria.org (general tourist site about Cantabria, mostly in Spanish)
⌨ www.galinor.es/galicia (the official tourist site for Galicia)

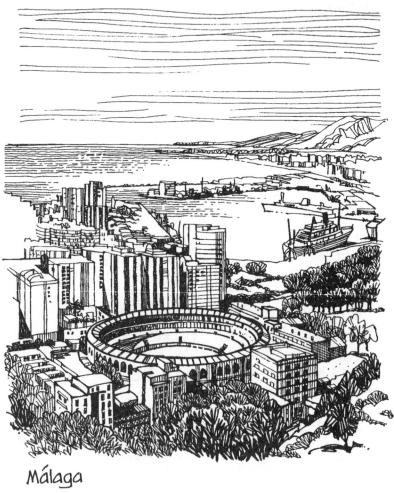

Málaga

APPENDICES

APPENDIX A: USEFUL ADDRESSES

Embassies & Consulates

Embassies are located in the capital Madrid and many countries also have consulates in other cities (see **Consulates** in relevant chapters and sections). Embassies and consulates are listed in the yellow pages under '*Embajadas*'. Note that some countries have more than one office in Madrid, and before writing or calling in person you should telephone to confirm that you have the correct office.

Australia: Paseo de la Castellana, 143, 28046 Madrid (☎ 915-790-428).

Austria: Paseo de la Castellana, 91, 28046 Madrid (☎ 915-565-315).

Belgium: Paseo de la Castellana, 18, 28046 Madrid (☎ 915 -776-300).

Canada: C/Núñez de Balboa, 35, 28001 Madrid (☎ 914-314-300).

Cyprus: C/Serrano, 43-45, 28006 Madrid (☎ 914-359-630).

Denmark: C/Claudio Coello, 91, 28006 Madrid (☎ 914-318-445, 🖳 www. embaja dadinamarca.es).

Finland: Paseo de la Castellana, 15, 28046 Madrid (☎ 913-196-172, 🖳 www.finlandia.org).

France: C/Salustiano Olózaga, 9, 28001 Madrid (☎ 914-355-560, 🖳 www. amba france.es).

Germany: C/Fortuny, 8, 28010 Madrid (☎ 913-196-310/185-866).

Greece: Avda. Doctor Arce, 24, 28002 Madrid (☎ 915-645-819).

Ireland: C/Claudio Coello, 73, 28001 Madrid (☎ 915-763-509).

Italy: C/Lagasca, 98, 28006 Madrid (☎ 915-776-529).

Luxembourg: C/Claudio Coello, 78, 28001 Madrid (☎ 914-359-164).

Malta: C/Maria de Molina, 39, 28006 Madrid (☎ 914-112-006).

The Netherlands: Avda. del Comandante Franco, 32, 28016 Madrid (☎ 913-590-914, 🖳 www.embajadapaisesbajos.es).

New Zealand: Plza. de la Lealtad, 2, 28014 Madrid (☎ 915-230-226).

Norway: Paseo de la Castellana, 31, 28046 Madrid (☎ 913-103-116).

Portugal: C/Pinar, 1, 28006 Madrid (☎ 915-617-800).

South Africa: C/Claudio Coello, 91, 28006 Madrid (☎ 914-356-688, 🖳 www.sudafrica.com).

Sweden: C/Caracas, 25, 28010 Madrid (☎ 913-081-535, 🖳 www.embaja dasuecia.es).

Switzerland: C/Núñez de Balboa, 35, 28001 Madrid (☎ 914-313-400, 🖳 www.eda.admin.ch/madrid_emb).

United Kingdom: C/de Fernando el Santo, 16, 28010 Madrid (☎ 913-190-208/190 200, 🖳 www.ukinspain.com).

United States of America: C/Serrano, 75, 28006 Madrid (☎ 915-774-000, 🖳 www-embusa.es).

British Provincial Consulates in Spain

Alicante: British Consulate, Plaza Calvo Sotelo, 1–2, 03001 Alicante (☎ 965-216-190, ✉ enquiries.alicante@fco.gov.uk).

Barcelona: British Consulate-General, Edificio Torre de Barcelona, Avda. Diagonal, 477-130, 08036 Barcelona (☎ 934-199-044, ✉ bcon@cyberbcn.com).

Bilbao: British Consulate-General, Alamada de Urquijo, 2-8, 48008 Bilbao (☎ 944-157-600, ✉ bcgbilbao@readysoft.es).

Granada: British Consulate, Carmen de San Cristobal, Ctra de Murcia s/n, 18010 Granada (☎ 958-274-724).

Ibiza: British Vice-Consulate, Avenida de Isidoro Macabich, 45, 07800 Ibiza (☎ 971-301-818, ✉ ibizacons@worldonline.es).

Madrid: British Consulate-General, Centro Colón, Marqués de la Ensenada, 16, 28004 Madrid (☎ 913-085-201).

Malaga: British Consulate, Edificio Eurocom, C/Mauricio Moro Pareto 2-2º, 29006 Malaga (☎ 952-352-300, ✉ malaga@fco.gov.uk).

Palma de Majorca: British Consulate, Plaza Mayor, 3D, 07002 Palma de Majorca (☎ 971-712-445, ✉ consulate@palma.mail.fco.gov.uk).

Minorca: Honorary British Vice-Consulate, Sa Casa Nova, Cami de Biniatap, 30, Es Castell, 07720 Minorca (☎ 971-363-373, ✉ deborah@in fotelecom.es).

Las Palmas: British Consulate, Edificio Cataluña, Luis Morote, 6-3, 35007 Las Palmas (☎ 928-262-508, ✉ laspalmasconsulate@ukinspain.com).

Santa Cruz de Tenerife: British Consulate, Plaza Weyler, 8-1, 38003 Santa Cruz de Tenerife (☎ 922-286-863, ✉ tenerifeconsulate@ukinspain.com).

Santander: Honorary British Consulate, Paseo de Pereda, 27, 39004 Santander (☎ 942-220-000, ✉ mpineiro@nexo.es).

Seville: The British Consulate is temporarily closed.

Vigo: British Consulate, Plaza Compostela, 23-6, 36201 Vigo (☎ 986-437-133, ✉ vigoconsulate@ukinspain.com).

Spanish Embassies Abroad

Australia and New Zealand: 15 Arkana St., Yarralumla, (PO Box 9076, Deakin), ACT 2600 (☎ 02-6273 3555, 💻 www.embaspain.com).

Canada: 74 Stanley Avenue, Ottawa, Ontario K1M 1P4 (☎ 613-747-2252, 💻 www. docuweb.ca/SpainInCanada).

United Kingdom: 39 Chesham Place, London SW1X 8SB (☎ 020-7235 5555).

United States of America: 2375 Pennsylvania Avenue, NW, 20037 Washington DC (☎ 202-452-0100, 💻 www.spainemb.org).

Spanish National Tourist Offices

Canada: 2 Bloor Street West, 34th Floor, Toronto, Ontario M4W 3E2 (☎ 416-961-3131, 💻 www.tourspain.toronto.on.ca).

UK: 22-23 Manchester Square, London W1M 5AP (☎ 020-7486 8077, 💻 www.tourspain.co.uk).

USA (💻 www.okpain.org)**:**

- **Chicago:** Water Tower Place, Suite 915 East, 845, North Michigan Avenue, Chicago, IL 60611 (☎ 312-642-1992).
- **Los Angeles:** 8383 Wilshire Blvd, Suite 960, Beverly Hills, CA 90211 (☎ 323-658-7188).
- **Miami:** 1221 Brickell Avenue, Miami, FL 33131 (☎ 305-358-1992).
- **New York:** 666 Fifth Avenue, New York, NY 10103 (☎ 212-265-8822).

Useful Telephone Numbers

Electricity

Electricity is primarily provided by two companies, depending on the region:

Endesa is the main company (💻 www.endesaoline.com), which provides electricity under the following company names:

- Fecsa in Catalonia (Barcelona, Costa Brava and Costa Dorada): ☎ 902-507-750.
- Gesa in the Balearic Islands: ☎ 971-226-262.
- Sevillana in Andalusia: ☎ 902-509-509.
- Unelco in the Canaries: ☎ 902-307-308.

Iberdrola (☎ 901-202-020, 💻 www.ciberdrola.com) provides electricity in the following regions: Asturias, the Basque Country, Cantabria, Catalonia, Comunidad Valenciana (including the Costa Blanca), Galicia and Madrid.

Gas

Most large cities have mains gas, although in smaller towns and country areas bottled gas is the only option. For information about the mains gas provider in a particular area, enquire at the local council offices (*Ayuntamiento*). Bottled gas is generally available from Repsol (☎ 901-100-100).

Water

Numerous water companies provide water and sewage services in Spain. For information about the provider in a particular area, enquire at the local council offices (*Ayuntamiento*).

Telephone

Since the deregulation of the telecommunications industry, the cost of national and international telephone calls in Spain has fallen dramatically and many companies now provide services. The former state monopoly company, Telefónica, still controls the lines and remains the principal provider.

Telefónica: general information including line contracts: ☎ 1004, 💻 www.telefonicaonline.net.

Retevisión: Telefónica's main competitor offering nation-wide services except in the Basque Country: ☎ 015, 💻 www.retevision.es.

Teleconnect: specialists in inexpensive international calls: ☎ 1685.

Tele 2: specialists in inexpensive nation-wide calls: ☎ 900-107-300.

Emergency Services

- Local Police: ☎ 092.
- National Police: ☎ 091.
- Civil Guard: ☎ 062.
- Medical Emergencies: ☎ 061.

Miscellaneous

Post Office (*Correos*): ☎ 902-197-197, 💻 www.correos.es.
Road traffic information: ☎ 900-123-505, 💻 www.dgt.es.
Spanish national railways (RENFE): ☎ 902-240-202, 💻 www.renfe.es.

APPENDIX B: FURTHER READING

The publications listed in this appendix are just a selection of the hundreds of books written about Spain. In addition to the general tourist guides listed below, guides covering individual cities and regions of Spain are listed under the area surveys throughout this book. The publication title is followed by the author's name and the publisher's name (in brackets). Note that some titles may be out of print but may still be obtainable from bookshops, libraries or second-hand bookshops. Books prefixed with an asterisk (*) are recommended by the author.

Living & Working in Spain

*The Bottlebrush Tree, Hugh Seymour-Davies (Black Swan)
**Buying a Home in Spain, David Hampshire (Survival Books)
Choose Spain, John Howells & Bettie Magee (Gateway)
*Driving Over Lemons, Chris Stewart (Sort Of Books)
Introducing Spain, B. A. McCullagh & S. Wood (Harrap)
Life in a Spanish Town, M. Newton (Harrap)
** Living & Working In Spain, David Hampshire (Survival Books)
*Madrid Inside Out, Artur Howard & Victoria Montero (Frank)
Simple Etiquette in Spain, Victoria Miranda McGuiness (Simple Books)
Spain: Business & Finance (Euromoney Books)
*You and the Law in Spain, David Searle (Santana)

General Tourist Guides

AA Essential Explorer Spain (AA)
Andalucía Handbook, Rowland Mead (Footprint)
*Andalucía: The Rough Guide (Rough Guides)
*Baedeker's Spain (Baedeker)
Berlitz Blueprint: Spain (Berlitz)
Berlitz Discover Spain, Ken Bernstein & Paul Murphy (Berlitz)
*Blue Guide to Spain: The Mainland, Ian Robertson (Ernest Benn)
*Cadogan Guides: Spain, Dana Facaros & Michael Pauls (Cadogan)
Collins Independent Travellers Guide Spain, Harry Debelius (Collins)
Daytrips Spain & Portugal, Norman Renouf (Hastings House Pub)

Excursions in Eastern Spain, Nick Inman & Clara Villanueva (Santana)
Excursions in Southern Spain, David Baird (Santana)
***Eyewitness Travel Guide: Spain**, Deni Bown (Dorling Kindersly)
Fielding's Paradors in Spain & Portugal, A. Hobbs (Fielding Worldwide)
***Fodor's Spain** (Fodor's)
***Fodor's Exploring Spain** (Fodor's Travel Publications)
***Frommer's Spain's Best-Loved Driving Tours**, Mona King (IDG Books)
Guide to the Best of Spain (Turespaña)
***Inside Andalusia**, David Baird (Santana)
The Insider's Guide to Spain, John de St. Jorre (Moorland)
***Insight Guides: Spain** (APA Publications)
Lazy Days Out in Andalucía, Jeremy Wayne (Cadogan)
***Let's Go Spain & Portugal** (Macmillan)
***Lonely Planet Spain** (Lonely Planet)
***Madrid**, Michael Jacobs (George Philip)
Madrid: A Traveller's Companion, Hugh Thomas (Constable)
***Michelin Green Guide Spain** (Michelin)
***Michelin Red Guide to Spain and Portugal** (Michelin)
Off the Beaten Track: Spain, Barbara Mandell & Roger Penn (Moorland)
***Paupers' Barcelona**, Miles Turner (Pan)
Rick Steves' Spain & Portugal, Rick Steves (John Muir Pubns)
***Rough Guide to Andalucía**, Mark Ellingham & John Fisher (Rough Guides)
The Shell Guide to Spain, David Mitchell (Simon & Schuster)
Spain: A Phaidon Cultural Guide (Phaidon)
Spain at its Best, Robert Kane (Passport)
Spain: Everything Under the Sun, Tom Burns (Harrap Columbus)
Spain on Backroads (Duncan Petersen)
***Spain: The Rough Guide**, Mark Ellingham & John Fisher (Rough Guides)
Special Places to Stay in Spain, Alistair Sawday (ASP)
Time Off in Spain and Portugal, Teresa Tinsley (Horizon)
Travellers in Spain: An Illustrated Anthology, David Mitchell (Cassell)
Welcome to Spain, RAN Dixon (Collins)
***Which? Guide to Spain** (Consumers' Association and Hodder & Stoughton)

Travel Literature

*As I Walked Out One Midsummer Morning, Laurie Lee (Penguin)

*Between Hopes and Memories: A Spanish Journey, Michael Jacobs (Picador)

*The Bible in Spain, George Borrow (Century Travellers Series)

*Cider With Rosie, Laurie Lee (Penguin)

Gatherings in Spain, Richard Ford (Dent Everyman)

*Handbook for Travellers in Spain, Richard Ford (Centaur Press)

Iberia, James A. Michener (Fawcett)

*Jogging Round Majorca, Gordon West (Black Swan)

In Search of Andalucía, Christopher Wawn & David Wood (Pentland Press)

*In Spain, Ted Walker (Corgi)

*A Rose for Winter, Laurie Lee (Penguin)

*Spanish Journeys: A Portrait of Spain, Adam Hopkins (Penguin)

*South from Granada, Gerald Brenan (Penguin)

*A Stranger in Spain, H. V. Morton (Methuen)

Two Middle-aged Ladies in Adalusia, Penelope Chetwode (Murray)

*A Winter in Majorca, George Sand

APPENDIX C: USEFUL WEBSITES

The following list contains some of the many websites dedicated to Spain. Websites about particular regions or areas of Spain are listed under the relevant area surveys.

About Spain (💻 www.aboutspain.net): information about specific regions in Spain.

All About Spain (💻 www.red2000.com): general tourist information about Spain.

Escape to Spain (💻 www.escapetospain.co.uk): general information and a property guide to the Costa Blanca, Costa Brava and Costa del Sol.

Ideal Spain (💻 www.idealspain.com): information about many aspects of living in Spain.

Life in Spain (💻 www.spain-info.com): general information about aspects of living in Spain.

Spain Alive (💻 www.spainalive.com): information about specific areas of Spain.

Spain Expat (💻 www.spainexpat.com): information about living in Spain, including an 'ask the legal expert' facility.

Spanish National Tourist Office (💻 www.tourspain.co.uk).

Survival Books (💻 www.survivalbooks.net): Survival Books are the publishers of this book and *Buying a Home in Spain*, *Living and Working an Spain*, and *The Wines of Spain*. The website includes useful tips for anyone planning to buy a home, live, work, retire or do business in Spain.

Travelling in Spain (💻 http://travelinginspain.com): information about Spanish cities with particular emphasis on Madrid.

TuSpain (💻 www.tuspain.com): general information about Spain with the emphasis on buying property and residential matters.

Typically Spanish (💻 www.typicallyspanish.com): information about a wide range of Spanish topics.

APPENDIX D: WEIGHTS & MEASURES

Spain uses the metric system of measurement. Nationals of a few countries (including the Americans and British) who are more familiar with the imperial system of measurement will find the tables on the following pages useful. Some comparisons shown are only approximate, but are close enough for most everyday uses. In addition to the variety of measurement systems used, clothes sizes often vary considerably with the manufacturer (as we all know only too well). Try all clothes on before buying and don't be afraid to return something if, when you try it on at home, you decide it doesn't fit (most shops will exchange goods or give a refund).

Women's Clothes

Continental	34	36	38	40	42	44	46	48	50	52
UK	8	10	12	14	16	18	20	22	24	26
USA	6	8	10	12	14	16	18	20	22	24

Pullovers

	Women's						Men's					
Continental	40	42	44	46	48	50	44	46	48	50	52	54
UK	34	36	38	40	42	44	34	36	38	40	42	44
USA	34	36	38	40	42	44	sm	medium		large		xl

Note: sm = small, xl = extra large

Men's Shirts

Continental	36	37	38	39	40	41	42	43	44	46
UK/USA	14	14	15	15	16	16	17	17	18	-

Men's Underwear

Continental	5	6	7	8	9	10
UK	34	36	38	40	42	44
USA	small	medium		large	extra large	

Children's Clothes

Continental	92	104	116	128	140	152
UK	16/18	20/22	24/26	28/30	32/34	36/38
USA	2	4	6	8	10	12

Children's Shoes

Continental	18	19	20	21	22	23	24	25	26	27	28	29	30	31	32
UK/USA	2	3	4	4	5	6	7	7	8	9	10	11	11	12	13

Continental	33	34	35	36	37	38
UK/USA	1	2	2	3	4	5

Shoes (Women's and Men's)

Continental	35	35	36	37	37	38	39	39	40	40	41	42	42	43	44	44
UK	2	3	3	4	4	5	5	6	6	7	7	8	8	9	9	10
USA	4	4	5	5	6	6	7	7	8	8	9	9	10	10	11	11

Weight

Avoirdupois	Metric	Metric	Avoirdupois
1 oz	28.35 g	1 g	0.035 oz
1 pound*	454 g	100 g	3.5 oz
1 cwt	50.8 kg	250 g	9 oz
1 ton	1,016 kg	500 g	18 oz
1 tonne	2,205 pounds	1 kg	2.2 pounds

* A metric 'pound' is 500g, g = gramme, kg = kilogramme

Length

British/US	Metric	Metric	British/US
1 inch	2.54 cm	1 cm	0.39 inch
1 foot	30.48 cm	1 m	3 feet 3.25 inches
1 yard	91.44 cm	1 km	0.62 mile
1 mile	1.6 km	8 km	5 miles

Note: cm = centimetre, m = metre, km = kilometre

Capacity

Imperial	Metric	Metric	Imperial
1 pint (USA)	0.47 litre	1 litre	1.76 UK pints
1 pint (UK)	0.57 litre	1 litre	0.26 US gallons
1 gallon (USA)	3.78 litre	1 litre	0.22 UK gallon
1 gallon (UK)	4.54 litre	1 litre	35.21 fluid oz

Square Measure

British/US	Metric	Metric	British/US
1 square inch	0.45 sq. cm	1 sq. cm	0.15 sq. inches
1 square foot	0.09 sq. m	1 sq. m	10.76 sq. feet
1 square yard	0.84 sq. m	1 sq. m	1.2 sq. yards
1 acre	0.4 hectares	1 hectare	2.47 acres
1 square mile	259 hectares	1 sq. km	0.39 sq. mile

Temperature

° Celsius	° Fahrenheit	
0	32	freezing point of water
5	41	
10	50	
15	59	
20	68	
25	77	
30	86	
35	95	
40	104	

Note: The boiling point of water is 100°C / 212°F.

Oven Temperature

Gas	Electric	
	°F	°C
-	225–250	110–120
1	275	140
2	300	150
3	325	160
4	350	180
5	375	190
6	400	200
7	425	220
8	450	230
9	475	240

For a quick conversion, the Celsius temperature is approximately half the Fahrenheit temperature.

Temperature Conversion

Celsius to Fahrenheit: multiply by 9, divide by 5 and add 32.
Fahrenheit to Celsius: subtract 32, multiply by 5 and divide by 9.

Body Temperature

Normal body temperature (if you're alive and well) is 98.4° Fahrenheit, which equals 37° Celsius.The map opposite shows the 17 autonomous regions and 49 provinces of Spain (listed below).

APPENDIX E: MAP OF REGIONS & PROVINCES

The map opposite shows the 17 autonomous regions and 49 provinces of Spain (listed below).

1. Coruña	26. Barcelona
2. Lugo	27. Tarragona
3. Pontevedra	28. Cáceres
4. Orense	29. Badajoz
5. Asturias	30. Guadalajara
6. León	31. Toledo
7. Palencia	32. Cuenca
8. Burgos	33. Ciudad Real
9. Zamora	34. Albacete
10. Valladolid	35. Madrid
11. Soria	36. Castellón
12. Salamanca	37. Valencia
13. Avila	38. Alicante
14. Segovia	39. Huelva
15. Cantabria	40. Seville
16. La Rioja	41. Córdoba
17. Vizcaya	42. Jaén
18. Guipúzcoa	43. Cadiz
19. Alava	44. Malaga
20. Navarra	45. Granada
21. Huesca	46. Almeria
22. Zaragossa	47. Murcia
23. Teruel	48. Baleares
24. Lérida (Lleida)	49. Canarias
25. Girona	

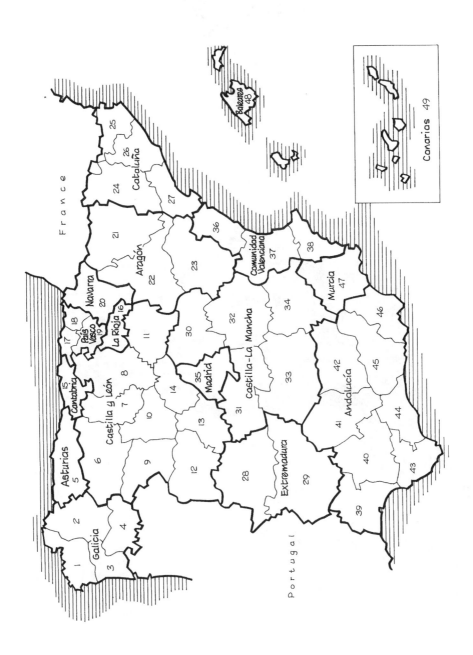

INDEX

BUYING A HOME IN SPAIN

Buying a Home in Spain is essential reading for anyone planning to purchase property in Spain and is designed to guide you through the jungle and make it a pleasant and enjoyable experience. Most importantly, it's packed with vital information to help you avoid the sort of disasters that can turn your dream home into a nightmare! Topics covered include:

- Avoiding problems
- Choosing the region
- Finding the right home & location
- Estate agents
- Finance, mortgages & taxes
- Home security
- Utilities, heating & air-conditioning
- Moving house & settling in
- Renting & letting
- Permits & visas
- Travelling & communications
- Health & insurance
- Renting a car & driving
- Retirement & starting a business
- And much, much more!

Buying a Home in Spain is the most comprehensive and up-to-date source of information available about buying property in Spain. Whether you want a detached house, townhouse or apartment, a holiday or a permanent home, this book will help make your dreams come true.

Buy this book and save yourself time, trouble and money!

Order your copies today by phone, fax, mail or e-mail from: Survival Books, PO Box 146, Wetherby, West Yorks. LS23 6XZ, United Kingdom (☎/🖷 +44 (0)1937-843523, ✉ orders@ survivalbooks.net, 🖳 www.survivalbooks.net).

ORDER FORM
ALIEN'S GUIDES / BEST PLACES / BUYING A HOME / WINES

Qty.	Title	Price (incl. p&p)*			Total
		UK	Europe	World	
	The Alien's Guide to Britain	£5.95	£6.95	£8.45	
	The Alien's Guide to France	£5.95	£6.95	£8.45	
	The Best Places to Buy a Home in France	£13.95	£15.95	£19.45	
	The Best Places to Buy a Home in Spain	£13.45	£14.95	£16.95	
	Buying a Home Abroad	£13.45	£14.95	£16.95	
	Buying a Home in Britain	£11.45	£12.95	£14.95	
	Buying a Home in Florida	£13.45	£14.95	£16.95	
	Buying a Home in France	£13.45	£14.95	£16.95	
	Buying a Home in Greece & Cyprus	£13.45	£14.95	£16.95	
	Buying a Home in Ireland	£11.45	£12.95	£14.95	
	Buying a Home in Italy	£13.45	£14.95	£16.95	
	Buying a Home in Portugal	£13.45	£14.95	£16.95	
	Buying a Home in Spain	£13.45	£14.95	£16.95	
	How to Avoid Holiday & Travel Disasters	£13.45	£14.95	£16.95	
	Maintaining & Renovating Your French Home	Autumn 2003			
	Rioja and its Wines	£11.45	£12.95	£14.95	
	The Wines of Spain	£15.95	£18.45	£21.95	
				Total	

Order your copies today by phone, fax, mail or e-mail from: Survival Books, PO Box 146, Wetherby, West Yorks. LS23 6XZ, UUK (☎/▤ +44 (0)1937-843523, ✉ orders@survivalbooks.net, 💻 www.survivalbooks.net). If you aren't entirely satisfied, simply return them to us within 14 days for a full and unconditional refund.

Cheque enclosed/please charge my Delta/Mastercard/Switch/Visa* card

Card No. __ __ __ __   __ __ __ __   __ __ __ __   __ __ __ __

Expiry date _____   **Issue number (Switch only)** _____

Signature _____   **Tel. No.** _____

NAME _____

ADDRESS _____

_____

_____

* Delete as applicable (price includes postage – airmail for Europe/world).

LIVING AND WORKING IN SPAIN

Living and Working in Spain is essential reading for anyone planning to spend some time in Spain including holiday-home owners, retirees, visitors, business people, migrants, students and even extraterrestrials! It's packed with over 400 pages of important and useful information designed to help you **avoid costly mistakes and save both time and money.** Topics covered include how to:

- Find a job with a good salary & conditions
- Obtain a residence permit
- Avoid and overcome problems
- Find your dream home
- Get the best education for your family
- Make the best use of public transport
- Endure motoring in Spain
- Obtain the best health treatment
- Stretch your euros further
- Make the most of your leisure time
- Enjoy the Spanish sporting life
- Find the best shopping bargains
- Insure yourself against most eventualities
- Use post office and telephone services
- Do numerous other things not listed above

Living and Working in Spain is the most comprehensive and up-to-date source of practical information available about everyday life in Spain. It isn't, however, a boring text book, but an interesting and entertaining guide written in a highly readable style.

Buy this book and discover what it's *really* like to live and work in Spain.

Order your copies today by phone, fax, mail or e-mail from: Survival Books, PO Box 146, Wetherby, West Yorks. LS23 6XZ, United Kingdom (☎/▤ +44 (0)1937-843523, ✉ orders@ survivalbooks.net, 🖥 www.survivalbooks.net).

ORDER FORM

LIVING & WORKING SERIES / RETIRING ABROAD

Qty.	Title	Price (incl. p&p)*			Total
		UK	**Europe**	**World**	
	Living & Working Abroad	£16.95	£18.95	£22.45	
	Living & Working in America	£14.95	£16.95	£20.45	
	Living & Working in Australia	£14.95	£16.95	£20.45	
	Living & Working in Britain	£14.95	£16.95	£20.45	
	Living & Working in Canada	£16.95	£18.95	£22.45	
	Living & Working in the Far East	Winter 2003			
	Living & Working in France	£14.95	£16.95	£20.45	
	Living & Working in Germany	£16.95	£18.95	£22.45	
	Living & Working in the Gulf States & Saudi Arabia	£16.95	£18.95	£22.45	
	Living & Working in Holland, Belgium & Luxembourg	£14.95	£16.95	£20.45	
	Living & Working in Ireland	£14.95	£16.95	£20.45	
	Living & Working in Italy	£14.95	£16.95	£20.45	
	Living & Working in London	£11.45	£12.95	£14.95	
	Living & Working in New Zealand	£14.95	£16.95	£20.45	
	Living & Working in Spain	£14.95	£16.95	£20.45	
	Living & Working in Switzerland	£14.95	£16.95	£20.45	
	Retiring Abroad	£14.95	£16.95	£20.45	
				Total	

Order your copies today by phone, fax, mail or e-mail from: Survival Books, PO Box 146, Wetherby, West Yorks. LS23 6XZ, UK (☎/🖳 +44 (0)1937-843523, ✉ orders@survivalbooks.net, 🖳 www.survivalbooks.net). If you aren't entirely satisfied, simply return them to us within 14 days for a full and unconditional refund.

Cheque enclosed/please charge my Delta/Mastercard/Switch/Visa* card

Card No. __ __ __ __   __ __ __ __   __ __ __ __   __ __ __ __

Expiry date_____   **Issue number (Switch only)** _____

Signature _____   **Tel. No.** _____

NAME _____

ADDRESS _____

_____

_____

* Delete as applicable (price includes postage – airmail for Europe/world).

NOTES

NOTES

Survival Books are essential reading for anyone planning to buy a home, live, work, retire or simply travel abroad. Our best-selling guides are the most comprehensive available, **containing up to three times as much information as similar books**, and are guaranteed to save you time, trouble and money!

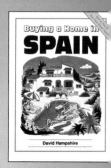

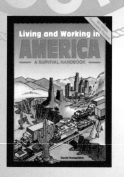

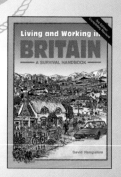

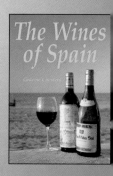

Order your copies today by using the order forms in this book, visiting our website (www.survivalbooks.net) or calling +44 (0)1937-843523